IMAGES
of America

SOLANA BEACH

On the Cover: This 1930s photograph shows the original Solana Beach Train Station, which was completed in 1924. Through constant communication with the Santa Fe Railroad, Ed Fletcher, one of the major developers of Solana Beach, persuaded the rail giant to help fund a station to serve the fledging suburb of San Diego. By the 1960s, the station had become obsolete. Solana Beach would not receive another station of its own until 1995, when it became a flourishing transit center for Amtrak and the San Diego County commuter rail, the *Coaster.* (Courtesy of the Mandeville Special Collections Library, University of California, San Diego.)

IMAGES
of America

SOLANA BEACH

Matthew Thompson and Hilary White

ARCADIA
PUBLISHING

ISBN 978-1-4671-3325-8

Published by Arcadia Publishing
Charleston, South Carolina

Printed in the United States of America

Library of Congress Control Number: 2014953878

For all general information, please contact Arcadia Publishing:
Telephone 843-853-2070
Fax 843-853-0044
E-mail sales@arcadiapublishing.com
For customer service and orders:
Toll-Free 1-888-313-2665

Visit us on the Internet at www.arcadiapublishing.com

I would like to dedicate this book to my favorite citizen of Solana Beach, my father, Tom Thompson.

Contents

Acknowledgments

A special thanks must go to the Solana Beach Civic and Historical Society; the San Dieguito Heritage Museum; the Solana Beach Department of Marine Safety; Mandeville Special Collections Library, University of California, San Diego; the San Diego History Center; David Ellenstein at North Coast Repertory Theatre; Aaron Rumley at North Coast Repertory Theatre; Julianne Eggold; Teresa Rincon and Tony's Jacal; and Fidel's Mexican Restaurant. All photographs not credited are part of the author's personal collection.

Thanks also to our editors at Arcadia Publishing, Alyssa Jones and Lily Watkins, for all their help, encouragement, and invaluable advice during the compilation of this book.

Introduction

Sunshine Beach: the Spanish-translated moniker for Solana Beach could not fit this shining city more than that. Since the time Native American Kumeyaay fished and foraged along the coast and gathered acorns, piñon nuts, and other edibles on the sloping hills, the area has always been a haven for home, recreation, and a way of life.

In 1769, while under Spanish control, Don Gaspar de Portola paved the first major roadway in California, El Camino Real, a 500-mile-long trail that stretched from San Diego to Monterey. The dusty superhighway of the past ran adjacent to modern-day Solana Beach. It would be an important link for the burgeoning township in the years leading up to its development.

Control of the area passed to Mexico when it gained independence from Spain in 1821. Many of the inhabitants were sons and grandsons of the original Spanish settlers, who became influential in government and were owners of enormous land areas known as ranchos. Many thousands of acres in what is now San Diego County became privately owned during the Mexican regime. In 1836, Don Juan Maria Osuna, then-mayor of the city of San Diego, claimed the 8,800 acres known as Rancho San Dieguito that would include all of modern-day Solana Beach.

Following the Mexican War with the United States, California became a US territory and on September 9, 1850, was admitted to the Union. The county of San Diego was established by the state legislature that same year, when the population of the entire county was numbered at 790, not counting the thousands of native Kumeyaay who had called the area their home for thousands of years. The first American homesteader in the vast San Luis Rey District was William A. Ewing, who took up 180 acres in the San Dieguito River Valley in 1862, although modern-day Solana Beach was uninhabited until a farmer named George H. Jones established the first of two ranches to cultivate lima beans in 1908.

The area encompassing Solana Beach began to develop slowly when adjacent Lake Hodges Dam was completed in 1918. The creation of the 12,000-acre Santa Fe Irrigation District ensured that the area from Rancho Santa Fe through Solana Beach would prosper and expand. In response to irrigation and the ability to tap freshwater, the coastline began to boom in the early 1920s. At this time, Solana Beach had no true shoreline, as the Pacific Ocean crashed into the cliff walls.

The "Surf Line" train route of the Atchison, Topeka and Santa Fe Railway (AT&SF) was completed in the 1880s and connected San Diego to neighboring Los Angeles, which allowed goods and services to be routed to the county. About this time, the Stevens family purchased hundreds of acres of what is now known as Solana Beach and Rancho Santa Fe. In 1922, Col. Ed Fletcher, an early community leader and developer, purchased 140 acres of the surrounding area to develop what is now known as downtown Solana Beach with the help of his brother-in-law Eugene Batchelder. Fletcher convinced the AT&SF to build a train station in the early 1920s.

George Jones took it upon himself to provide access to the beach in order to spur real estate development. Fletcher Cove was created by eroding tons of earth that formed the coastal bluff using a single fire hose with hydraulic water pressure. The beach was opened with great fanfare, including horse races, on July 4, 1925. It was also around this time that the area informally changed its name from Lockwood Mesa to Solana Beach.

Fletcher envisioned the area as an up-and-coming suburb of San Diego, but the coming of the Great Depression and World War II postponed that vision until the booming economy took hold once again the 1950s.

The Bill Jack Scientific Instrument Company was formed in 1949 and was housed in Quonset huts, the quirky structures that currently house local businesses in the Cedros Design Center and served as a design element for the 1995 train station. The simple structures were originally constructed as small industrial centers that built reconnaissance photographic equipment, motors, tachometers, helmets, and police equipment. As the largest employer in the area, the workers at the Bill Jack Plant began to purchase land and build homes in the area, creating the suburb of housing that still exists today.

After World War II, Solana Beach created a chamber of commerce and a sanitation and fire district. For a 10-year period between 1950 and 1960, the community underwent tremendous growth. Marview Heights, originally owned by the Santa Fe Irrigation District and later sold as individual homes by Fred Howland Ford and his brother, gave impetus to local residential development. Eden Gardens, one of the oldest residential areas of Solana Beach, was a community formed by Mexican farmers who were hired by owners of large ranches in Rancho Santa Fe. These farmers wanted their families nearby, hence the formation of La Colonia (the colony). The name Eden Gardens came later from a land developer who thought it would be a good marketing tool.

By 1986, San Diego County had grown commercially and artistically, and in 1986 Solana Beach achieved cityhood within the county of San Diego. Today, it is home to more than 13,000 residents. With a major train station, professional theater, and premiere music venue, the tiny town on the edge of the Pacific Ocean has become a jewel of progress. Within its borders, art and design thrive in the Cedros Design District, the music scene flourishes at the Belly Up, and professional actors tread the boards at North Coast Repertory Theatre. Outdoor enthusiasts can bask in the Mediterranean climate at the beach or along the award-winning Rail Trail for walkers and bicyclists.

The citizens and civic leaders of the little four-square-mile hamlet known as Solana Beach are continually striving to make one of Southern California's hidden gems a world-class experience for all.

One

LOCKWOOD MESA AND THE KUMEYAAY
THE LAND BEFORE TIME

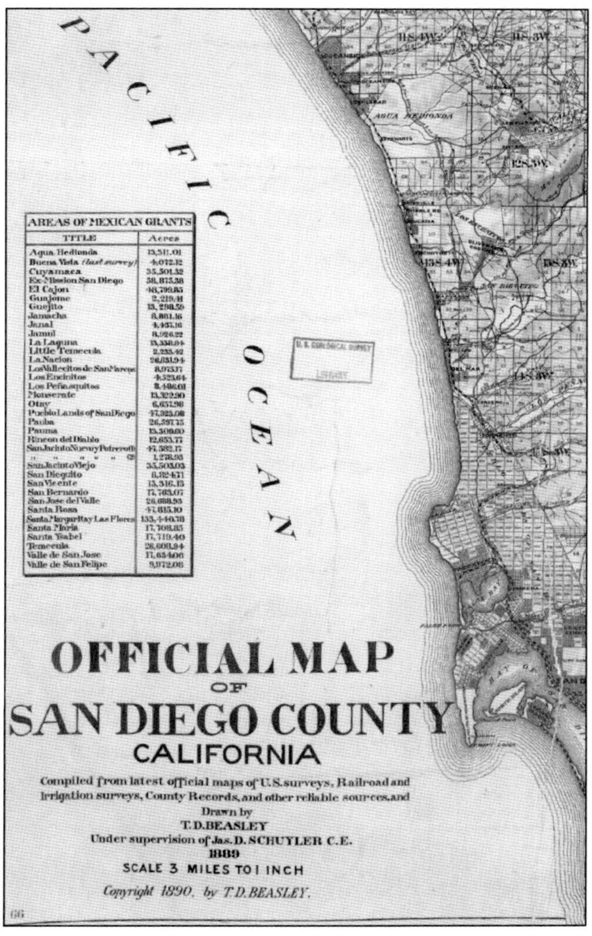

This 1889 map was produced by the US Geological Survey. Note the dotted line that denotes the railroad, which utilizes the identical route from Oceanside to downtown San Diego used today. (Courtesy of the US Geological Survey.)

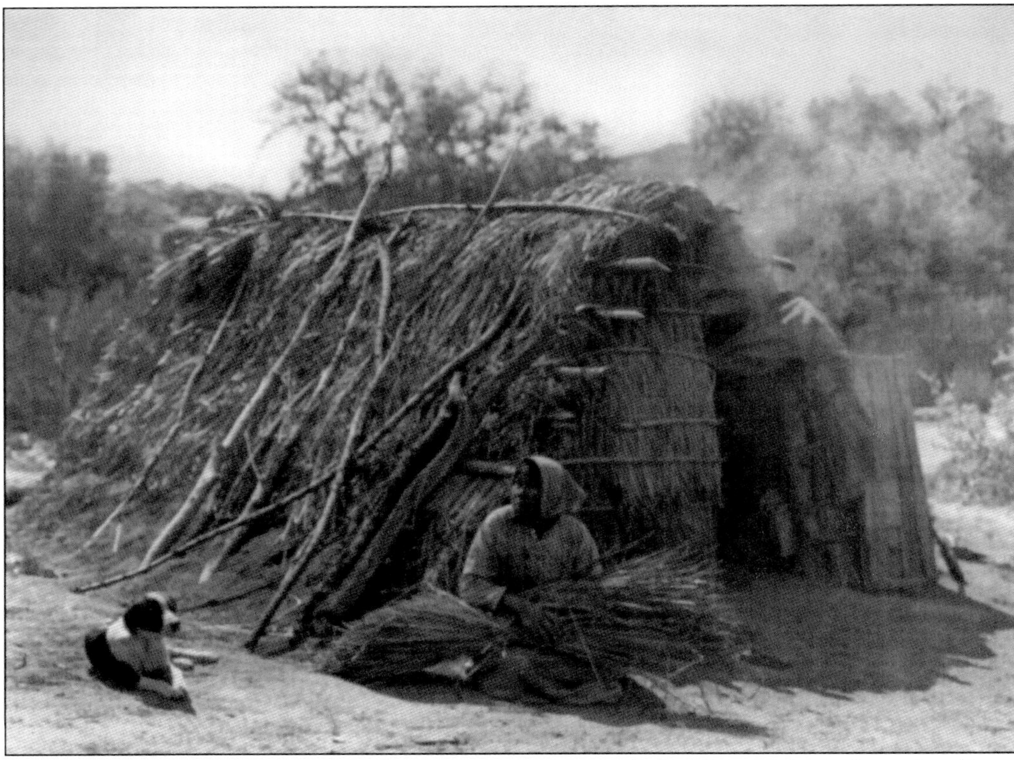

The native Kumeyaay inhabited areas throughout San Diego County to as far south as Ensenada, Mexico. The term Kumeyaay means, "those who face the water from a cliff." The Kumeyaay consist of two related groups, the Ipai and Tipai. Both Ipai and Tipai mean "people." The San Diego River separated the two coastal groups' traditional homelands. This 1883 photograph shows a Kumeyaay woman gathering thatching materials in San Diego County. In 1875, Pres. Ulysses Grant created reservations in the area, and additional lands were placed under trust patent status after the passage of the 1891 Act for the Relief of Mission Indians. (Courtesy of the Edward S. Curtis Collection, Library of Congress.)

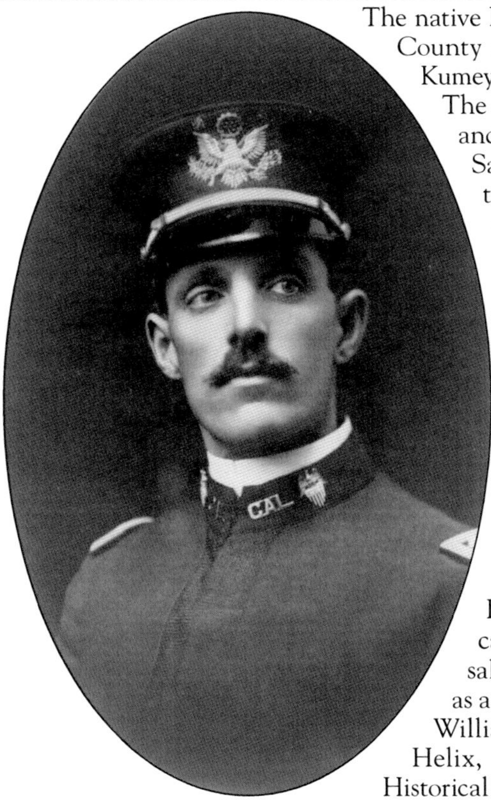

In 1888, Col. Ed Fletcher, father of Solana Beach, came to San Diego, where he started as a produce salesman. In 1901, he entered the real estate business as a land agent and started a partnership in 1908 with William Gross, which developed Grossmont, Mount Helix, and Del Mar. (Courtesy of the Solana Beach Historical Society.)

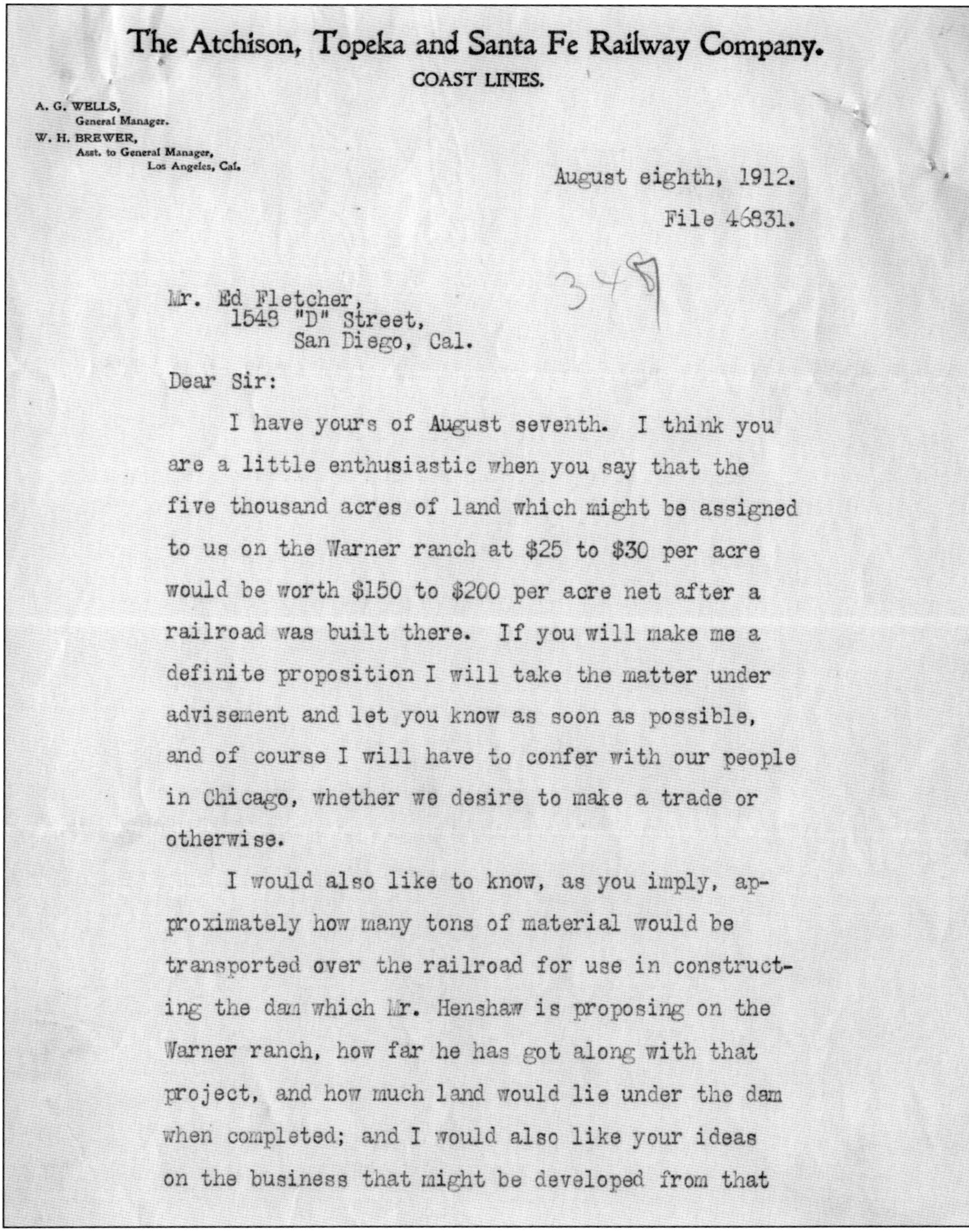
The Atchison, Topeka and Santa Fe Railway Company.
COAST LINES.

A. G. WELLS,
General Manager.
W. H. BREWER,
Asst. to General Manager,
Los Angeles, Cal.

August eighth, 1912.
File 46831.

349

Mr. Ed Fletcher,
1548 "D" Street,
San Diego, Cal.

Dear Sir:

I have yours of August seventh. I think you are a little enthusiastic when you say that the five thousand acres of land which might be assigned to us on the Warner ranch at $25 to $30 per acre would be worth $150 to $200 per acre net after a railroad was built there. If you will make me a definite proposition I will take the matter under advisement and let you know as soon as possible, and of course I will have to confer with our people in Chicago, whether we desire to make a trade or otherwise.

I would also like to know, as you imply, approximately how many tons of material would be transported over the railroad for use in constructing the dam which Mr. Henshaw is proposing on the Warner ranch, how far he has got along with that project, and how much land would lie under the dam when completed; and I would also like your ideas on the business that might be developed from that

Fletcher became interested in road building and saw to it that many such projects were completed. An avid road builder and highway-development advocate, Fletcher was later active in having state and US highways built to San Diego, including Highway 101, which ran right through Solana Beach. Commerce and travel into coastal North County of San Diego from the north was primarily via rail. After Del Mar received its own station, Fletcher decided Solana Beach was worthy of its own stop. Ever the real estate mogul, this 1912 letter to Fletcher from the Atchison, Topeka & Santa Fe Railway Company shows his optimism that the land around the station would more than quadruple in value. The railroad company begged to differ. (Courtesy of the Mandeville Special Collections Library, University of California, San Diego.)

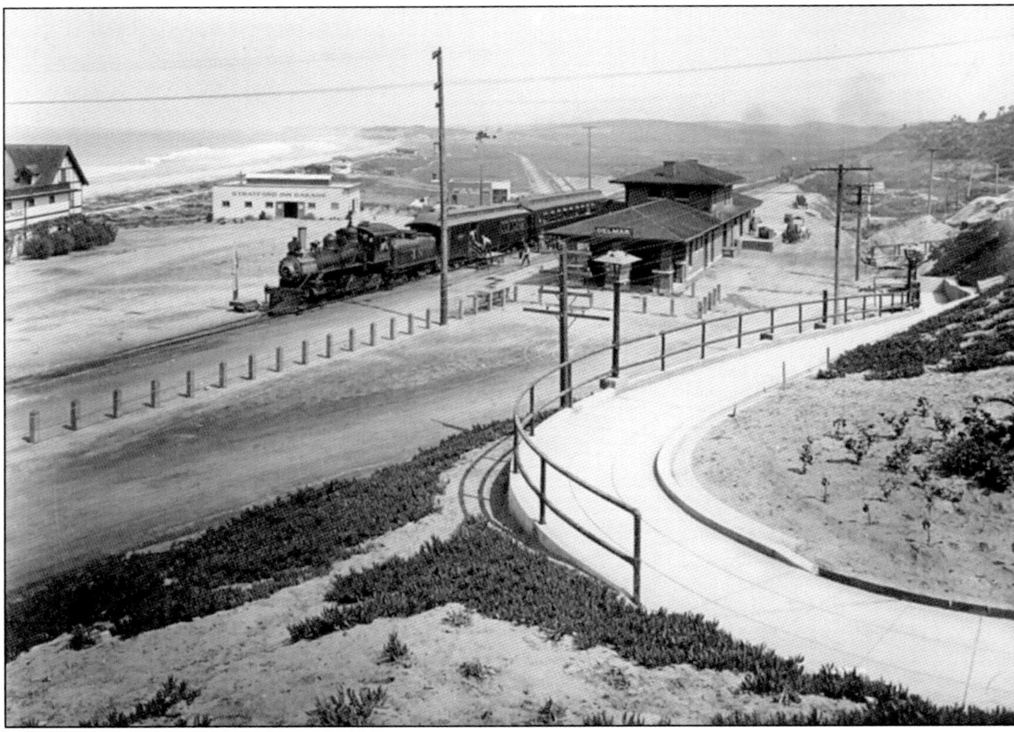

This 1910 photograph of the newly constructed Del Mar Train Station shows how undeveloped the surrounding areas of the unincorporated county were. In the distance, the rocky cliffs and rolling hills near the top would become Solana Beach in just a few short years. Solana Beach received its own train station in 1924. (Courtesy of the Del Mar Historical Society.)

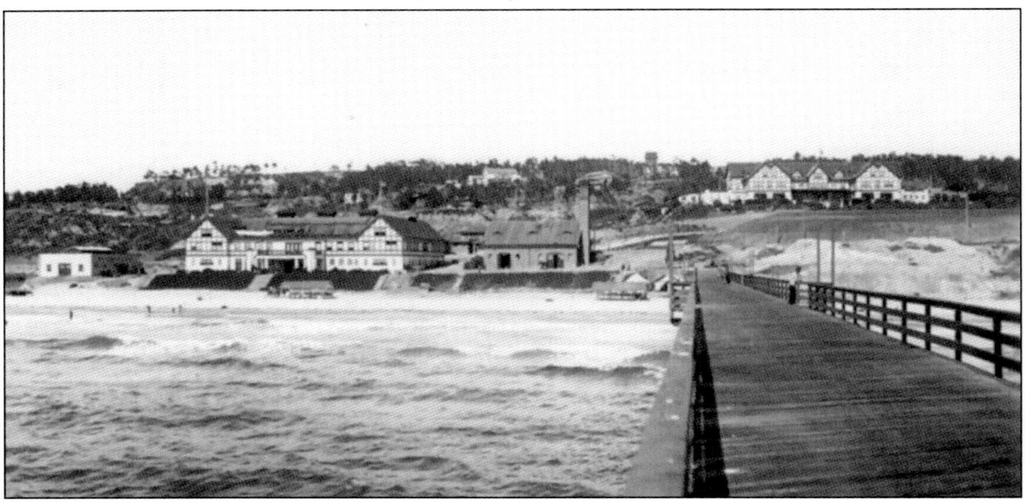

This 1917 photograph shows the Stratford Inn, a three-story hotel in Del Mar. Just south of Solana Beach, Del Mar was a destination for celebrities and vacationers coming from Los Angeles and parts north. The center of Del Mar was mapped to be at the intersection of Fifteenth Street and Grand Avenue (now Camino del Mar). The Stratford Inn was built on the northwest corner, with a saltwater plunge, a powerhouse, and a garage to house the newly popular automobile. Built in 1910, the Stratford Inn Garage is now the site of Jake's Del Mar restaurant. (Courtesy of the Del Mar Historical Society.)

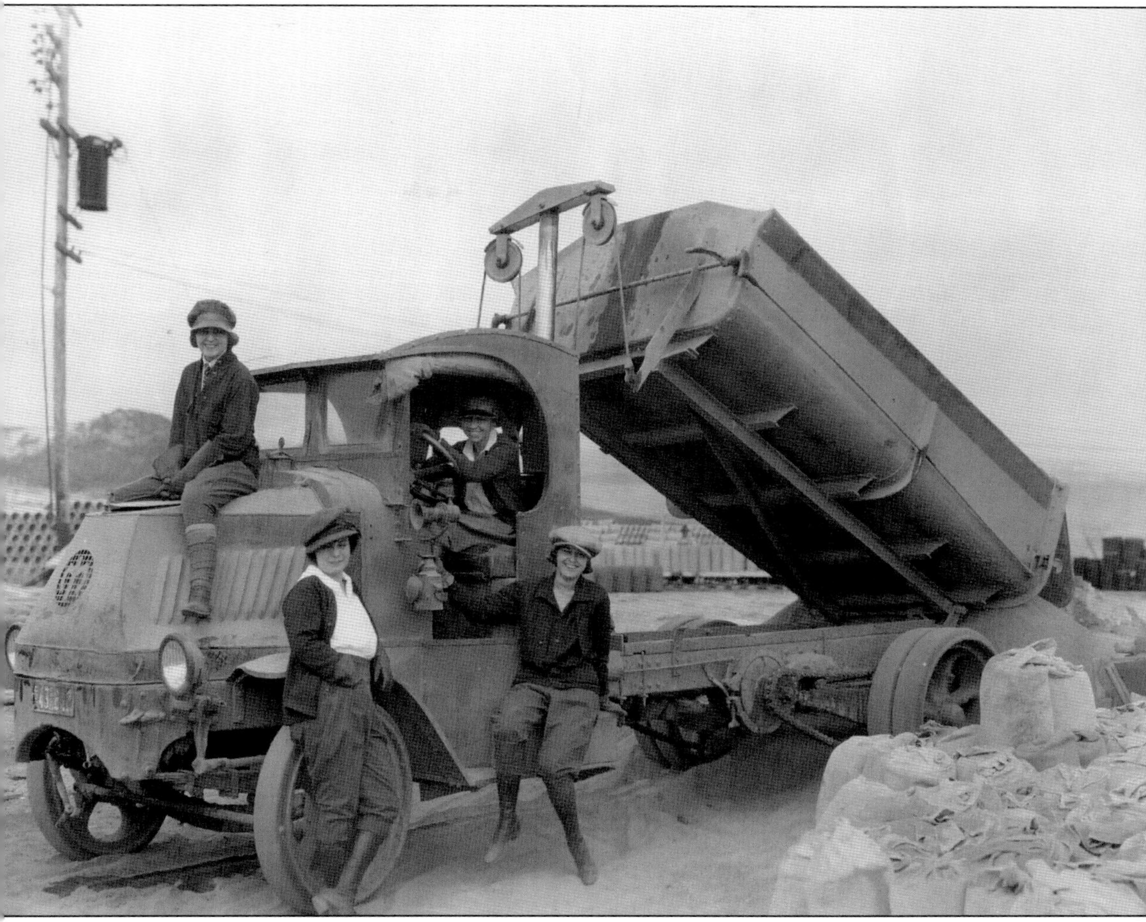

This early-1900s photograph shows the beginnings of what would become the area known as Rancho Santa Fe, located east of Solana Beach. At this time, water had to be pumped directly from the ground, so being away from the coast was actually more beneficial. In the upper right is the Pacific Ocean and what is now Solana Beach. (Courtesy of the Rancho Santa Fe Historical Society.)

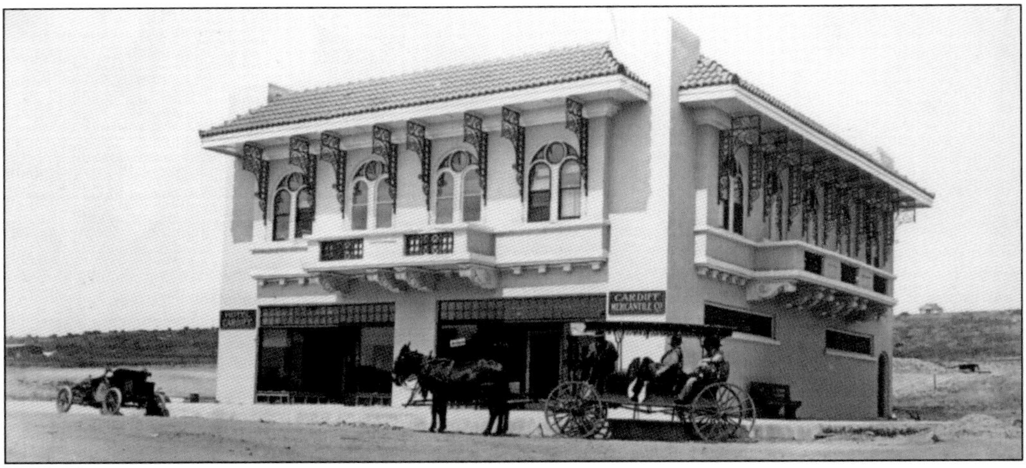

Pictured here in the 1910s is the Cullen Building Hotel, also known as the Cardiff Mercantile Building. The hotel was built by Frank Cullen, developer of Cardiff-by-the-Sea. (Courtesy of the San Dieguito Heritage Museum.)

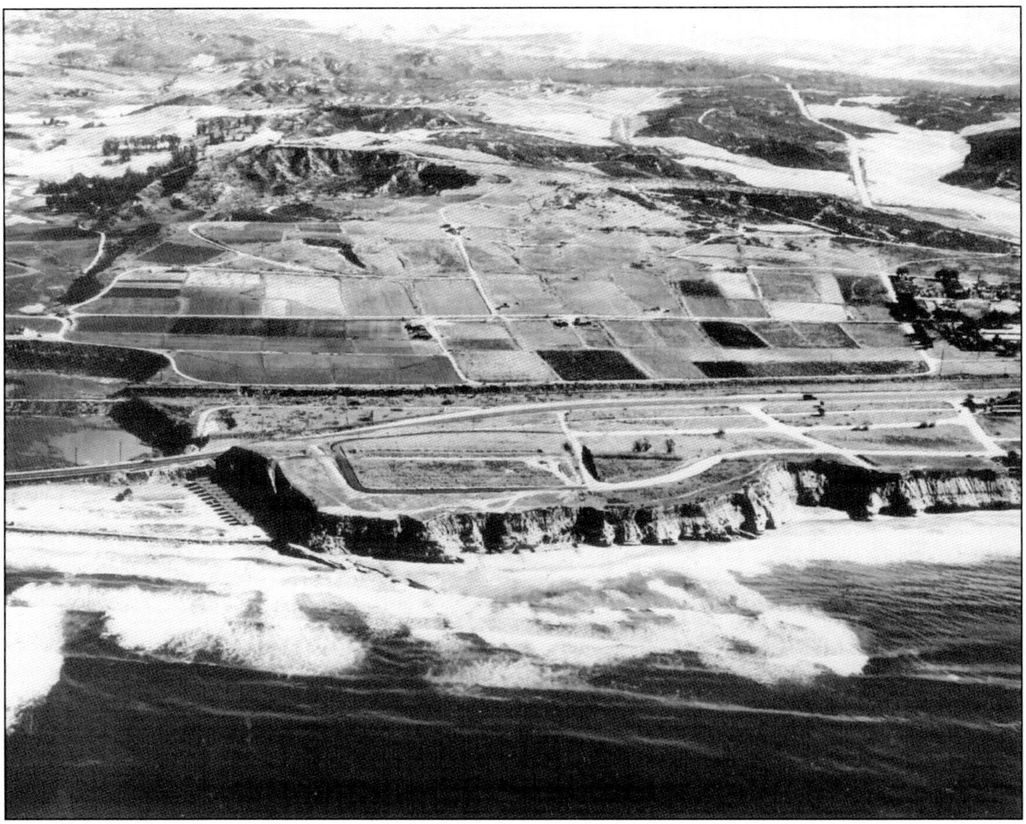

This aerial photograph from the 1920s features the coastline of what is now northern Solana Beach. Note the nascent roads that Fletcher had a hand in developing in the area above the bluffs where some of the most prominent homes in the city now stand. Solana Beach was born on this highway, officially designated US Highway 101 in 1925, the primary north-south route from San Diego to Los Angeles that connects the rest of the state with the Mexican border. (Courtesy of the Mandeville Special Collections Library, University of California, San Diego.)

Two

Ed Fletcher's Progressive Dream

The Roaring Twenties

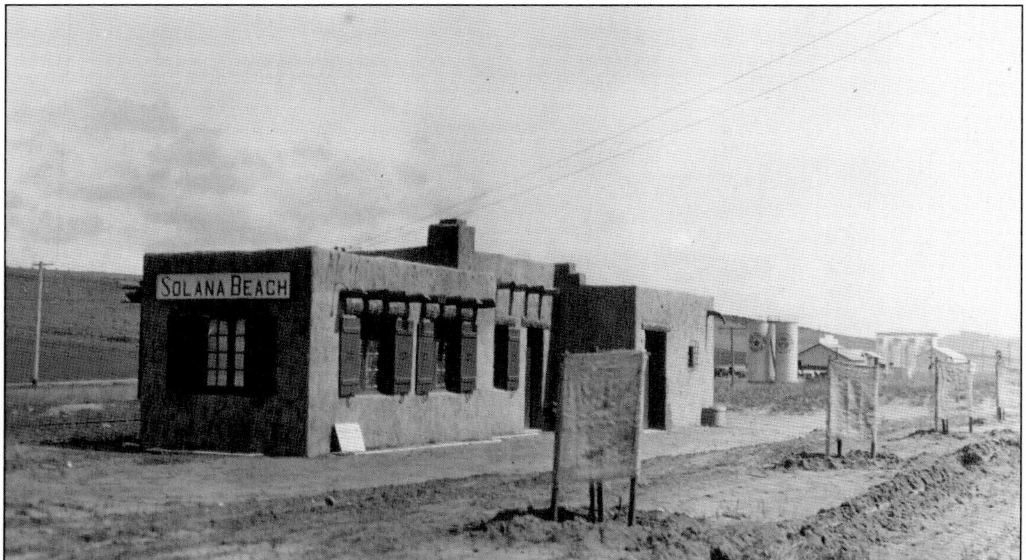

This photograph, looking southeast, depicts the nearly completed Solana Beach Train Station in the foreground. Standard Oil Company can be seen on the far right. (Courtesy of the Mandeville Special Collections Library, University of California, San Diego.)

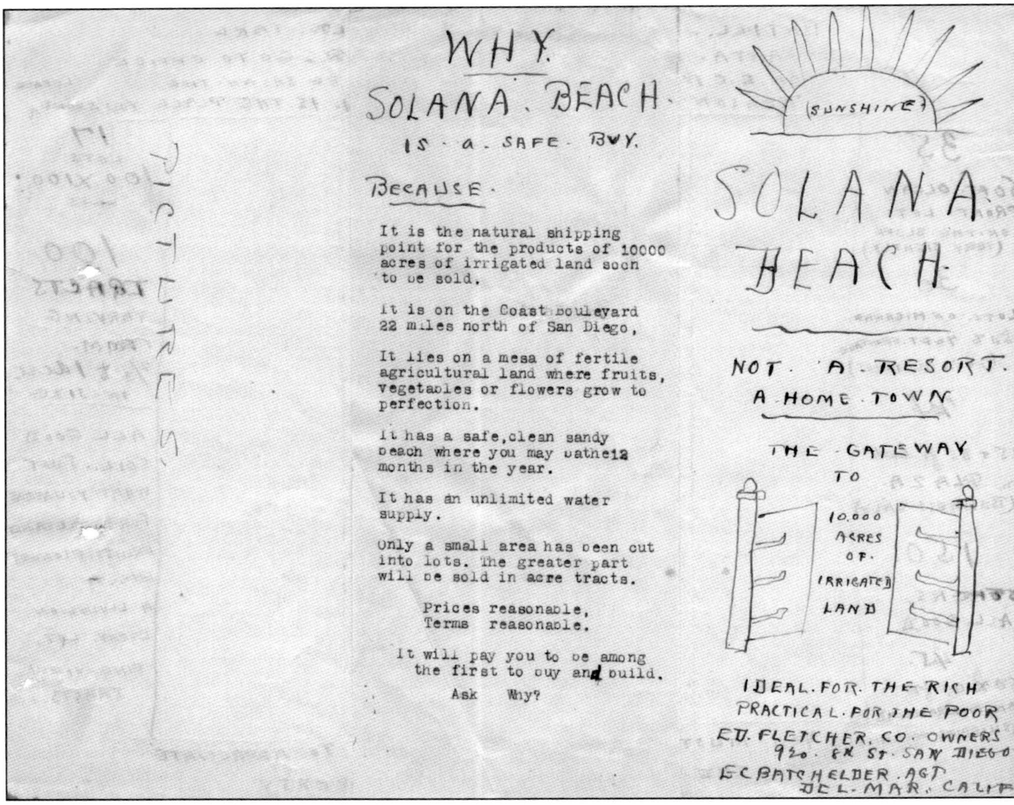

This partially hand-drawn marketing brochure from the early 1920s touts the desirability of Solana Beach for prospective investors. Like Hollywoodland, the name Solana Beach was selected as part of a marketing tool to buy lots in the area. The back of the brochure (below) was to feature a full-color illustrated map. The handwritten note at the top of the page instructs visitors to take the train to Del Mar, as Solana Beach's own train station would not be built for several years. (Both, courtesy of the Mandeville Special Collections Library, University of California, San Diego.)

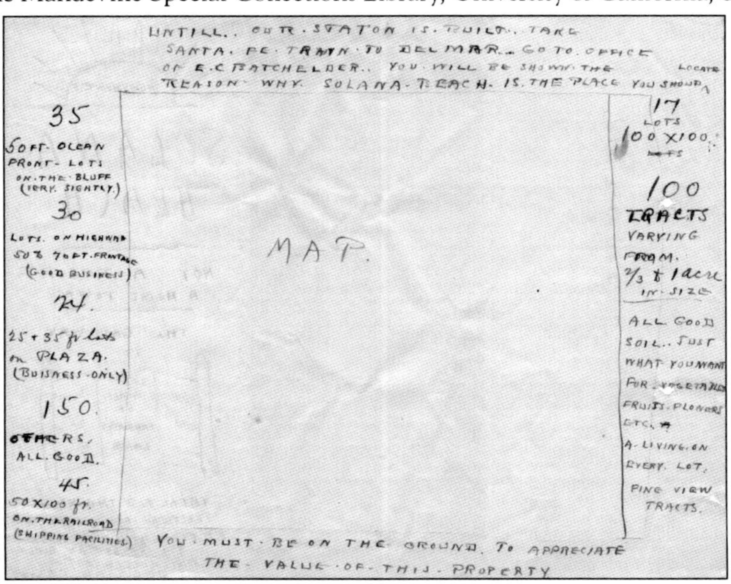

This 1928 grant deed details the sale of a 1.25-acre lot for $3,125 by Fletcher to Mrs. M.F. Baumgardner. The various lots were named after potential crops that could be grown there, in this case, avocado. (Courtesy of the Mandeville Special Collections Library, University of California, San Diego.)

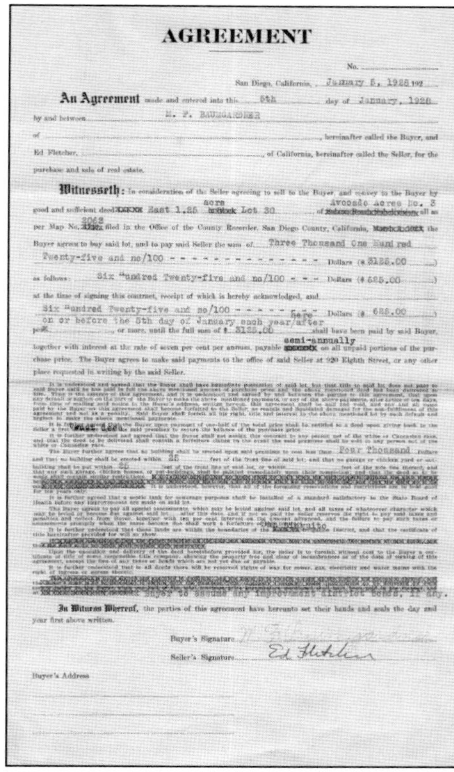

AGREEMENT

No.

San Diego, California, January 5, 1928 192

An Agreement made and entered into this 5th day of January, 1928 by and between M. F. BAUMGARDNER of , hereinafter called the Buyer, and Ed Fletcher, , of California, hereinafter called the Seller, for the purchase and sale of real estate.

Witnesseth: In consideration of the Seller agreeing to sell to the Buyer, and convey to the Buyer by good and sufficient deed XXXXX East 1.25 acre Lot 30 of Avocado Acres No. 3, all as per Map No. 2068 filed in the Office of the County Recorder, San Diego County, California, the Buyer agrees to buy said lot, and to pay said Seller the sum of Three Thousand One Hundred Twenty-five and no/100 - - - - - - - - - - - - - - Dollars ($ 3125.00) as follows: Six Hundred Twenty-five and no/100 - - - Dollars ($ 625.00) at the time of signing this contract, receipt of which is hereby acknowledged, and Six Hundred Twenty-five and no/100 - - - - - - Dollars ($ 625.00) on or before the 5th day of January each year/after here per , or more, until the full sum of $ 3125.00 shall have been paid by said Buyer, together with interest at the rate of seven per cent per annum, payable semi-annually on all unpaid portions of the purchase price. The Buyer agrees to make said payments to the office of said Seller at 920 Eighth Street, or any other place requested in writing by the said Seller.

In Witness Whereof, the parties of this agreement have hereunto set their hands and seals the day and year first above written.

Buyer's Signature

Seller's Signature Ed Fletcher

Buyer's Address

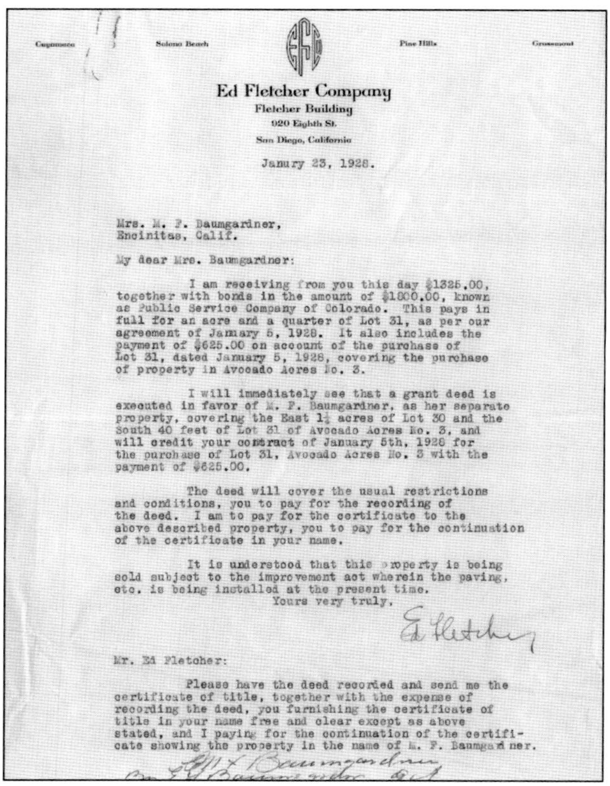

Cuyamaca Solana Beach Pine Hills Grossmont

Ed Fletcher Company
Fletcher Building
920 Eighth St.
San Diego, California

Janury 23, 1928.

Mrs. M. F. Baumgardner,
Encinitas, Calif.

My dear Mrs. Baumgardner:

I am receiving from you this day $1325.00, together with bonds in the amount of $1800.00, known as Public Service Company of Colorado. This pays in full for an acre and a quarter of Lot 31, as per our agreement of January 5, 1928. It also includes the payment of $625.00 on account of the purchase of Lot 31, dated January 5, 1928, covering the purchase of property in Avocado Acres No. 3.

I will immediately see that a grant deed is executed in favor of M. F. Baumgardner, as her separate property, covering the East 1¼ acres of Lot 30 and the South 40 feet of Lot 31 of Avocado Acres No. 3, and will credit your contract of January 5th, 1928 for the purchase of Lot 31, Avocado Acres No. 3 with the payment of $625.00.

The deed will cover the usual restrictions and conditions, you to pay for the recording of the deed. I am to pay for the certificate to the above described property, you to pay for the continuation of the certificate in your name.

It is understood that this property is being sold subject to the improvement act wherein the paving, etc. is being installed at the present time.

Yours very truly,

Ed Fletcher

Mr. Ed Fletcher:

Please have the deed recorded and send me the certificate of title, together with the expense of recording the deed, you furnishing the certificate of title in your name free and clear except as above stated, and I paying for the continuation of the certificate showing the property in the name of M. F. Baumgardner.

M. F. Baumgardner

The corresponding letter to Baumgardner from Fletcher lists the details of the purchase agreement. (Courtesy of the Mandeville Special Collections Library, University of California, San Diego.)

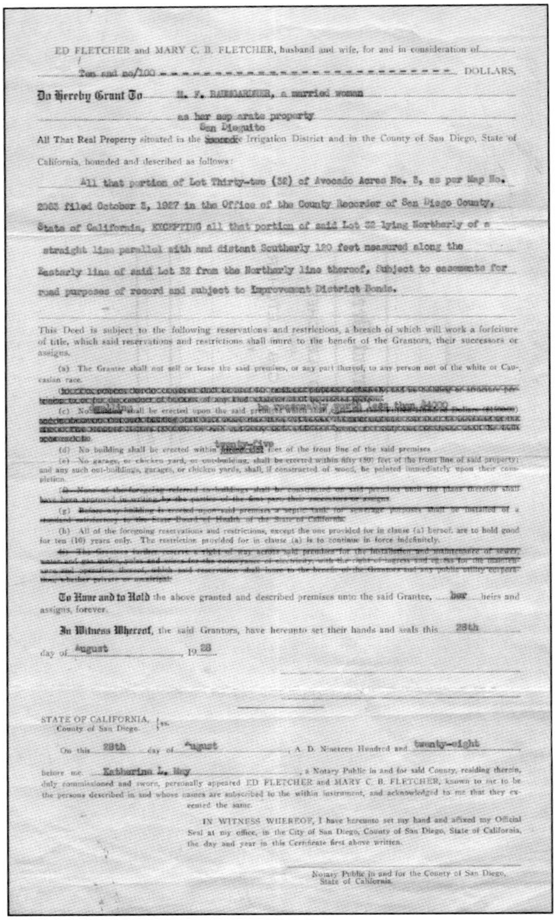

ED FLETCHER and MARY C. B. FLETCHER, husband and wife, for and in consideration of

Ten and no/100 - DOLLARS,

Do Hereby Grant To M. F. BAUMGARDNER, a married woman

as her sep arate property

All That Real Property situated in the San Dieguito Irrigation District and in the County of San Diego, State of California, bounded and described as follows:

All that portion of Lot Thirty-two (32) of Avocado Acres No. 3, as per Map No. 2063 filed October 3, 1927 in the Office of the County Recorder of San Diego County, State of California, EXCEPTING all that portion of said Lot 32 lying Northerly of a straight line parallel with and distant Southerly 120 feet measured along the Easterly line of said Lot 32 from the Northerly line thereof, Subject to easements for road purposes of record and subject to Improvement District Bonds.

This Deed is subject to the following reservations and restrictions, a breach of which will work a forfeiture of title, which said reservations and restrictions shall inure to the benefit of the Grantors, their successors or assigns.

(a) The Grantee shall not sell or lease the said premises, or any part thereof, to any person not of the white or Caucasian race.

[illegible]

(c) No building shall be erected upon the said premises which shall be reasonably worth less than $4000 [illegible]

(d) No building shall be erected within twenty-five feet of the front line of the said premises.

(e) No garage, or chicken yard, or out-building, shall be erected within fifty (50) feet of the front line of said property; and any such out-buildings, garages, or chicken yards, shall, if constructed of wood, be painted immediately upon their completion.

[illegible]

[illegible]

(h) All of the foregoing reservations and restrictions, except the one provided for in clause (a) hereof, are to hold good for ten (10) years only. The restriction provided for in clause (a) is to continue in force indefinitely.

[illegible]

To Have and to Hold the above granted and described premises unto the said Grantee, her heirs and assigns, forever.

In Witness Whereof, the said Grantors, have hereunto set their hands and seals this 28th day of August, 1928

STATE OF CALIFORNIA, County of San Diego. } ss.

On this 28th day of August, A. D. Nineteen Hundred and twenty-eight before me Katharine L. Hay, a Notary Public in and for said County, residing therein, duly commissioned and sworn, personally appeared ED FLETCHER and MARY C. B. FLETCHER, known to me to be the persons described in and whose names are subscribed to the within instrument, and acknowledged to me that they executed the same.

IN WITNESS WHEREOF, I have hereunto set my hand and affixed my Official Seal at my office, in the City of San Diego, County of San Diego, State of California, the day and year in this Certificate first above written.

Notary Public in and for the County of San Diego, State of California.

The land grant for the sale was filed on October 3, 1927, with the county recorder of San Diego. (Courtesy of the Mandeville Special Collections Library, University of California, San Diego.)

This is the front of a grant deed that Ed and Mary Fletcher would send out to prospective buyers. (Courtesy of the Mandeville Special Collections Library, University of California, San Diego.)

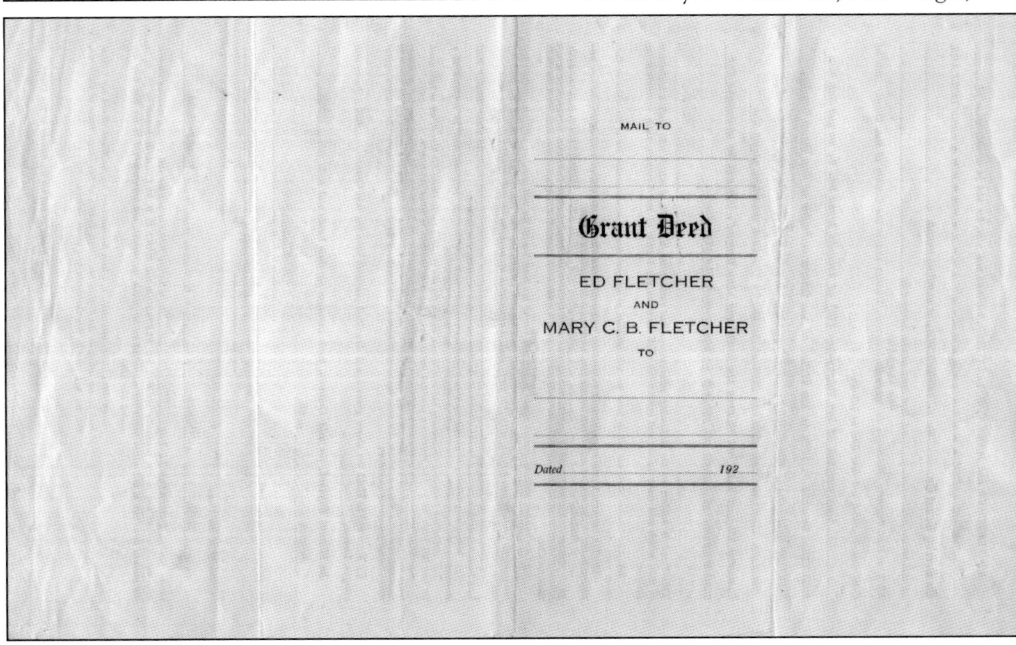

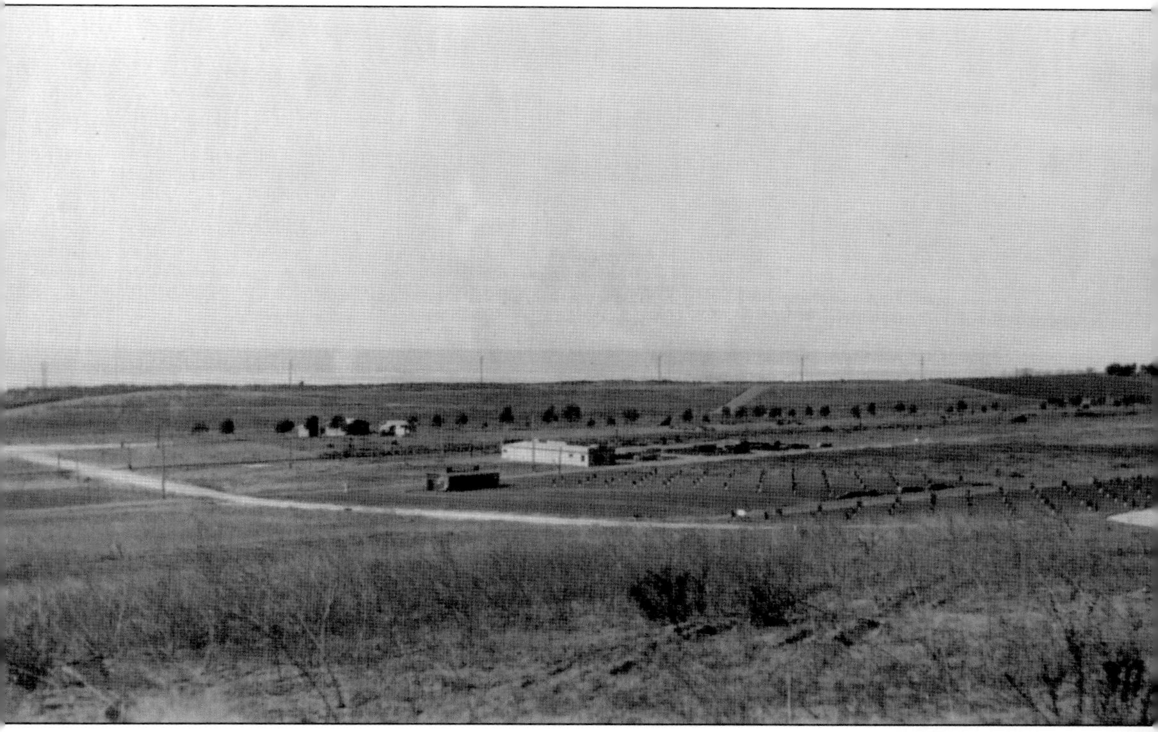

This early-1920s photograph looking west toward the Pacific Ocean shows vast expanses of land, along with several lots Fletcher was attempting to sell. Looking closely, one can spot the railroad and, just beyond that, an unpaved road that is now US Route 101. (Courtesy of the Mandeville Special Collections Library, University of California, San Diego.)

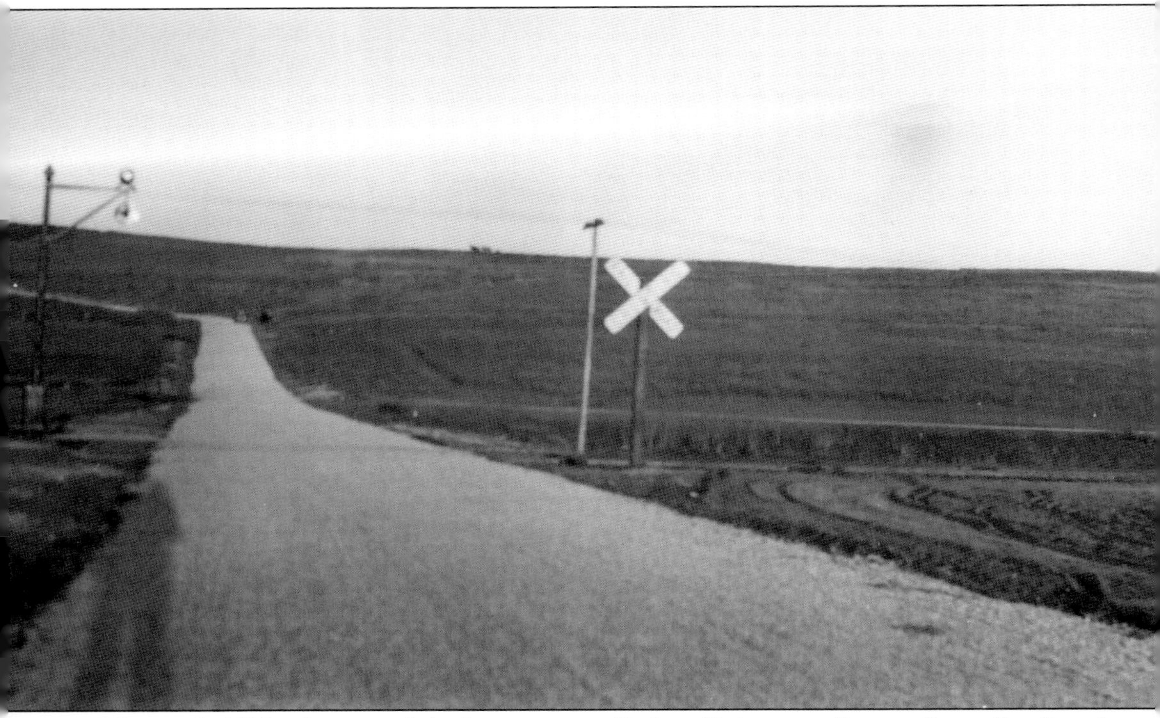

This early-1920s photograph looking east up Skyline Drive, now Lomas Santa Fe, directly corresponds to the 1923 letter that Fletcher wrote to the Atchison, Topeka & Santa Fe Railway Company about the need for an automated flagman, anticipating the population growth that necessitated it. Note in the lower left the shadow of the photographer on the gravel road. (Courtesy of the Mandeville Special Collections Library, University of California, San Diego.)

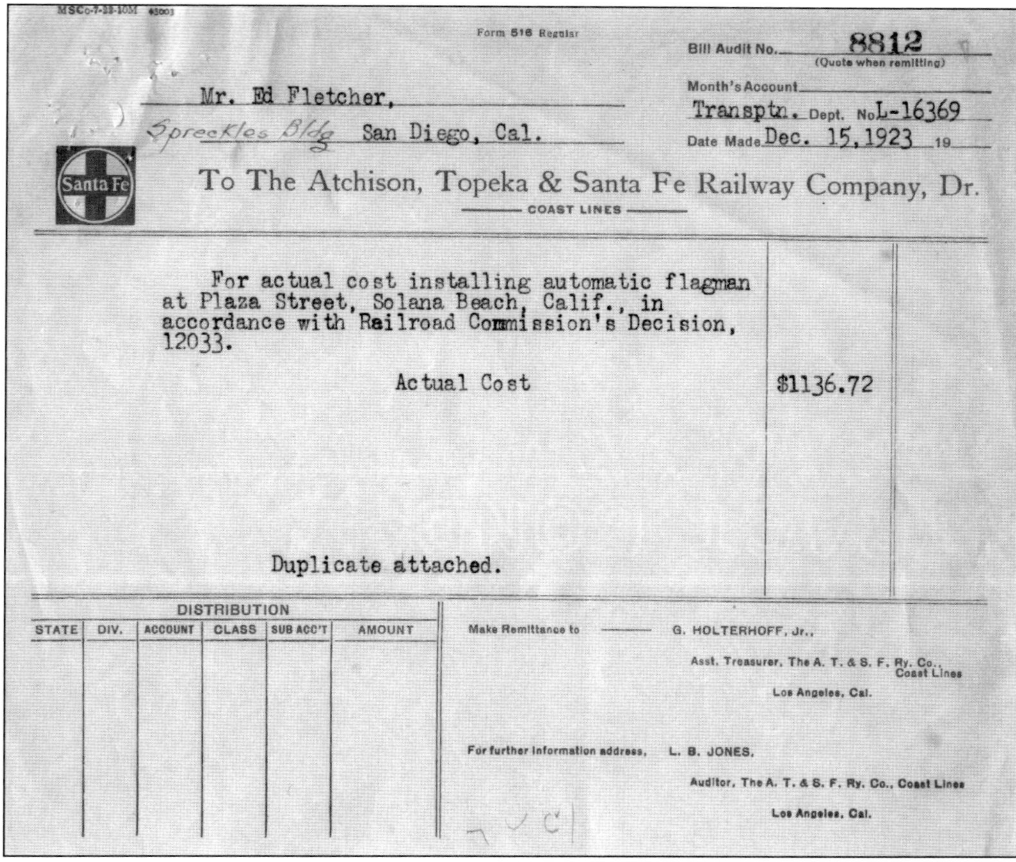

Form 516 Regular

Bill Audit No. 8812 (Quote when remitting)

Month's Account Transptn. Dept. No. L-16369

Date Made Dec. 15, 1923 19

Mr. Ed Fletcher,
Spreckles Bldg San Diego, Cal.

To The Atchison, Topeka & Santa Fe Railway Company, Dr.

COAST LINES

For actual cost installing automatic flagman at Plaza Street, Solana Beach, Calif., in accordance with Railroad Commission's Decision, 12033.

Actual Cost $1136.72

Duplicate attached.

DISTRIBUTION

STATE	DIV.	ACCOUNT	CLASS	SUB ACC'T	AMOUNT

Make Remittance to G. HOLTERHOFF, Jr., Asst. Treasurer, The A. T. & S. F. Ry. Co., Coast Lines, Los Angeles, Cal.

For further information address, L. B. JONES, Auditor, The A. T. & S. F. Ry. Co., Coast Lines, Los Angeles, Cal.

This 1923 letter from the Atchison, Topeka & Santa Fe Railway Company shows the cost of installing an automatic flagman prior to the opening of the railway station the following year. (Courtesy of the Mandeville Special Collections Library, University of California, San Diego.)

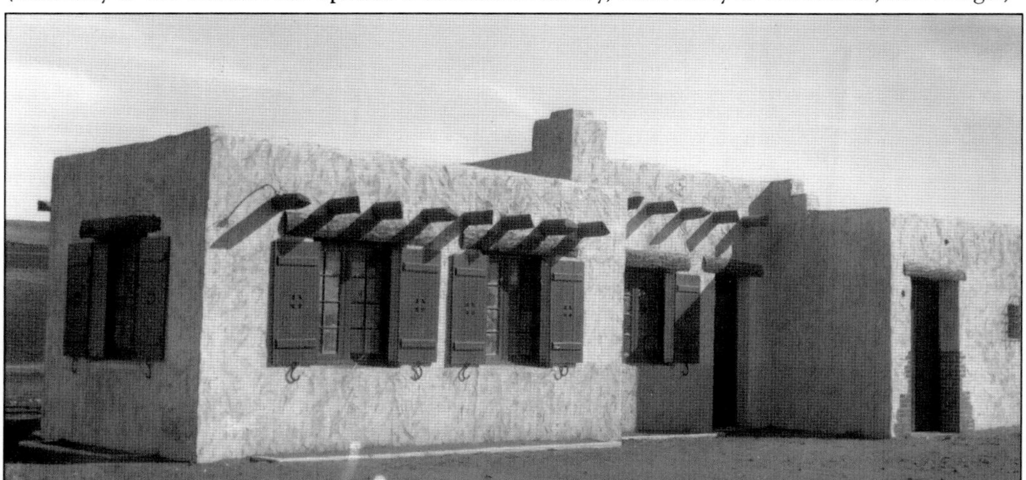

This photograph from 1924 features the newly completed adobe-style train station. The Solana Beach sign had not yet been erected. (Courtesy of the Mandeville Special Collections Library, University of California, San Diego.)

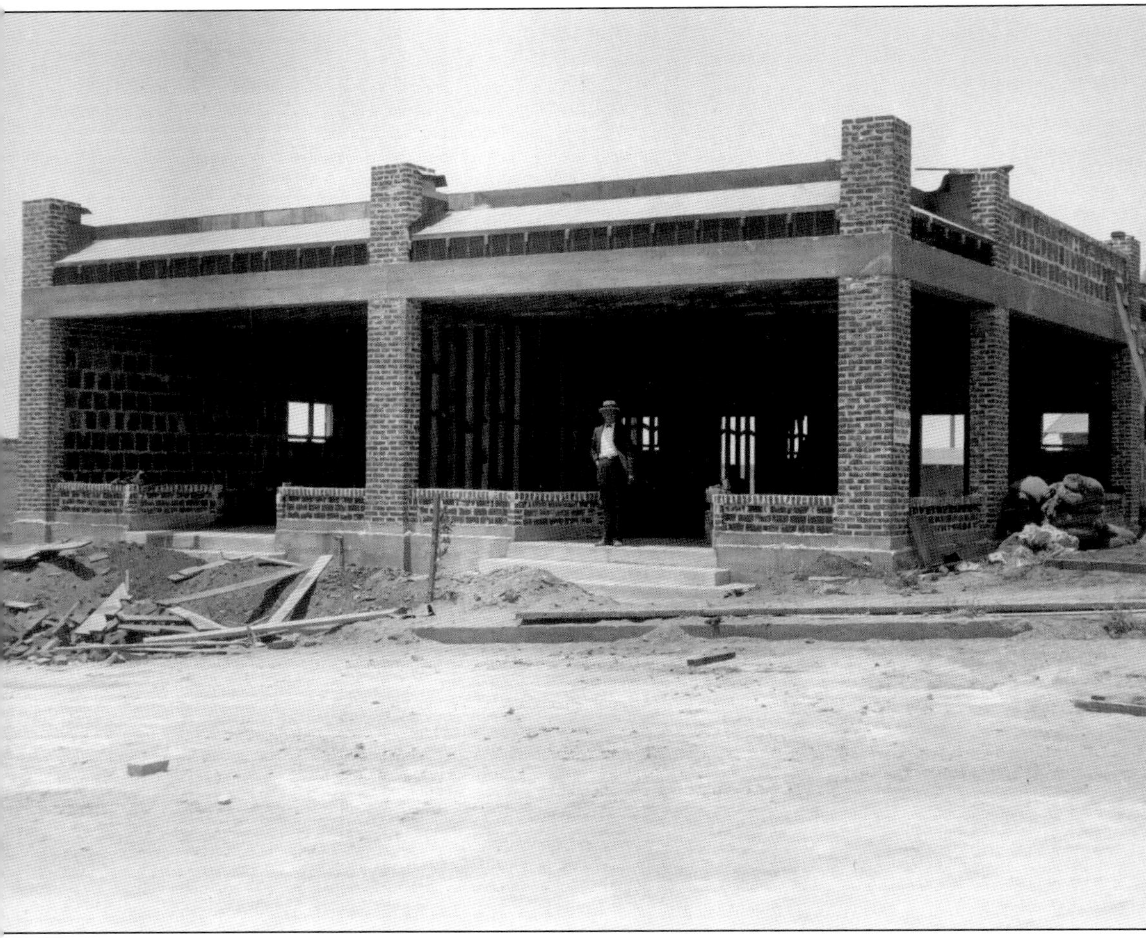

Fletcher stands in the building that would become his office and the bank in the Solana Beach Plaza, at the corner of Highway 101 and Plaza Street. (Courtesy of the Mandeville Special Collections Library, University of California, San Diego.)

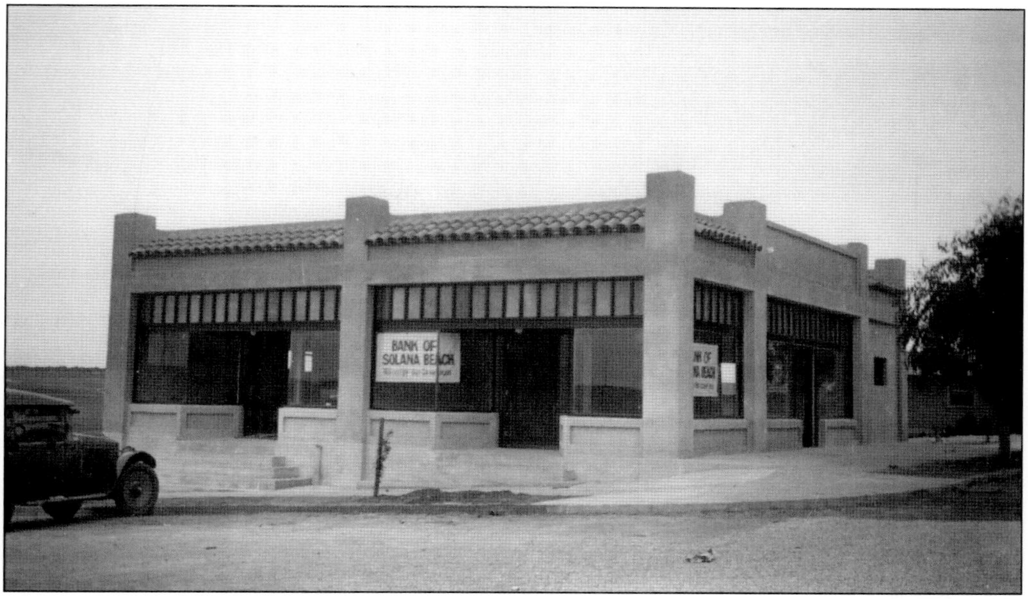

Pictured here is the nearly completed Bank of Solana Beach and Fletcher's office. (Courtesy of the Mandeville Special Collections Library, University of California, San Diego.)

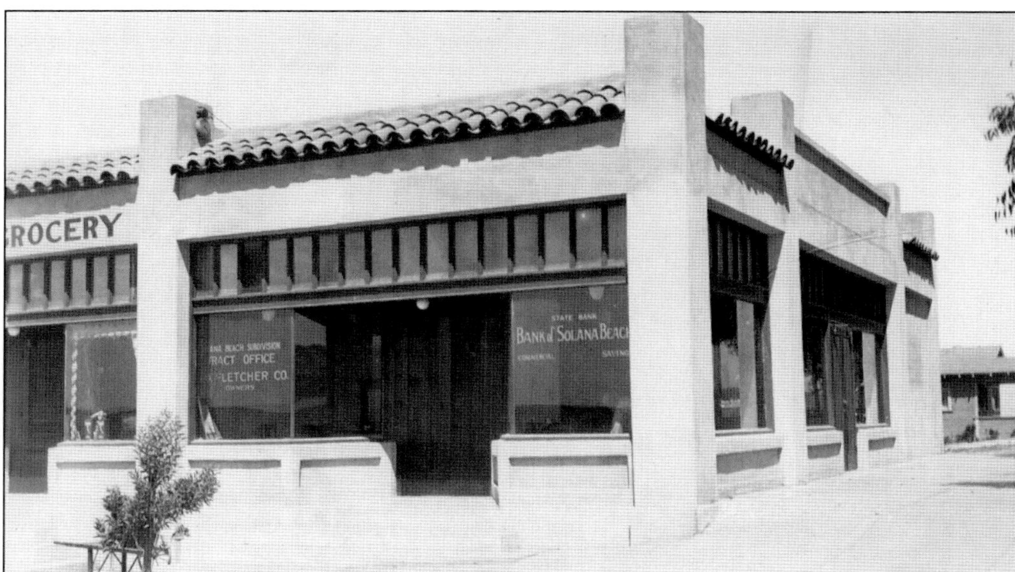

This is another early-1920s photograph of Fletcher's commercial center, including the bank, which he subsequently sold to the Bank of America. (Courtesy of the Mandeville Special Collections Library, University of California, San Diego.)

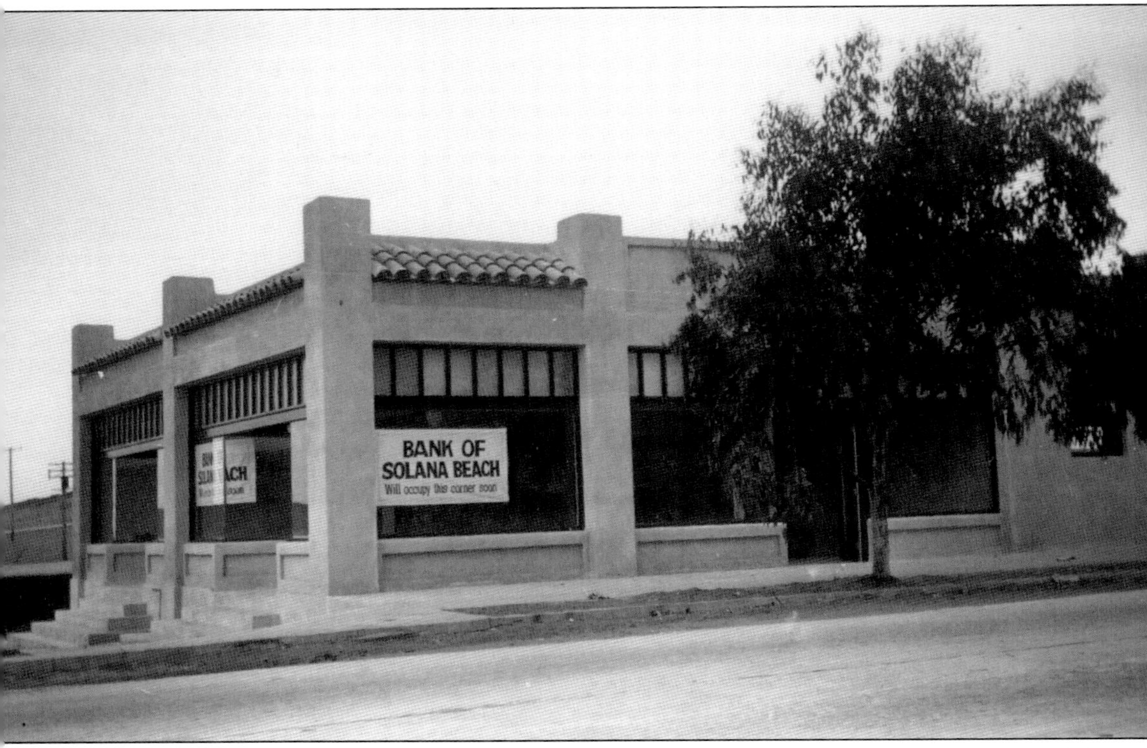

Fletcher's commercial ventures spurred the development of additional businesses in and around this area of Solana Beach. With the onset of the Great Depression, Fletcher subsequently lost a large portion of his real estate holdings, including 800 contiguous acres running to Rancho Santa Fe. (Courtesy of the Mandeville Special Collections Library, University of California, San Diego.)

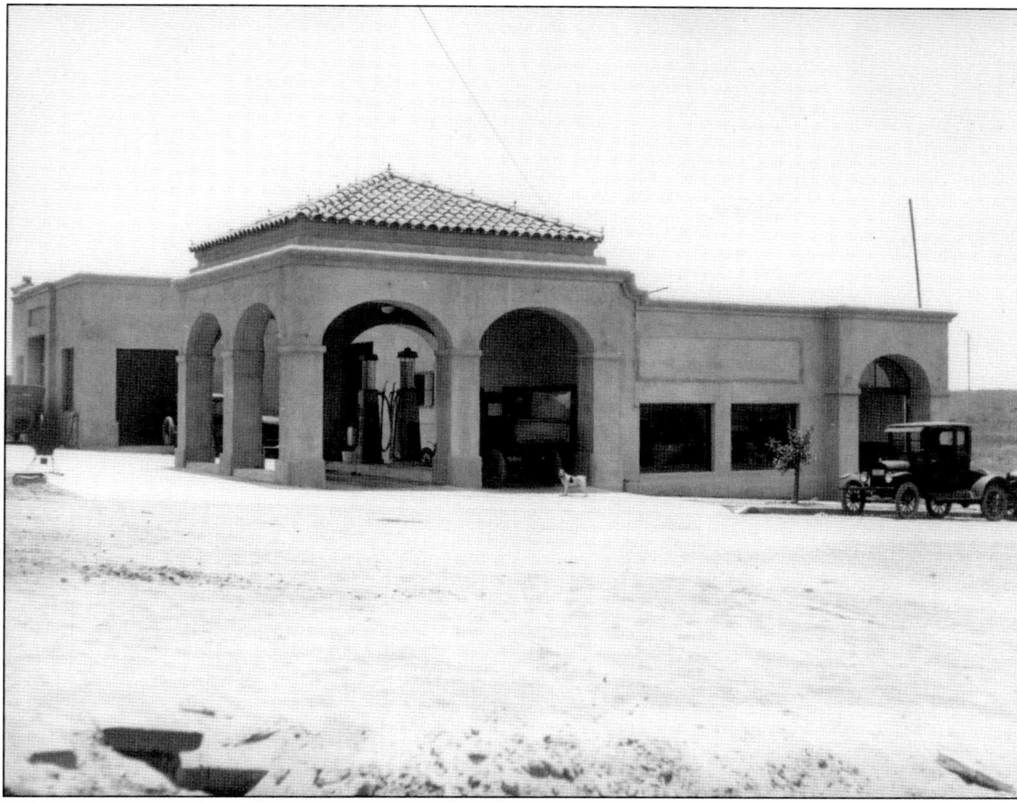

This early-1920s photograph shows the fueling station situated within the plaza. (Courtesy of the Mandeville Special Collections Library, University of California, San Diego.)

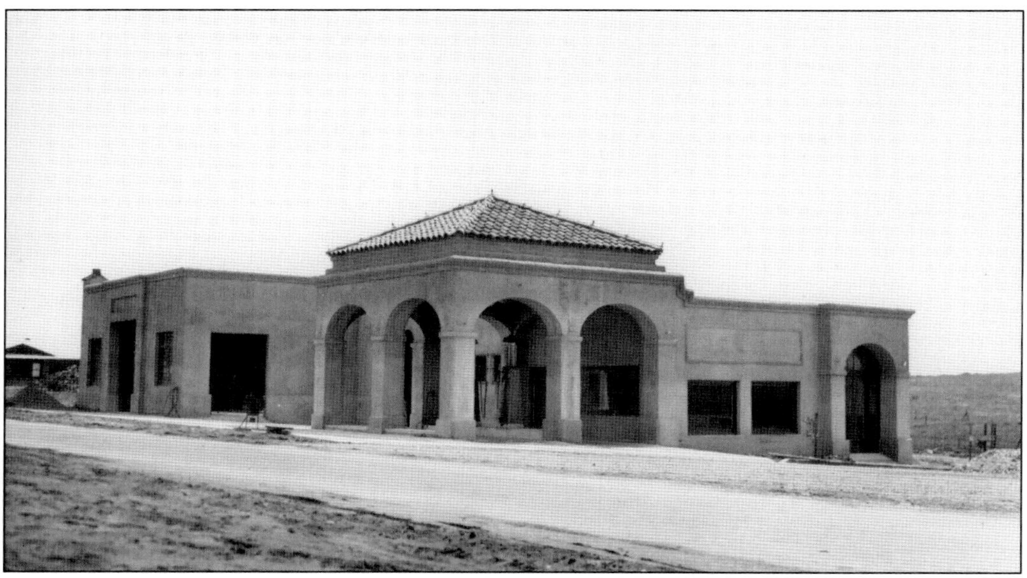

This is another shot of the pumping station at the plaza. (Courtesy of the Mandeville Special Collections Library, University of California, San Diego.)

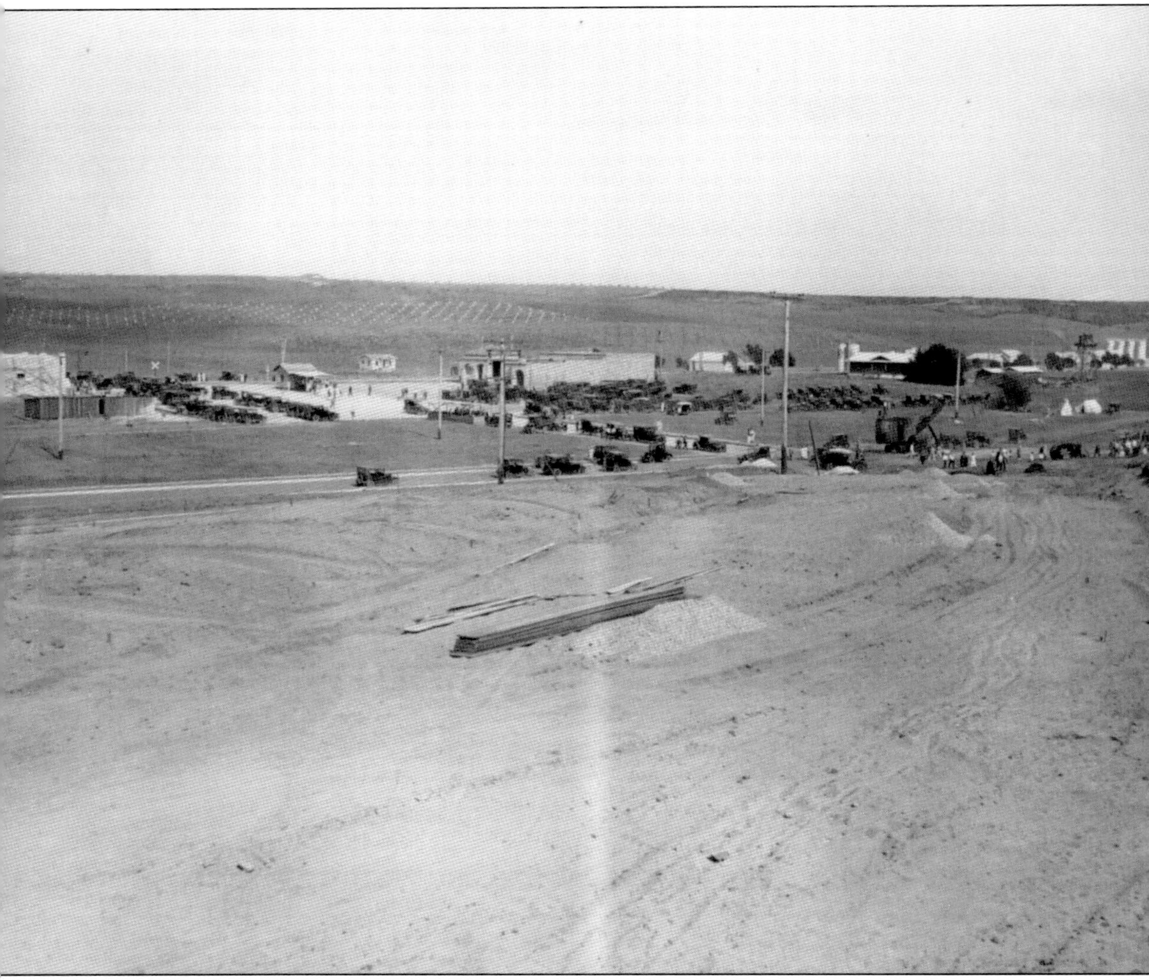

This 1920s photograph, taken from the bluff of what is now Pacific Avenue, captures the ongoing construction of Fletcher Cove, as well as citizens purchasing new lots in the plaza. (Courtesy of the Mandeville Special Collections Library, University of California, San Diego.)

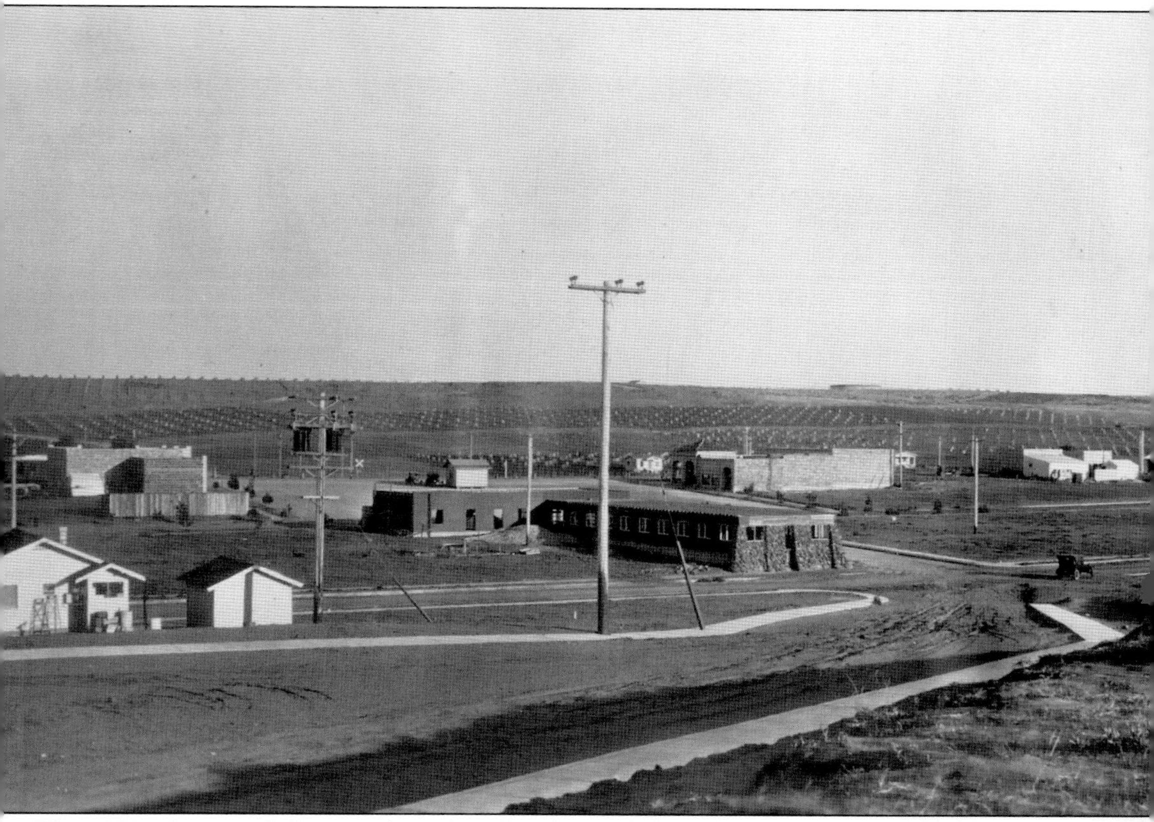

This 1920s photograph features the Solana Beach Hotel, the cobblestone building in the center of the image, on the corner Plaza Street and South Sierra Avenue. The view looks down from Pacific Avenue where the Solana Beach Community Center now stands. To the far right are four white posts, which marked what would become the entrance to Fletcher Cove. (Courtesy of Mandeville Special Collections Library, University of California, San Diego.)

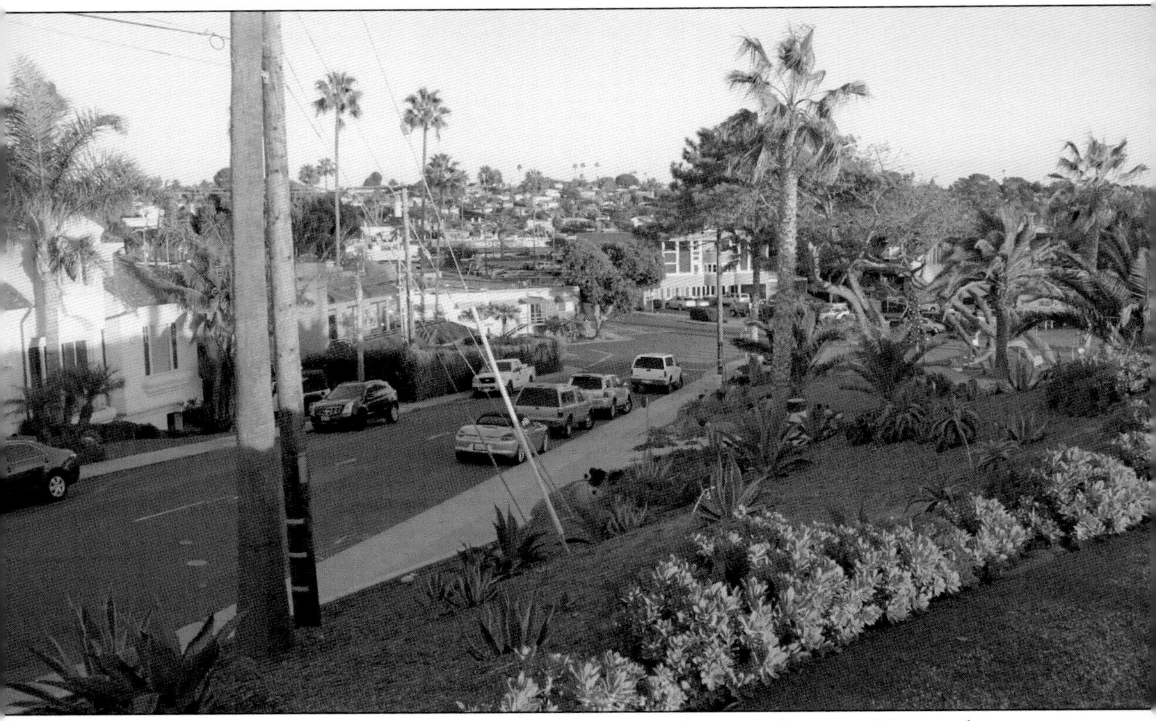

Taken from roughly the same angle as the previous photograph some 70 years later, one can still see the Solana Beach Hotel, which now houses the chamber of commerce. (Courtesy of the Julianne Eggold.)

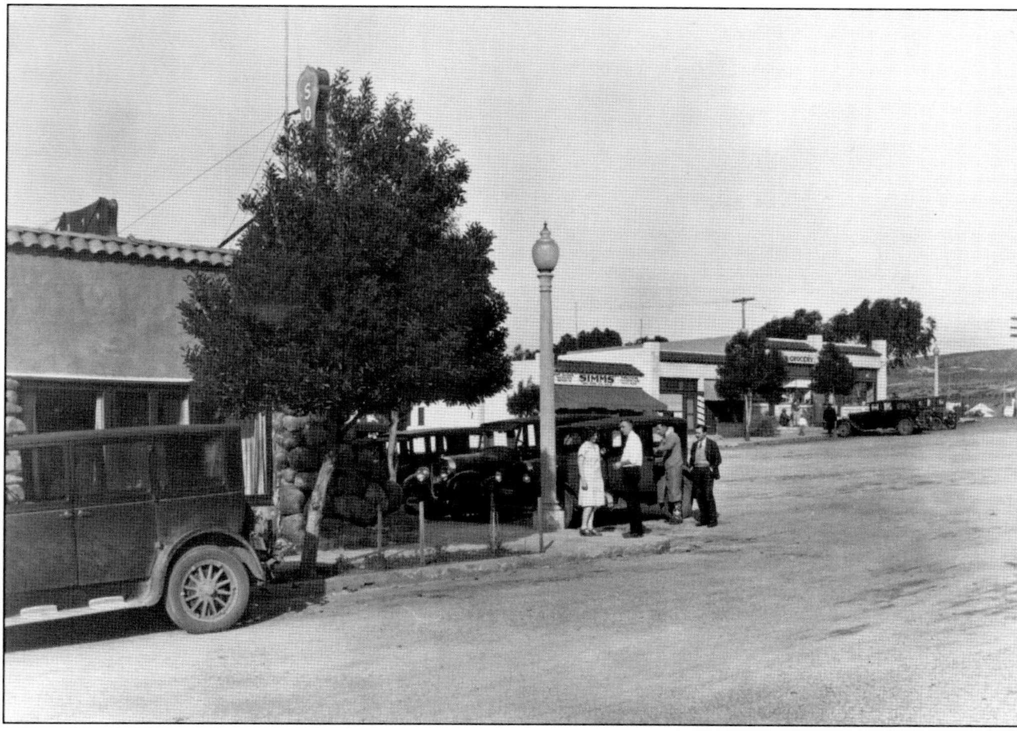

This late-1920s shot, taken just south of Highway 101 and looking northeast, shows the Solana Beach Hotel on the left and the plaza. (Courtesy of the Mandeville Special Collections Library, University of California, San Diego.)

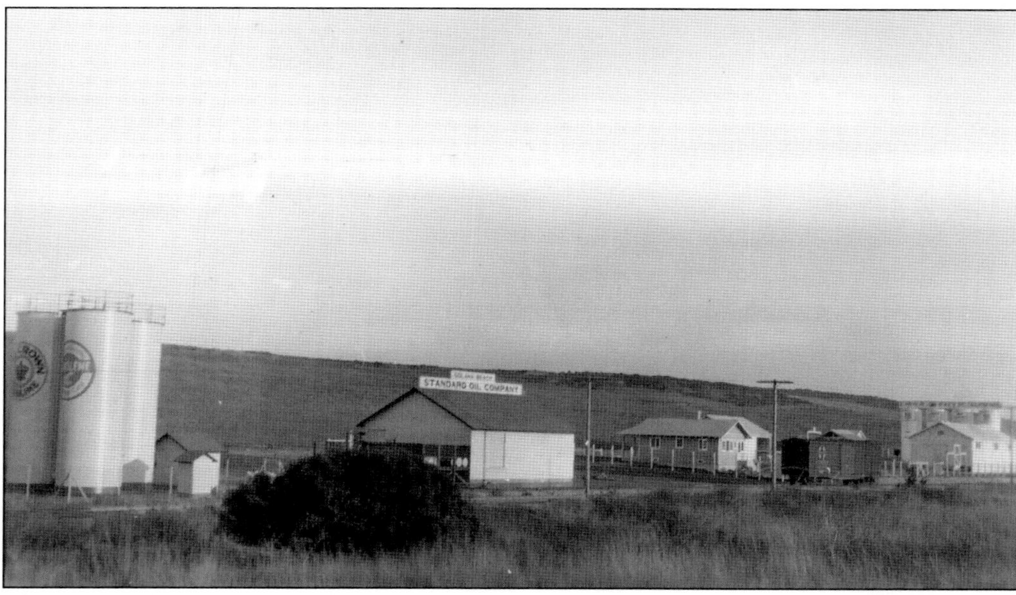

This 1920s photograph, which looks south along South Cedros Drive, reveals how various corporate industries were beginning to settle in Solana Beach, Standard Oil being one of them. Wedged between Highway 101 and the rail line, these structures sat just south of the original Solana Beach Train Station, where the oil could easily be offloaded. (Courtesy of the Mandeville Special Collections Library, University of California, San Diego.)

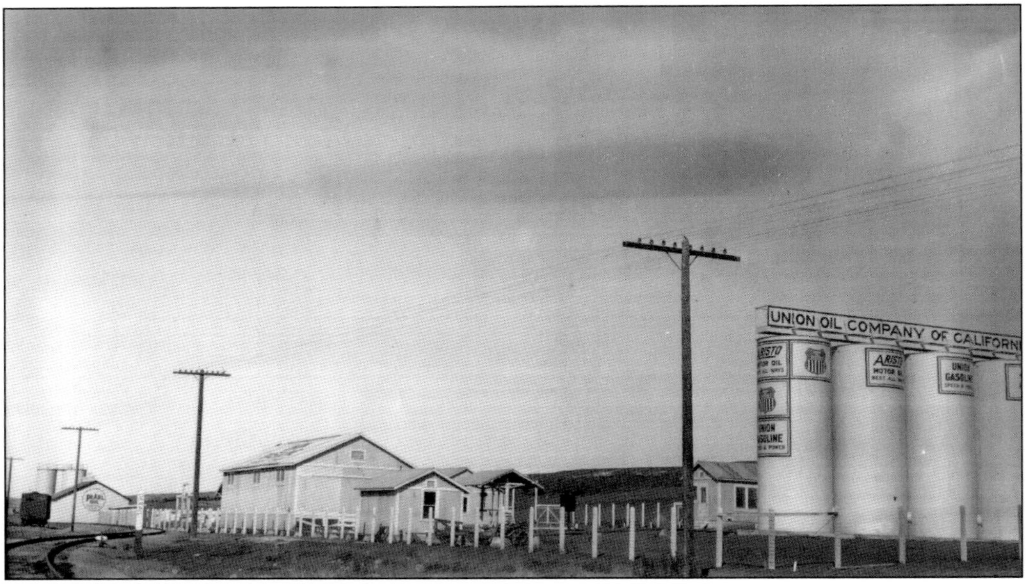

Pictured here is the Union Oil Company of California, situated along the tracks. (Courtesy of the Mandeville Special Collections Library, University of California, San Diego.)

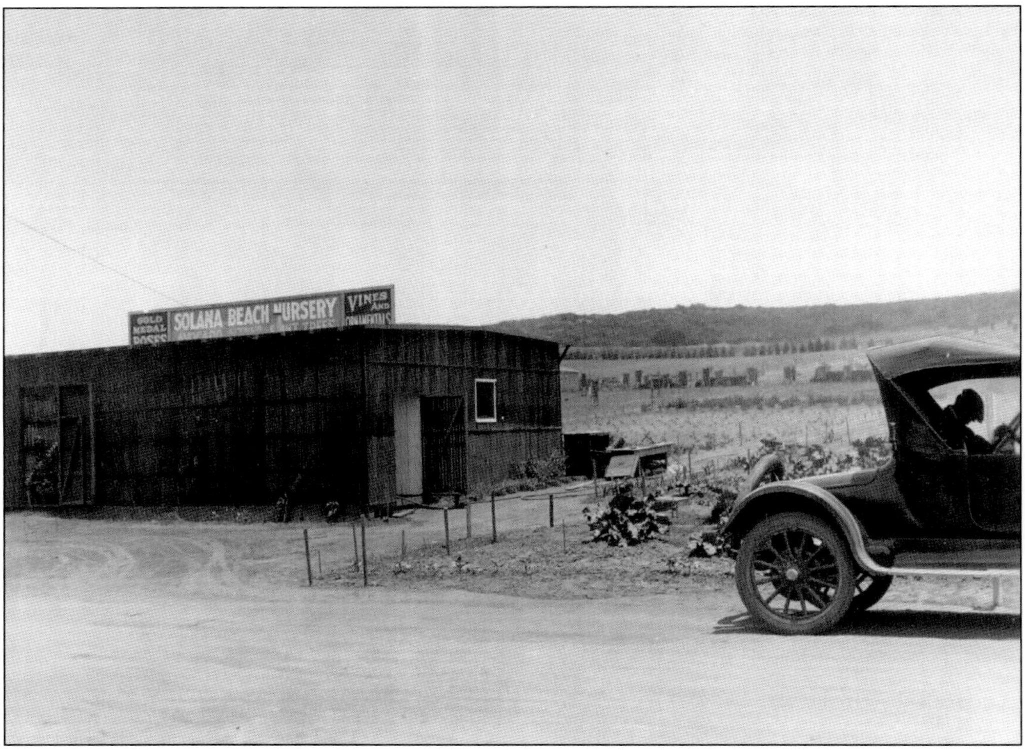

Solana Beach was touted as a rural agricultural suburb of San Diego to prospective buyers. The local nursery in this 1920s photograph offered seeds and other agricultural products for prospective farmers. Note the vast amount of open land looking east. (Courtesy of the Mandeville Special Collections Library, University of California, San Diego.)

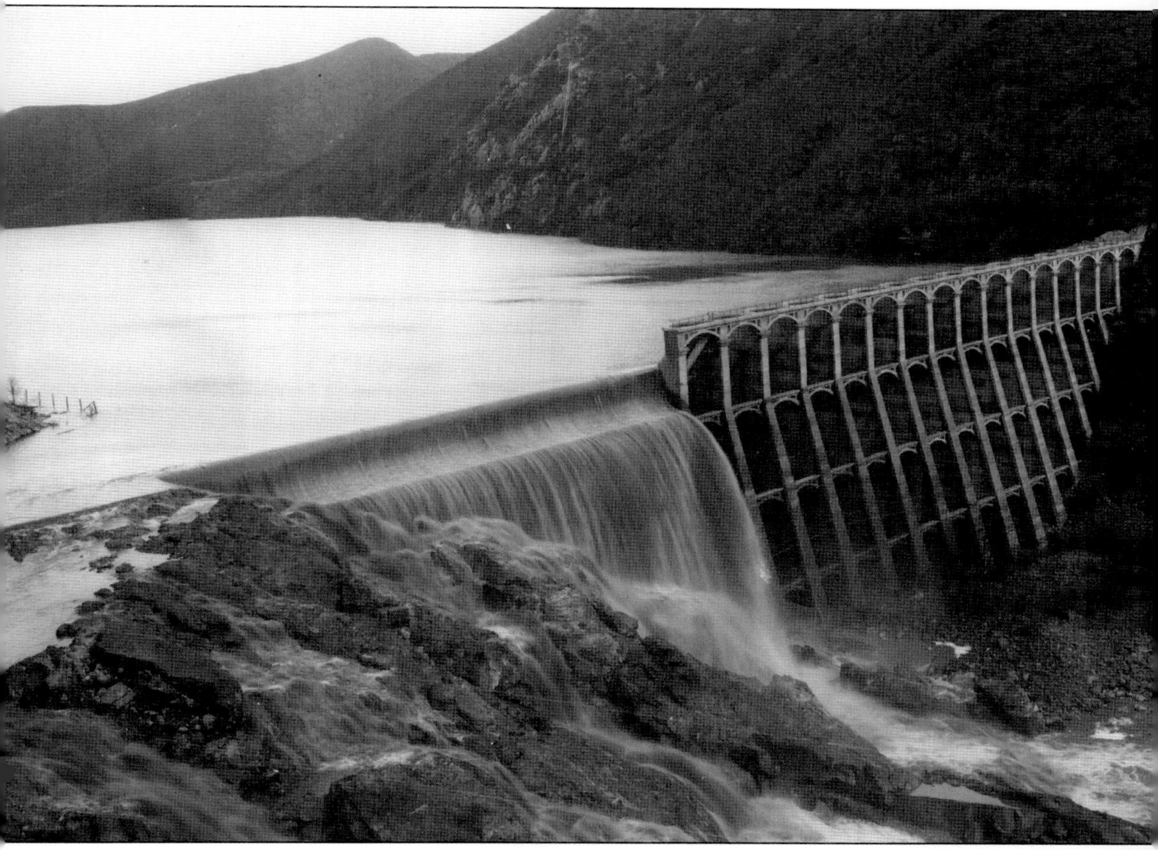

Ed Fletcher was instrumental in developing the majority of San Diego County's water systems, including creating Lake Hodges, a man-made reservoir that sits on the San Dieguito River. The lake was named after William Hodges, then vice president of the railroad company. The Lake Hodges Dam, constructed by the San Dieguito Mutual Water Company/Santa Fe Land Improvement Company and financed by the Santa Fe Railroad, was completed in 1918 and immediately began to bring water to all areas of North County, including Solana Beach. In 1922, Colonel Fletcher purchased 201 acres at $200 per acre from farmer George H. Jones to develop the town of Solana Beach.

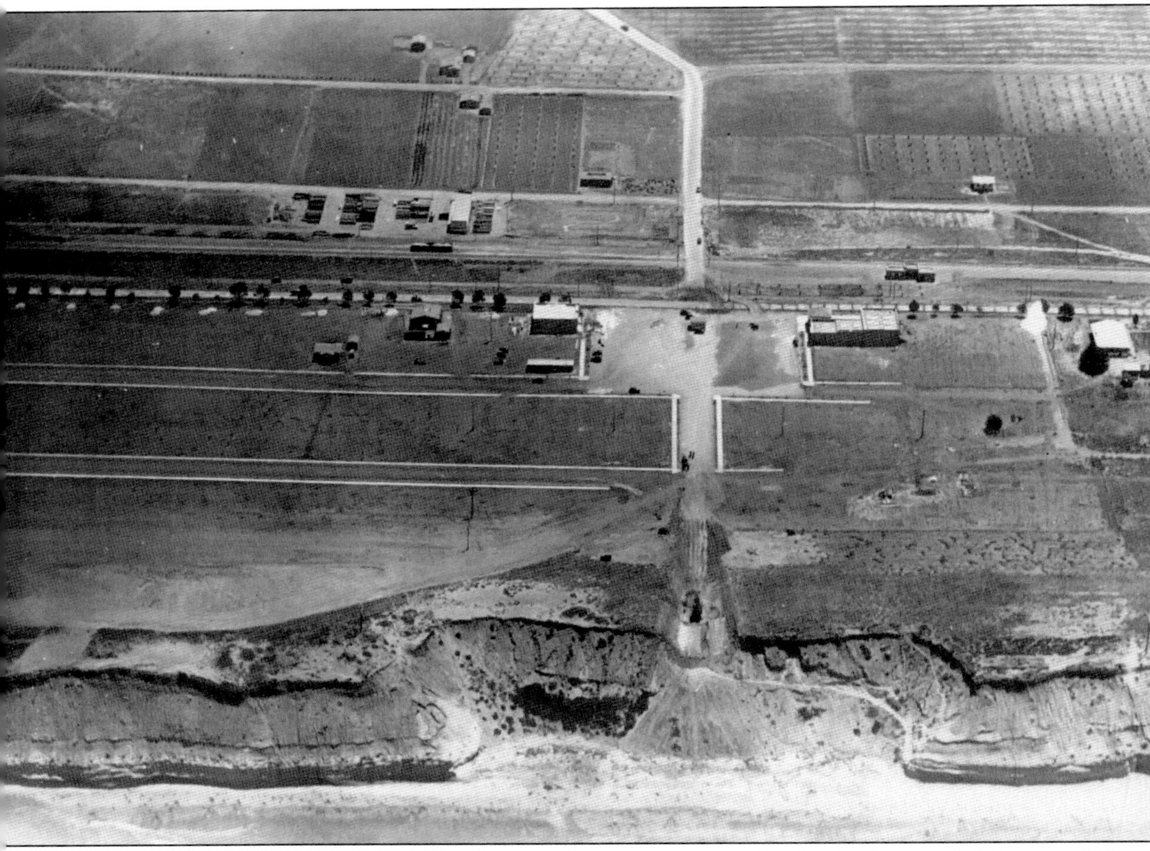

This aerial view features Fletcher Cove under construction. In the background, Highway 101 is now a paved road. Skyline Drive, which became Lomas Santa Fe east of Highway 101 and Plaza Street west of the 101, is still a dusty, dirt road. The train station is just southeast of the large plaza area. (Courtesy of the Mandeville Special Collections Library, University of California, San Diego.)

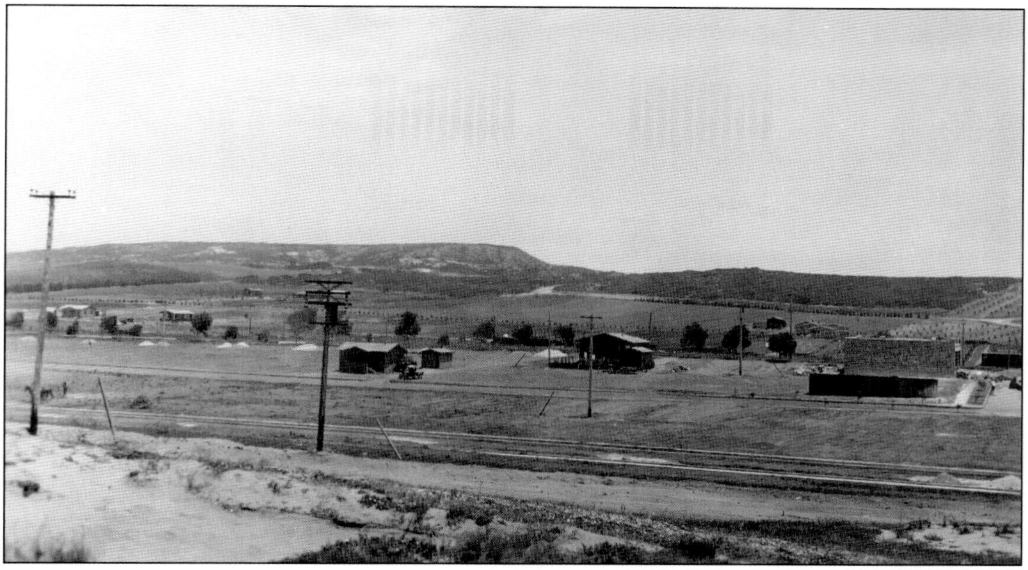

This photograph looks slightly northeast, gleaning the northern section of the plaza to the right. (Courtesy of the Mandeville Special Collections Library, University of California, San Diego.)

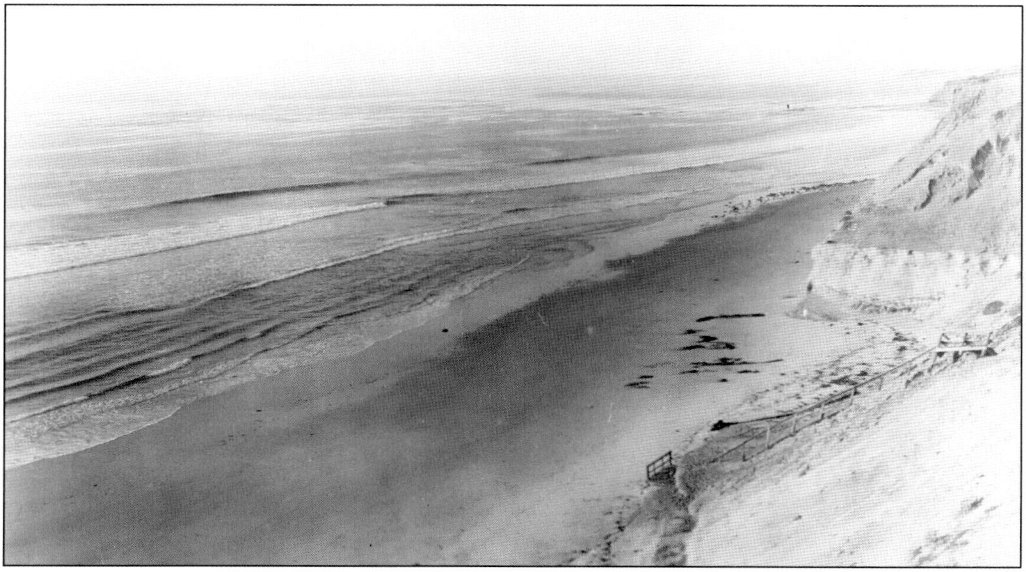

This is an early 1920s photograph of what would become Fletcher Cove. Note the wooden staircase to access the beach. (Courtesy of the Mandeville Special Collections Library, University of California, San Diego.)

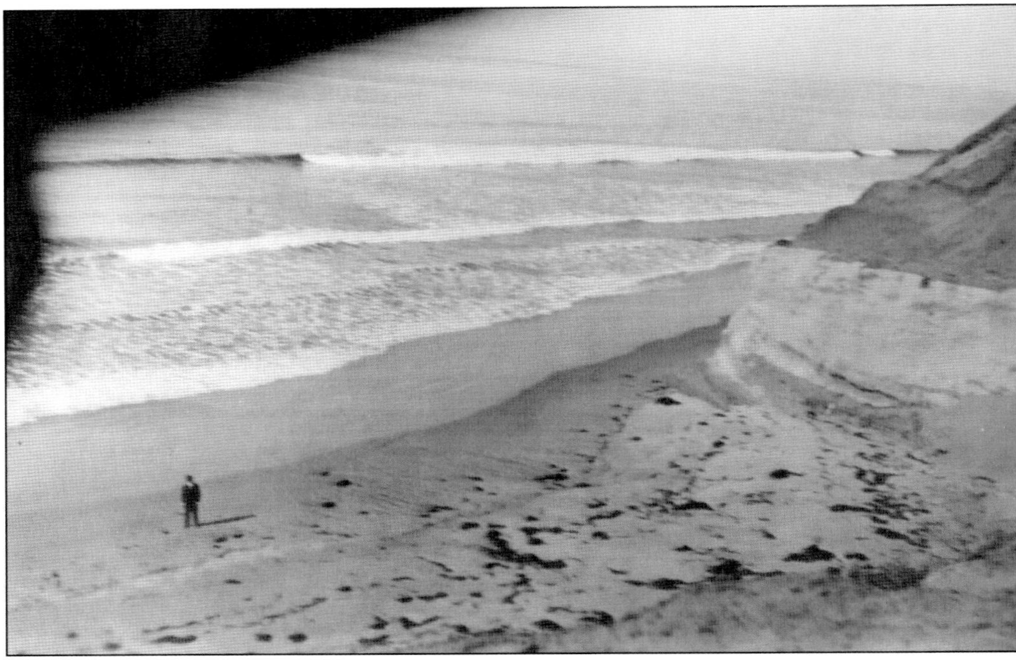

This view looks northwest from the embankment before the construction of the cove was completed. (Courtesy of the Mandeville Special Collections Library, University of California, San Diego.)

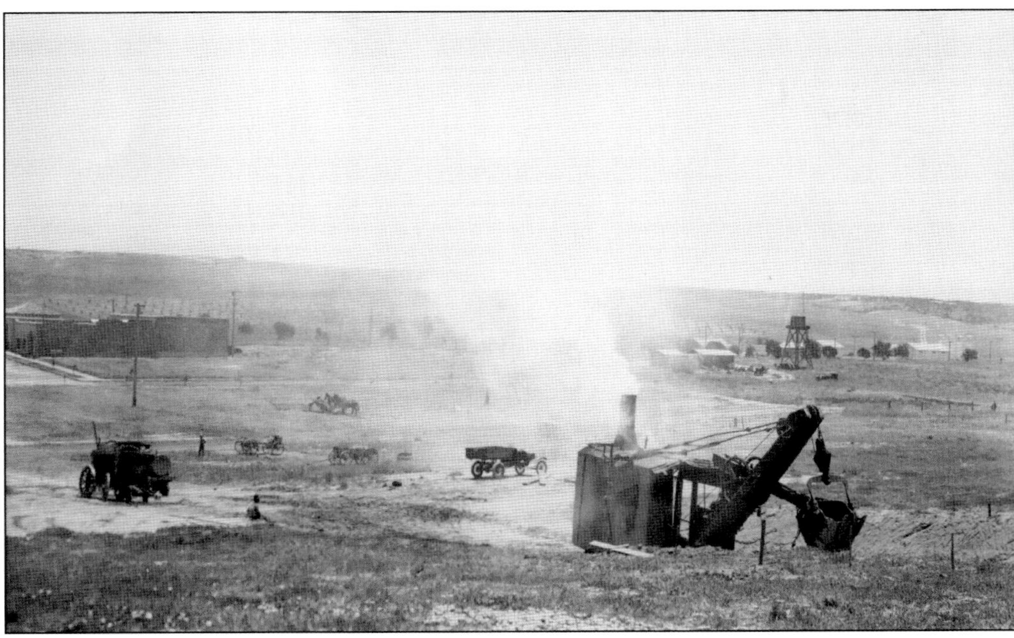

This 1924 photograph, looking southeast, shows a steam shovel carving out the pathway to the beach and what would become Fletcher Cove. (Courtesy of the Mandeville Special Collections Library, University of California, San Diego.)

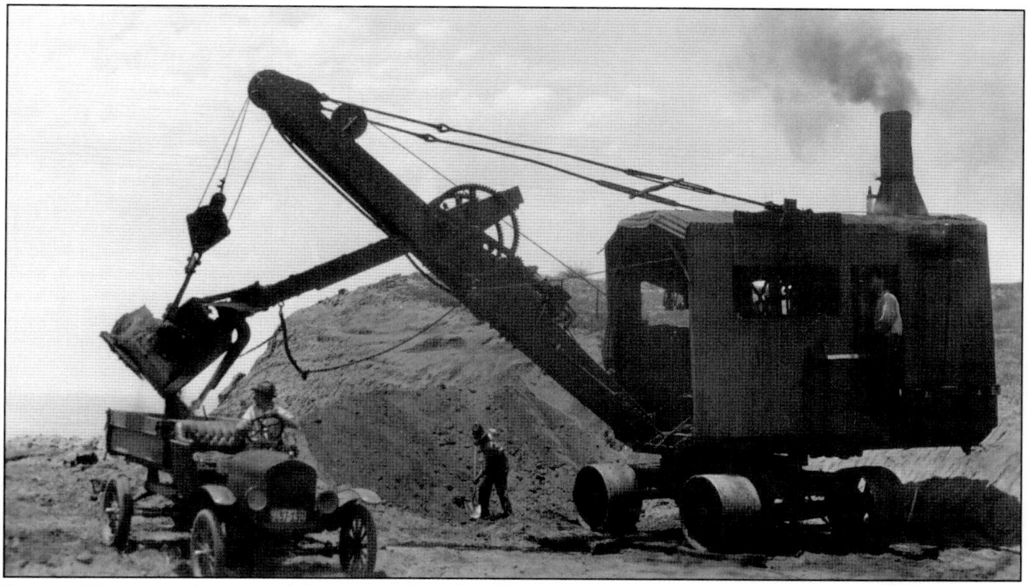
Pictured here is a close-up of the steam shovel and men working on the cove construction. (Courtesy of the Mandeville Special Collections Library, University of California, San Diego.)

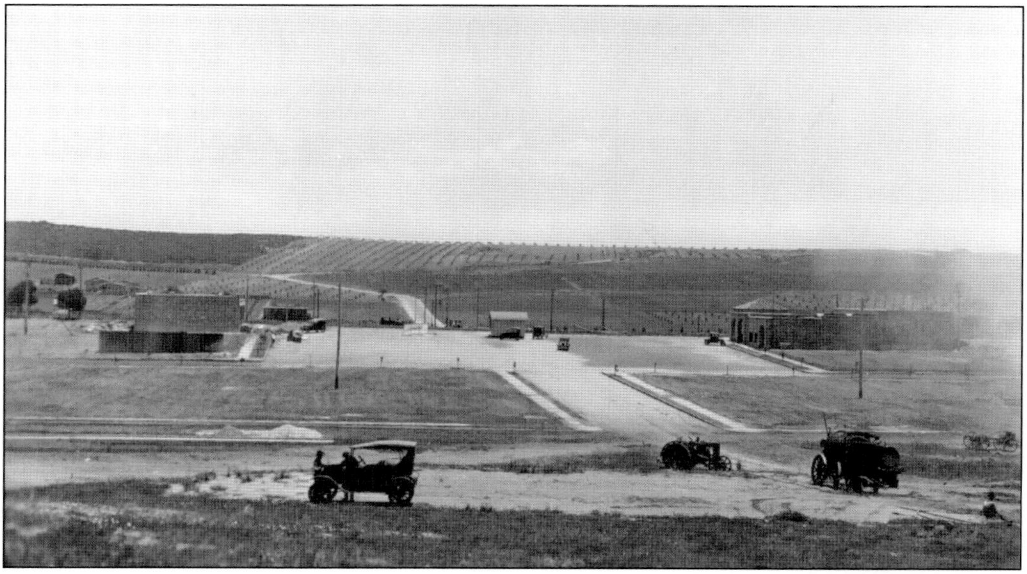
This photograph looks directly east past the plaza, Highway 101, and the train station. In the center of the image is the plaza with Fletcher's temporary real estate office that was used on opening day. (Courtesy of the Mandeville Special Collections Library, University of California, San Diego.)

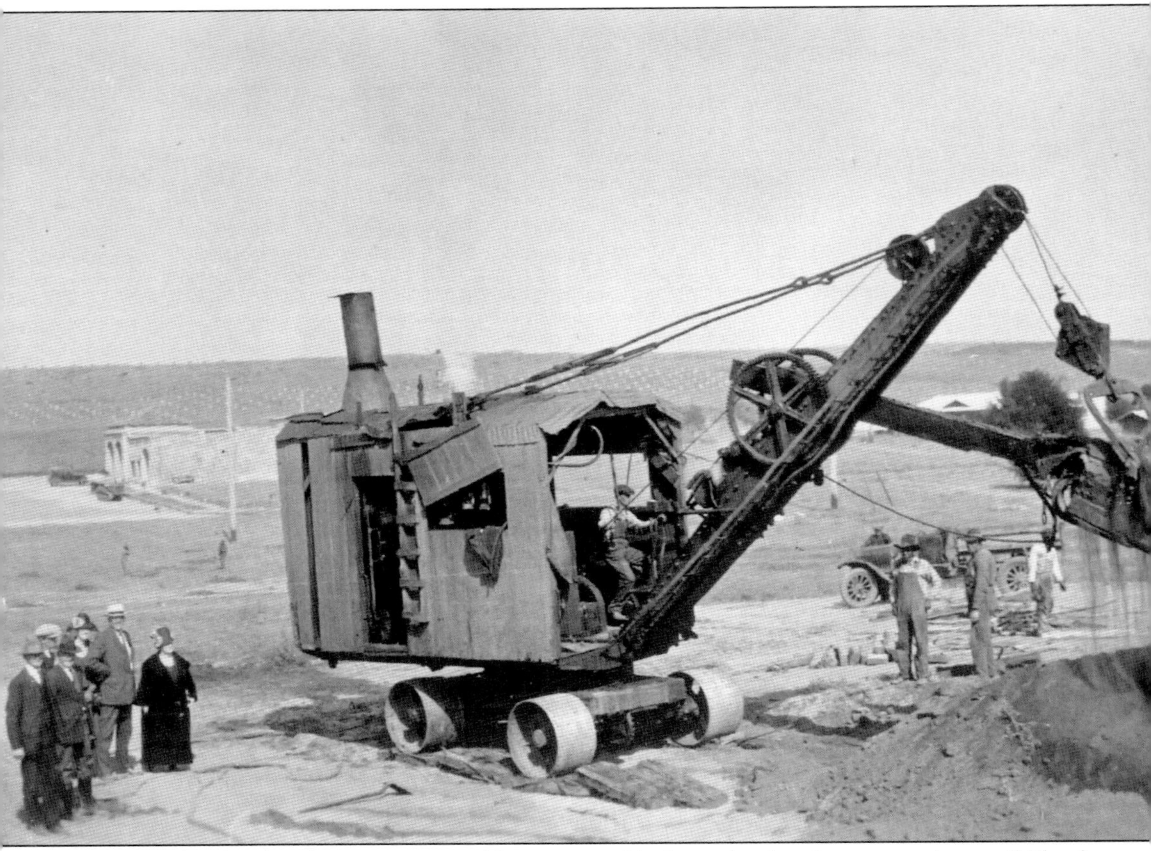

Ironically, the shoreline was not visible or accessible from this beach community until Fletcher developed a plan. Fletcher and his wife, Mary, are pictured here in 1924 with a small group of people observing a steam shovel lifting the first scoops of dirt that would eventually lead to a cut in the bluffs and formation of the beach. Using the water from Lake Hodges Dam, it took one man using hydraulic pressure three months to melt away the soil to create Fletcher Cove. (Courtesy of the Mandeville Special Collections Library, University of California, San Diego.)

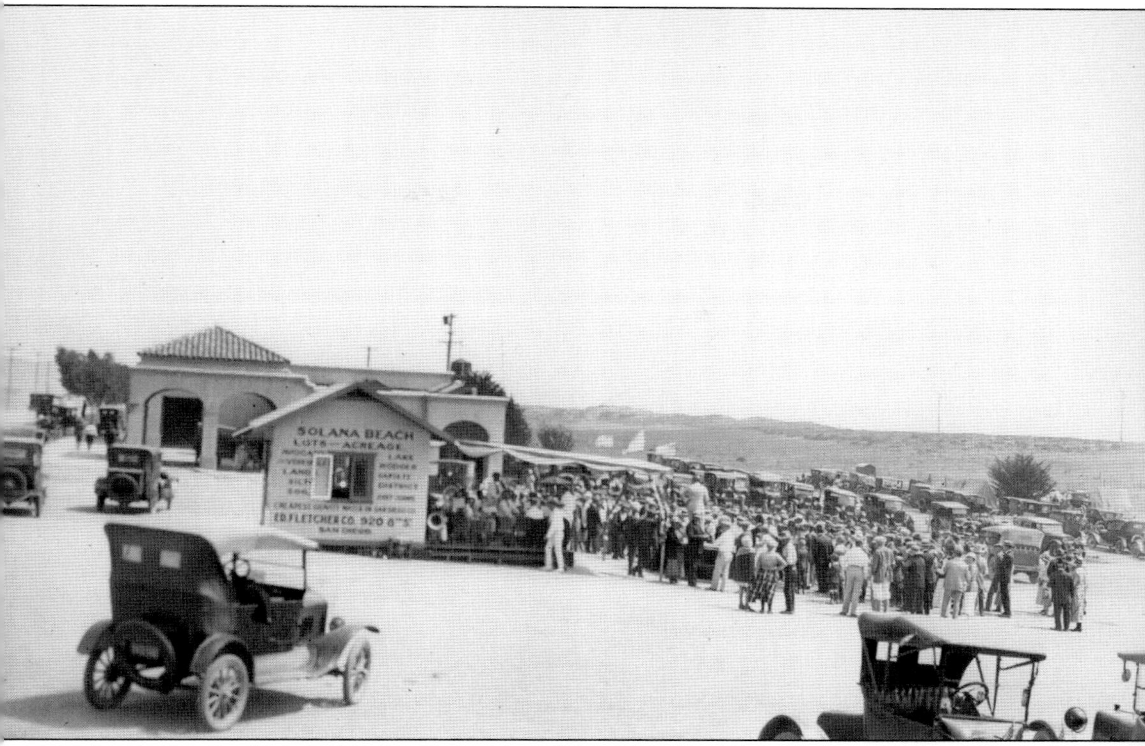

This bustling scene depicts the plaza on opening day and a prime opportunity for the enterprising Fletcher to advertise his lots for sale. (Courtesy of the Mandeville Special Collections Library, University of California, San Diego.)

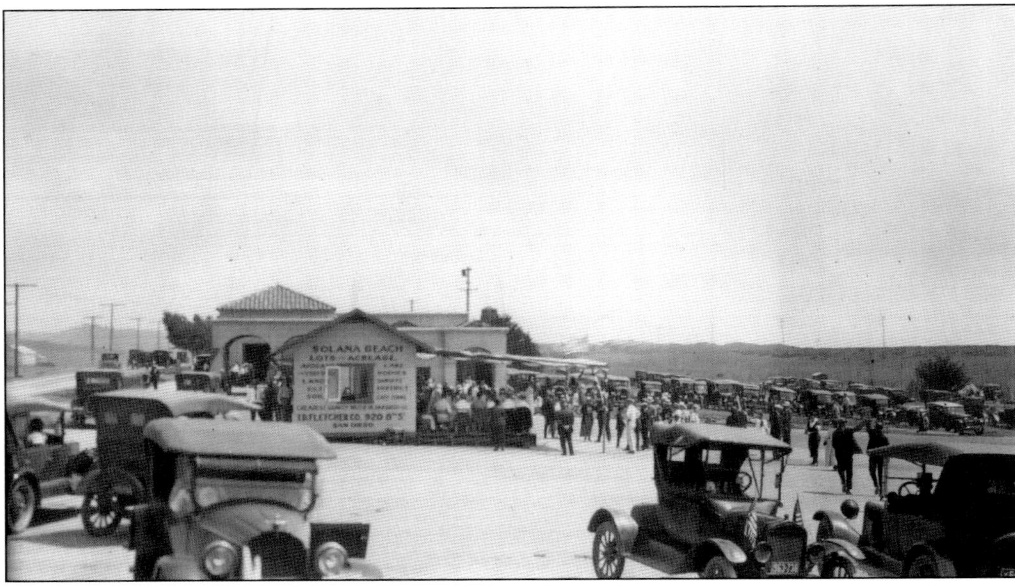

The plaza's opening day attracted locals and people from all over San Diego and Orange Counties. (Courtesy of the Mandeville Special Collections Library, University of California, San Diego.)

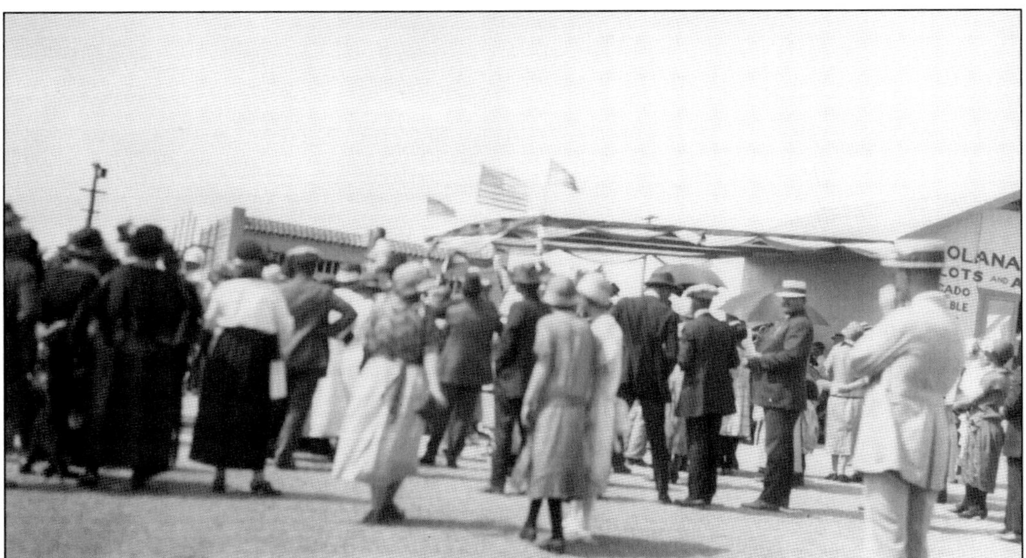

Another view of the plaza opening shows a close-up of the well-dressed crowd, the men smartly attired in suits and boater hats and the women in lightweight frocks suitable for the Mediterranean climate of Southern California. (Courtesy of the Mandeville Special Collections Library, University of California, San Diego.)

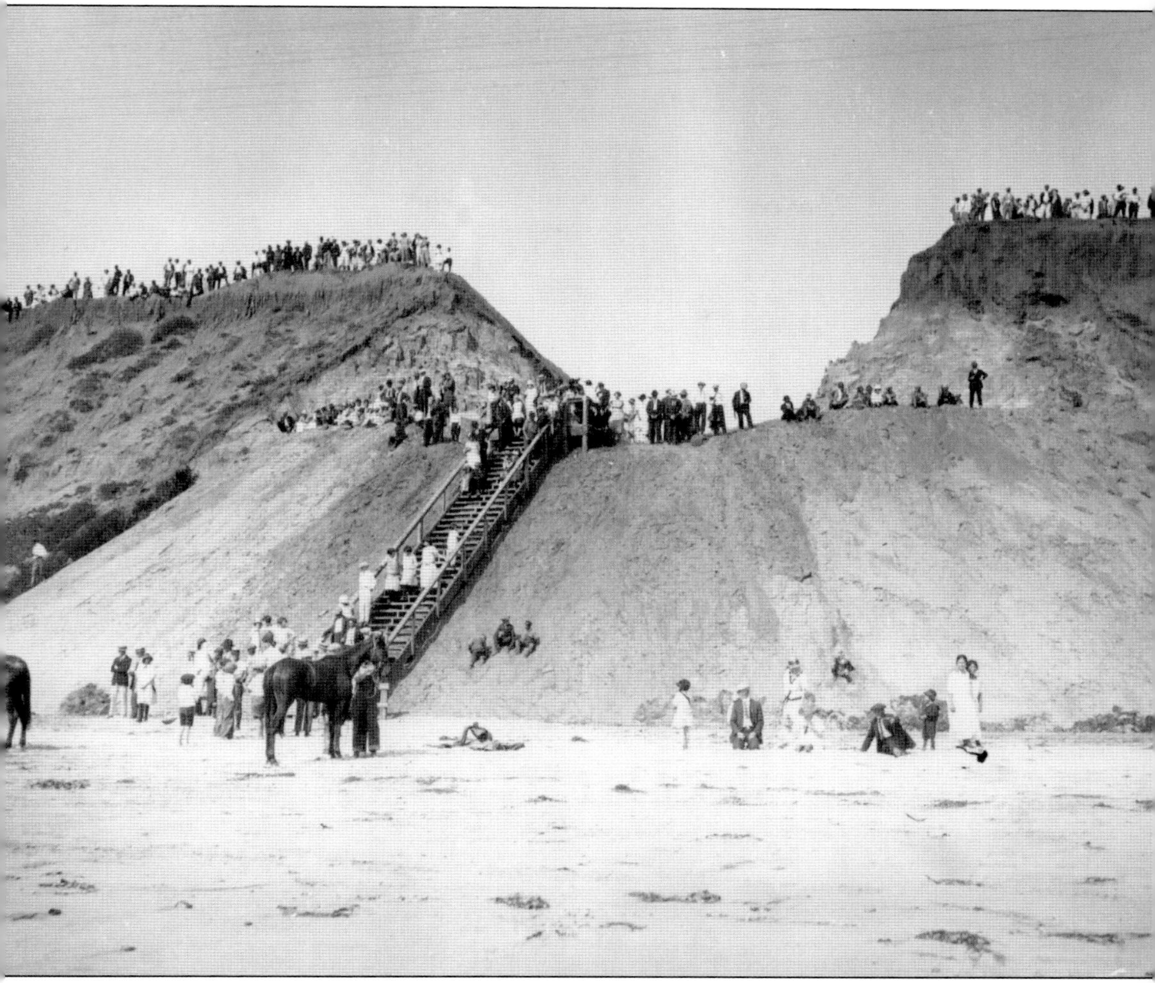

On July 4, 1924, the official opening of Fletcher Cove was celebrated. Sydney Chaplin, Charlie Chaplin's brother and an Encinitas resident, was one of the celebrities in attendance. Ceremonial speeches were given at a grandstand in the plaza before everyone relocated to the beach for the actual celebration. The glamorous festivities, with celebrities and horse races along the beach, drew hundreds of people from all over the county who spent the day picnicking on the shore. (Courtesy of the Mandeville Special Collections Library, University of California, San Diego.)

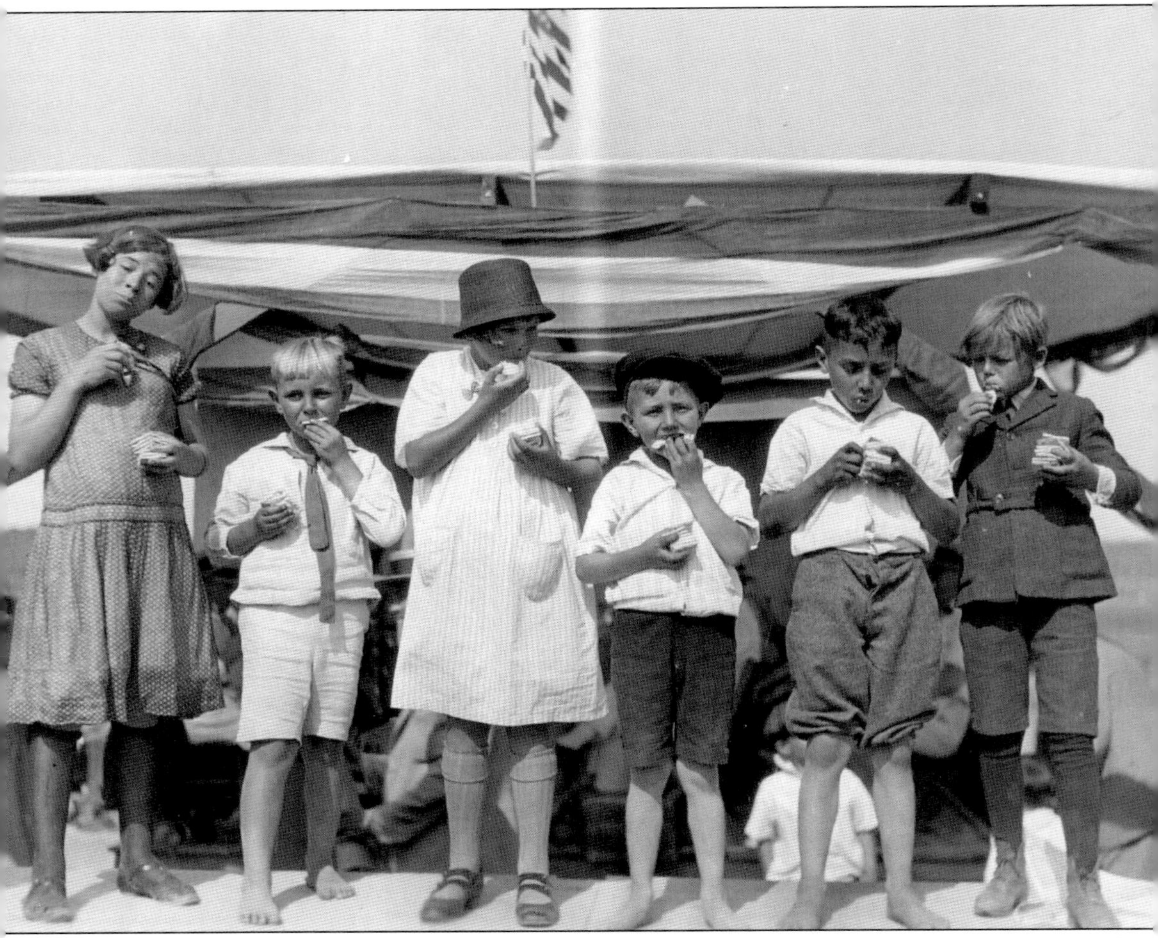

Children enjoy a tasty treat during the Fourth of July festivities in Solana Beach. (Courtesy of the Mandeville Special Collections Library, University of California, San Diego.)

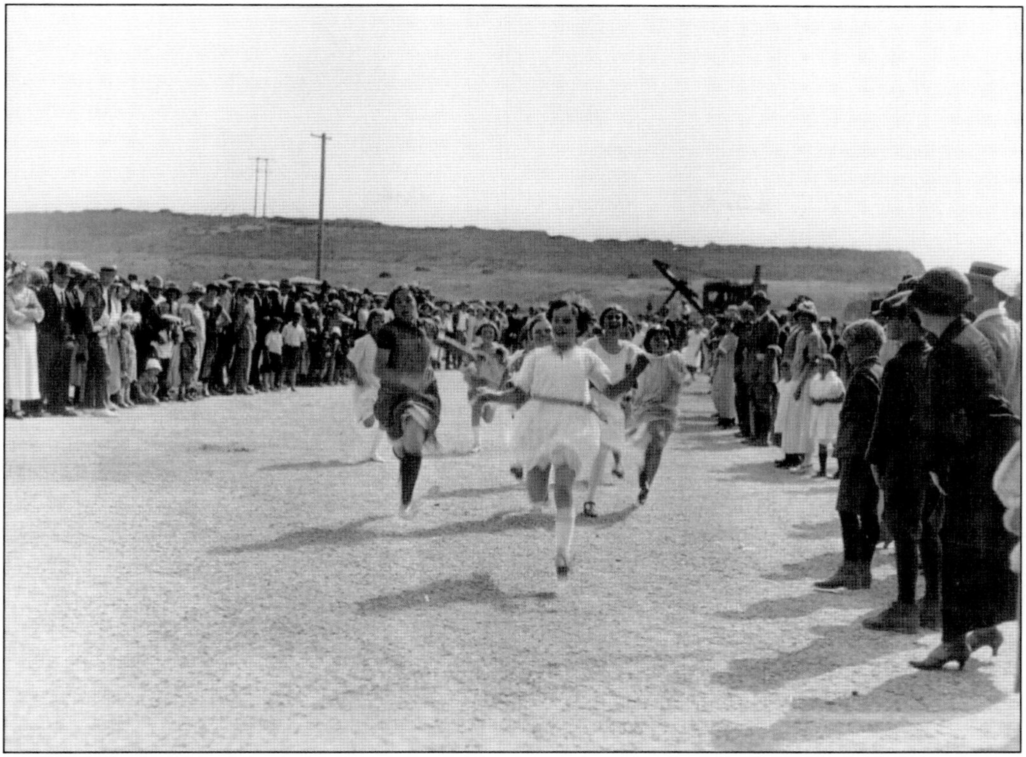

Fourth of July festivities included a footrace east along what is now Lomas Santa Fe. (Courtesy of the Mandeville Special Collections Library, University of California, San Diego.)

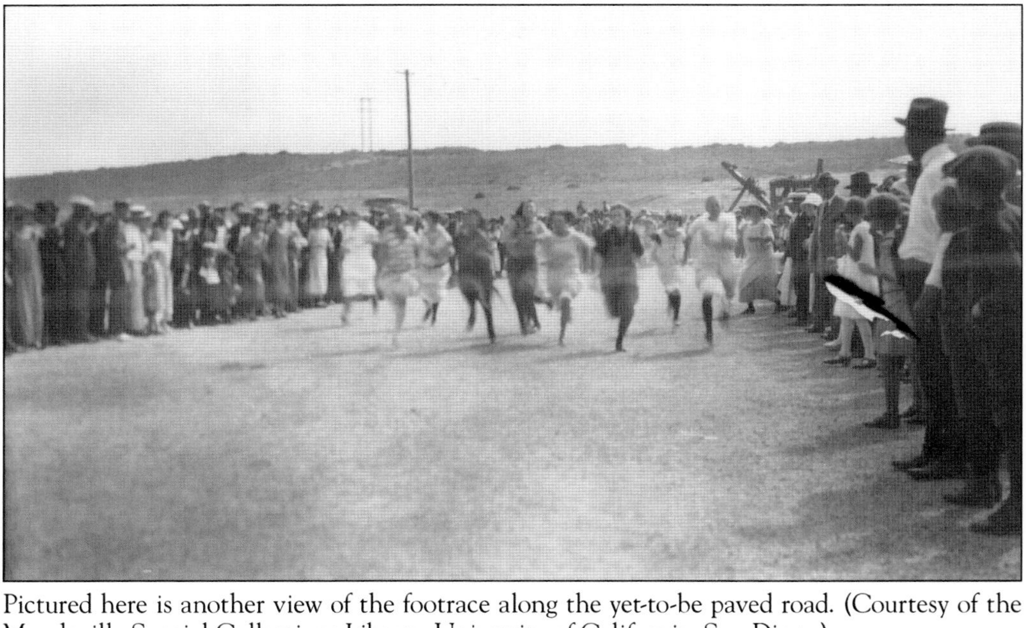

Pictured here is another view of the footrace along the yet-to-be paved road. (Courtesy of the Mandeville Special Collections Library, University of California, San Diego.)

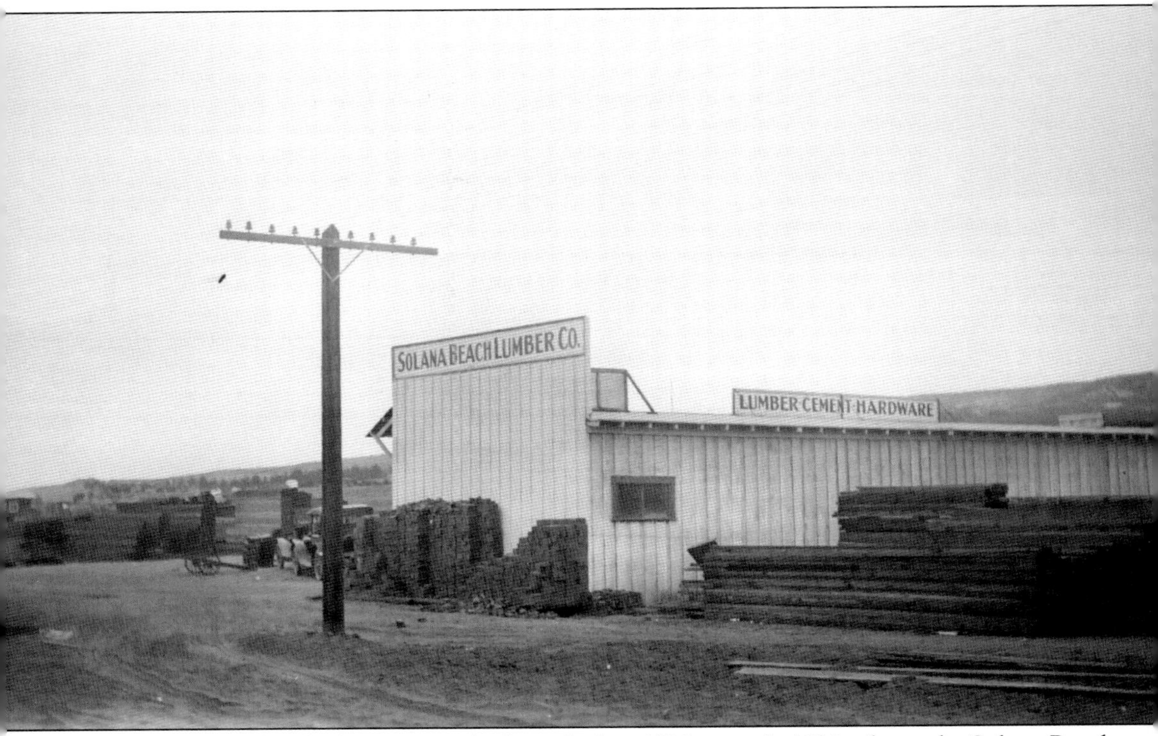

This photograph, which appears to be from the late 1920s or early 1930s, shows the Solana Beach lumberyard, established by Herschel Larrick Sr. in 1923. All building materials had to be shipped in via train or truck since many of the trees that grew in the area were nonnative eucalyptus that were planted during the early 1900s. (Courtesy of the Mandeville Special Collections Library, University of California, San Diego.)

Herschel Larrick Sr. is pictured here standing in front of the lumberyard. (Courtesy of the San Dieguito Heritage Museum.)

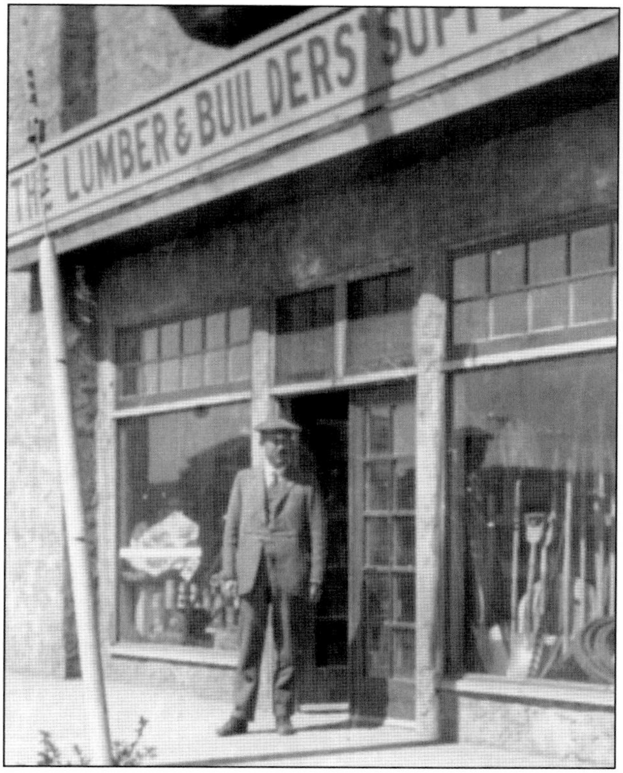

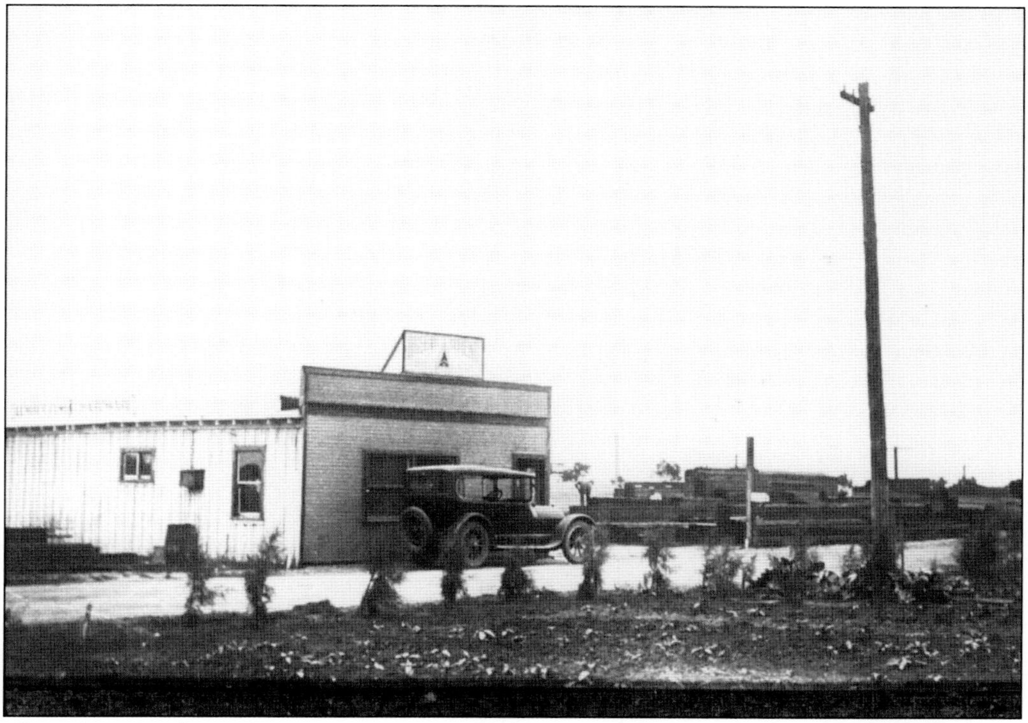

The Solana Beach Lumber Company was established in the 1920s to provide housing materials and it did so until it closed in the early 1980s. (Courtesy of the San Dieguito Heritage Museum.)

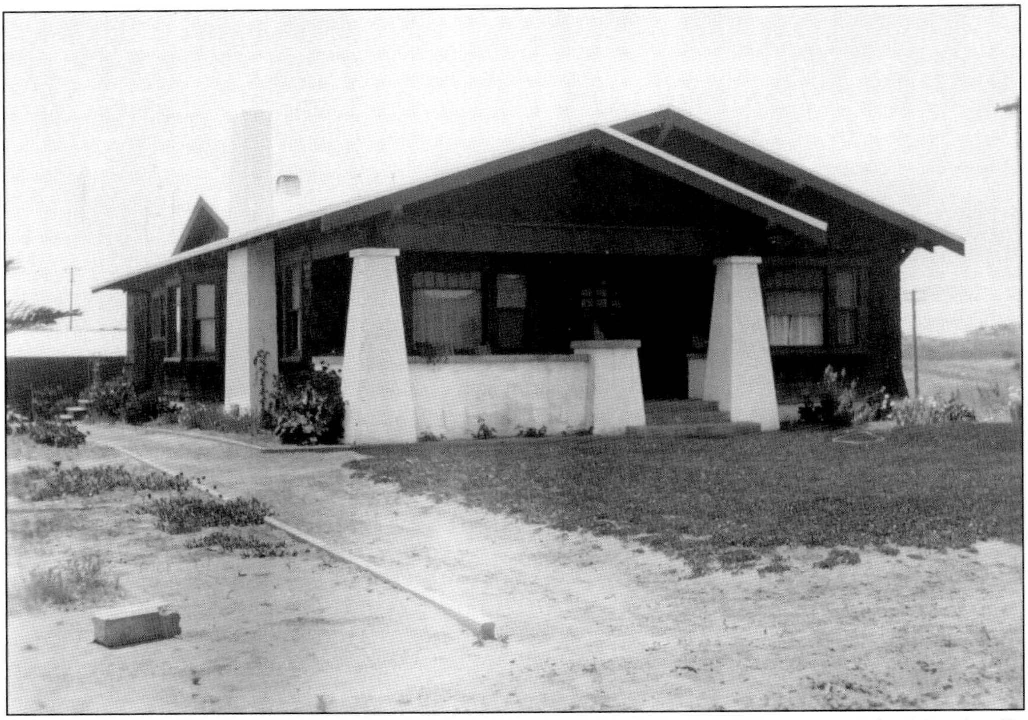

A Craftsman-style home, typical of the era, sits on one of Fletcher's lots. (Courtesy of the Mandeville Special Collections Library, University of California, San Diego.)

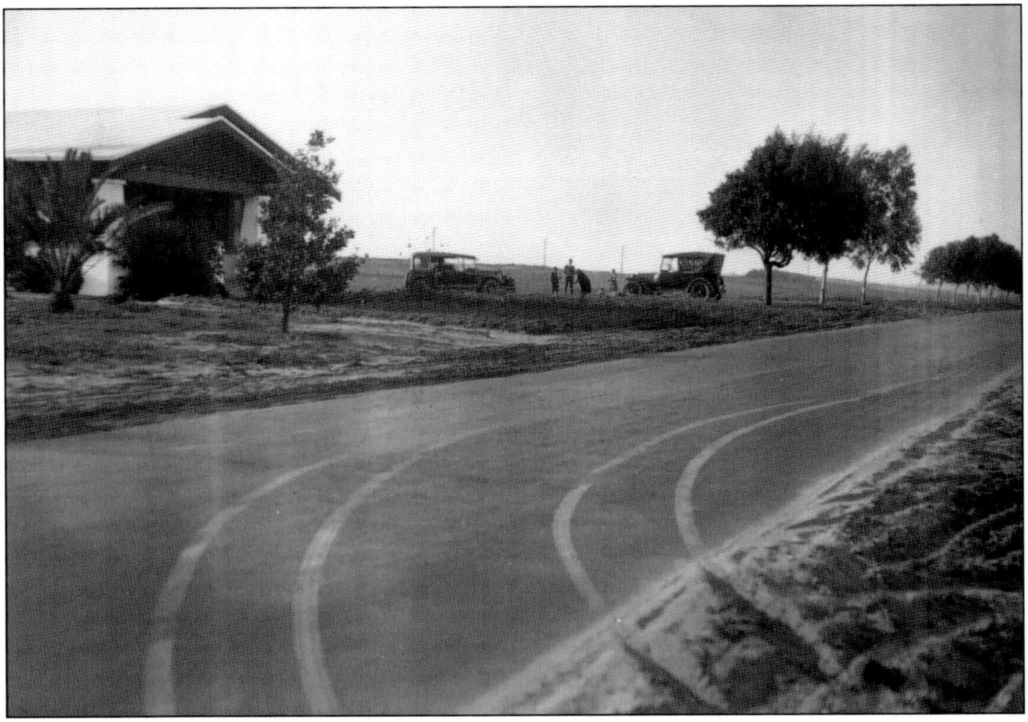

This is another view of the Craftsman home. (Courtesy of the Mandeville Special Collections Library, University of California, San Diego.)

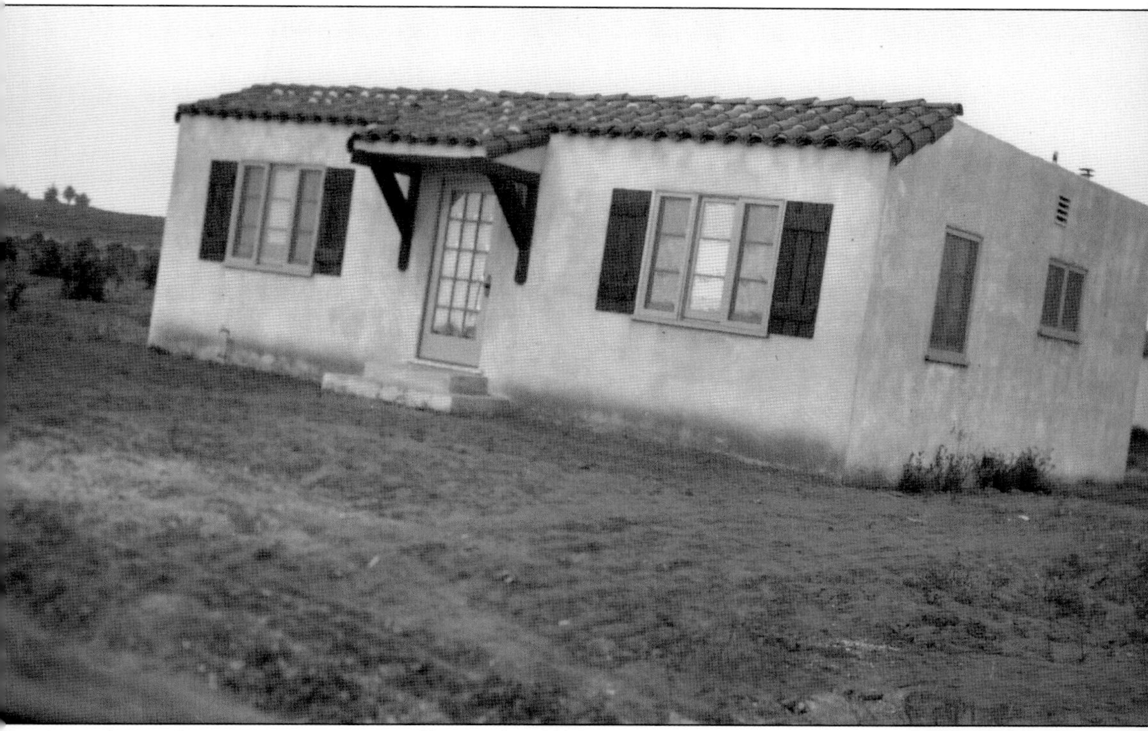

Some home designs were exceptionally simple, such as this boxy structure with a Spanish-tile roof. (Courtesy of the Mandeville Special Collections Library, University of California, San Diego.)

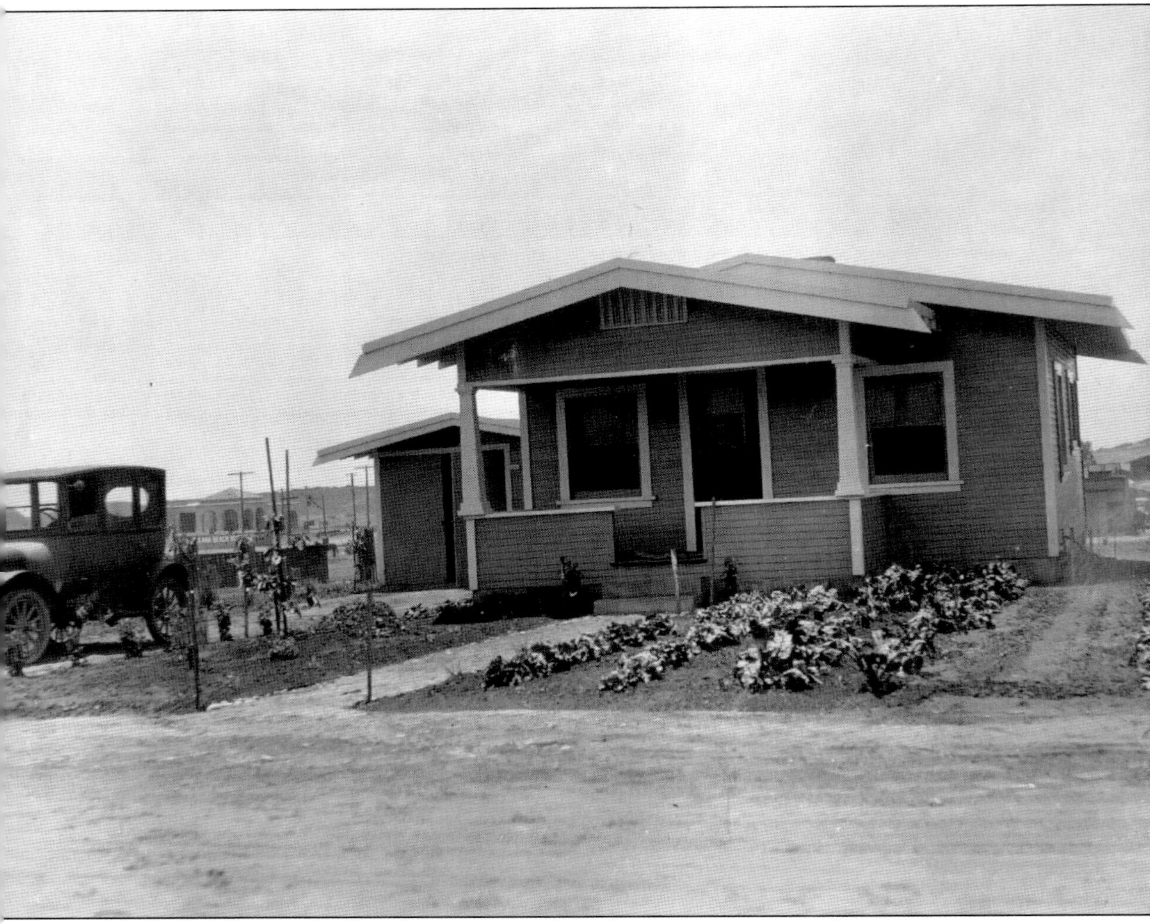

Solana Beach offered a rural, middle-class life: a lot to build one's own home, an area to grow food, and a driveway to park a Model T, as indicated by this 1920s photograph. (Courtesy of the Mandeville Special Collections Library, University of California, San Diego.)

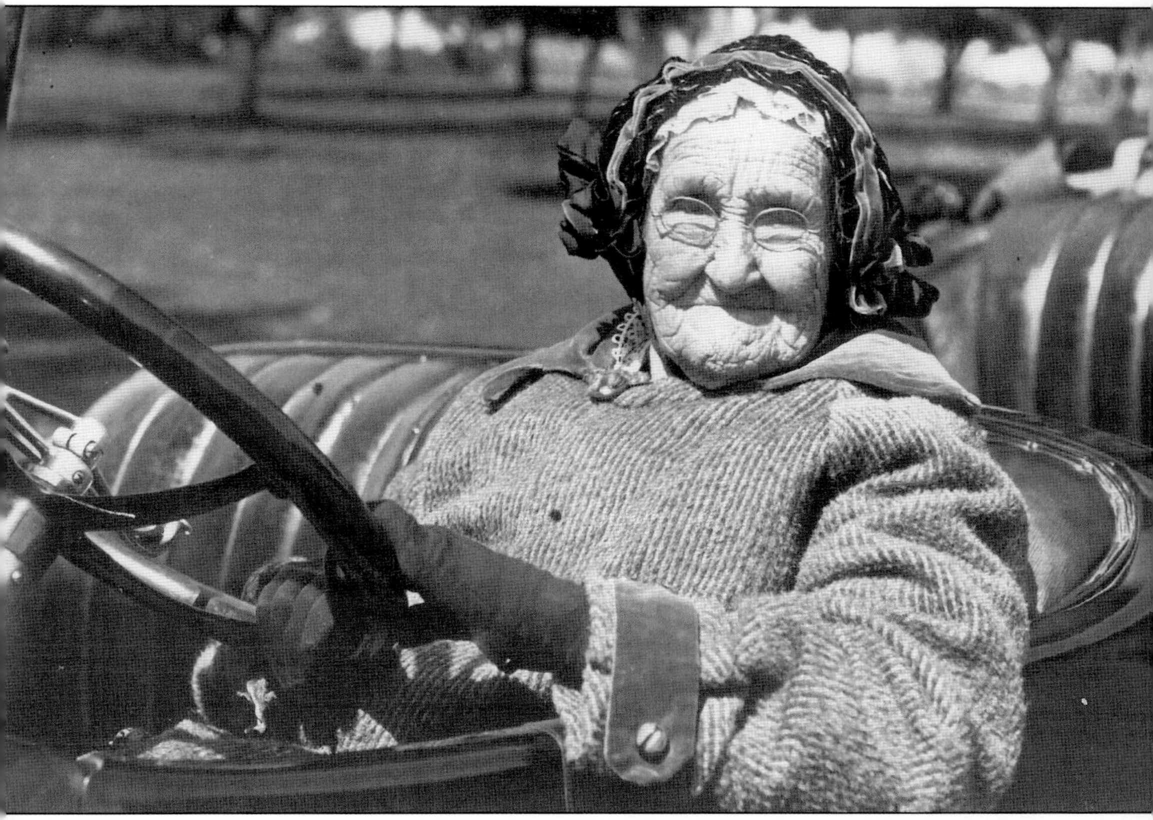

Pictured here is Solana Beach celebrity Susannah Stevens, affectionately known as "Grandma Stevens." Grandma Stevens had been featured in newspapers in San Diego and Los Angeles by the time she reached her 100th birthday. (Courtesy of the Solana Beach Civic and Historical Society.)

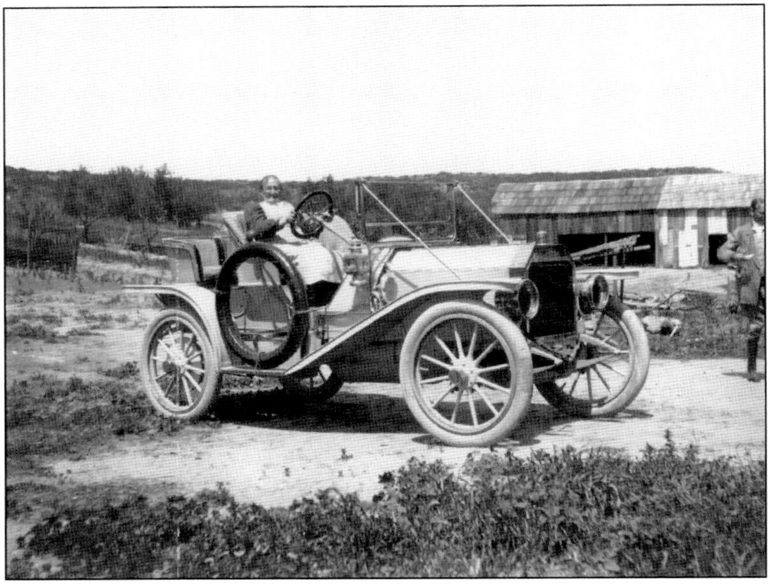

Susannah and her husband, James, celebrated their 60th anniversary with a party on the Del Mar beach in 1906. James died in 1907, and Susannah lived in the ranch house known as Steven's House, the oldest residence in Solana Beach, until her death in 1927, a few days shy of her 106th birthday. (Courtesy of the Solana Beach Civic and Historical Society.)

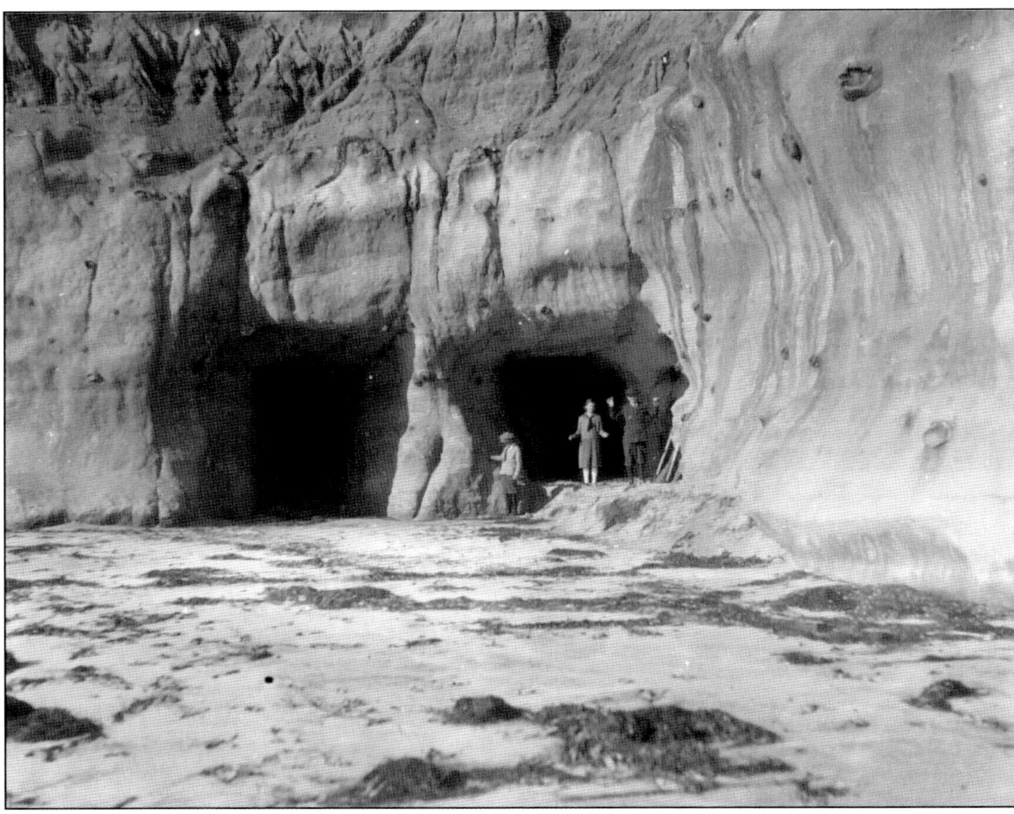

This early-1920s photograph shows the natural erosion of the cliffs along the Solana Beach shoreline. Natural caves once dotted the seascape. Today, many of the caves have been filled in or have naturally eroded. (Courtesy of the Mandeville Special Collections Library, University of California, San Diego.)

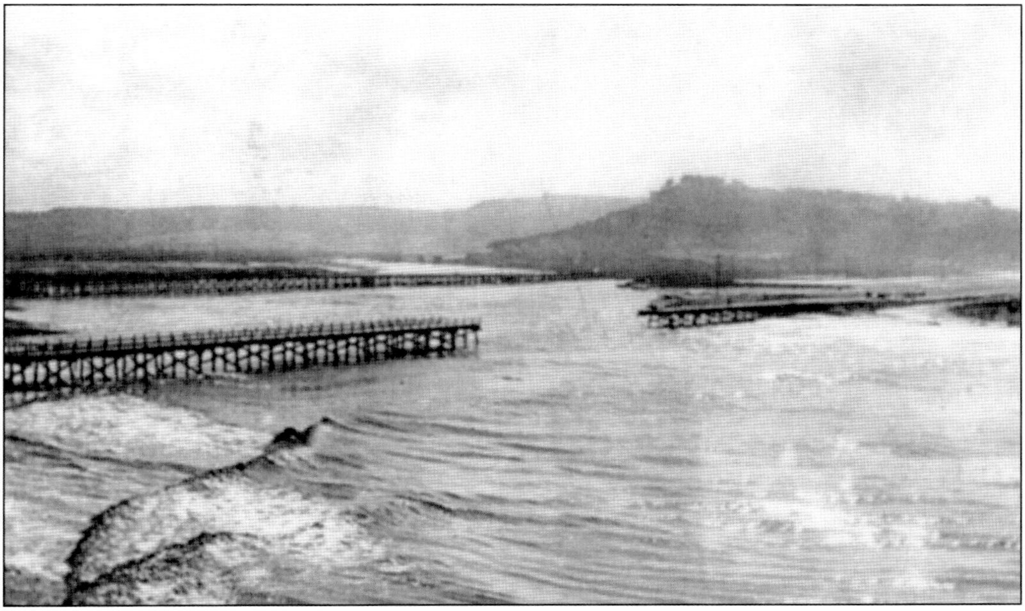

This view of Highway 101, in the center of the photograph, features the portion of the bridge connecting Del Mar to Solana Beach that was washed away in a 1927 flood. Luckily, the railroad sustained only minor damage.

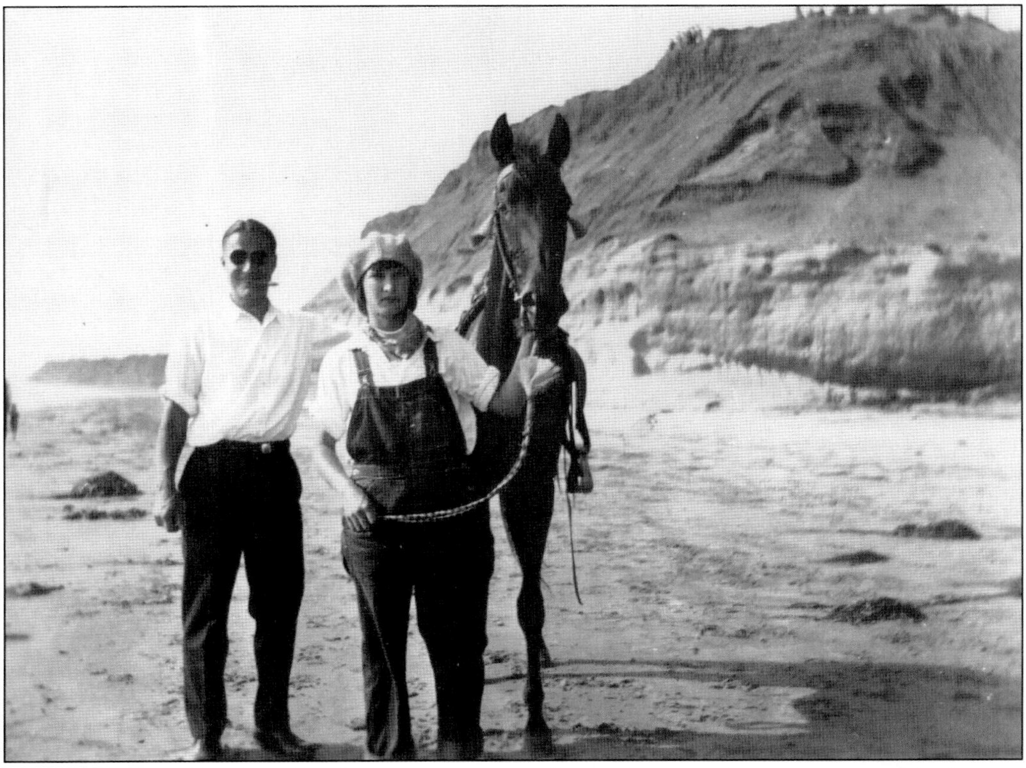

Until World War II, Solana Beach was an exceptionally rural society. Horse owners could ride their horses right on the beach. (Courtesy of the Mandeville Special Collections Library, University of California, San Diego.)

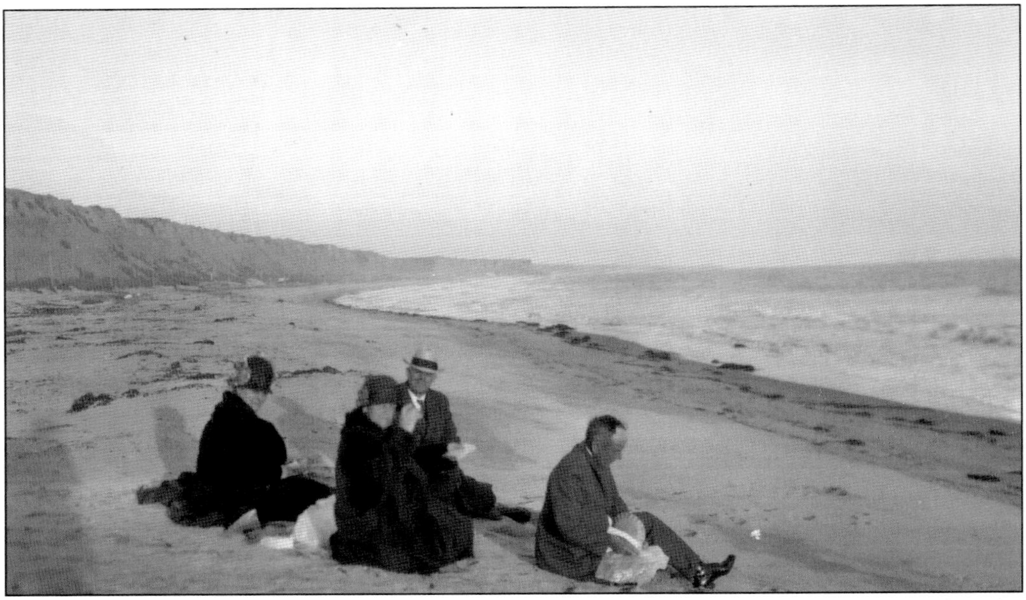

This photograph, which faces south, shows residents of Solana Beach, who often escaped to the beach that was accessible year-round. (Courtesy of the Mandeville Special Collections Library, University of California, San Diego.)

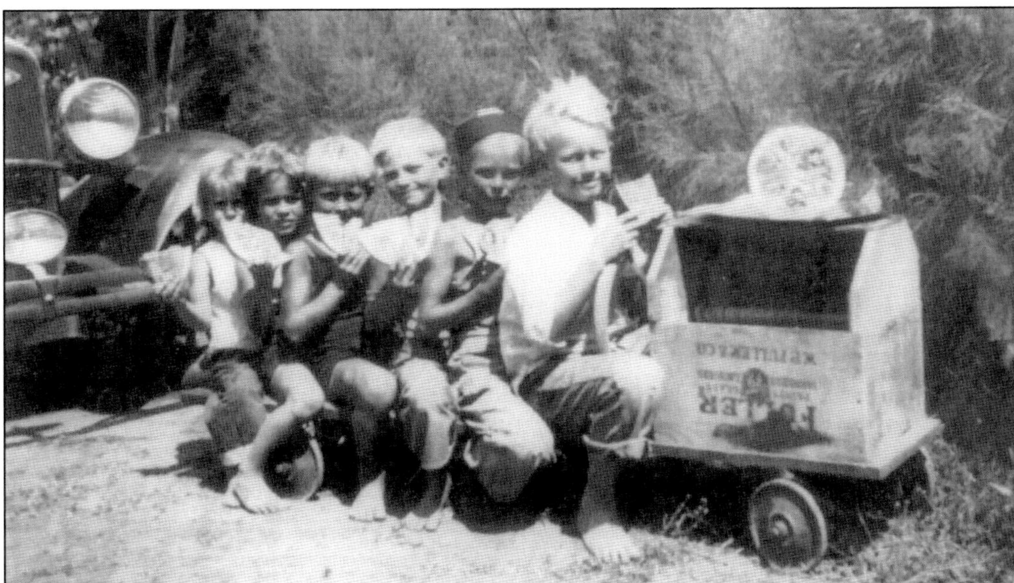

Pictured here in 1929 are, from right to left, George Wilkens, Bob King, Jack Anderson, Bob Wilkens, Jim King, and Pat King. George and Bob Wilkens were the sons of Gustav George Wilkens, known as "Duke," who opened a small supply store in Solana Beach in 1933. When the Del Mar Racetrack opened in 1937, the Wilkenses made daily deliveries to the track and catered to celebrities in nearby areas as well, including Bing Crosby, Harry James, Betty Grable, and Victor Mature. As the decade closed, the growth of Solana Beach would slow with the impending stock-market crash and Great Depression. (Courtesy of the Mandeville Special Collections Library, University of California, San Diego.)

Three

Development of Solana Beach

The 1930s and 1940s

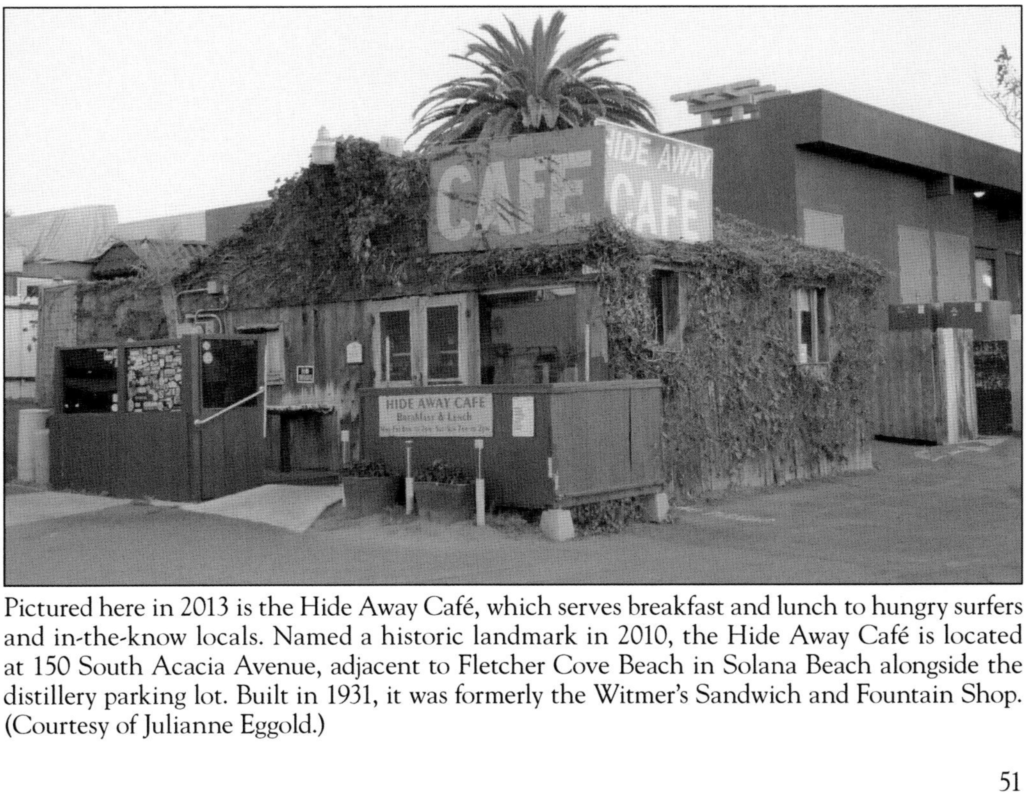

Pictured here in 2013 is the Hide Away Café, which serves breakfast and lunch to hungry surfers and in-the-know locals. Named a historic landmark in 2010, the Hide Away Café is located at 150 South Acacia Avenue, adjacent to Fletcher Cove Beach in Solana Beach alongside the distillery parking lot. Built in 1931, it was formerly the Witmer's Sandwich and Fountain Shop. (Courtesy of Julianne Eggold.)

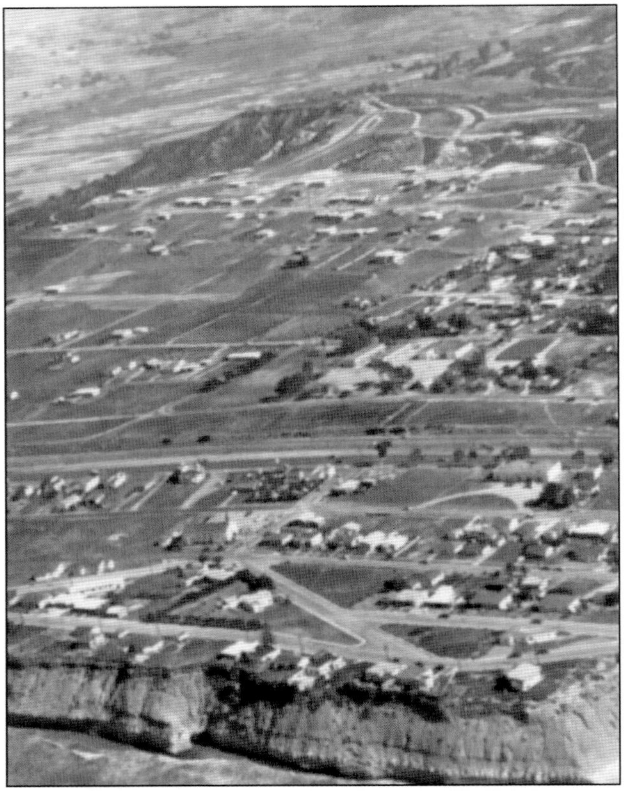

This aerial shot looks east, just north of Fletcher Cove. Note the building in lower right of the photograph, where the community center would later be built. (Courtesy of the Mandeville Special Collections Library, University of California, San Diego.)

The oldest surviving residence in Solana Beach, the Stevens House in La Colonia Park, houses the Solana Beach Heritage Museum. Built in 1887 overlooking the San Dieguito Estuary on a site near the present La Vida Del Mar, the house was slated for demolition in the late 1980s. However, the house subsequently was donated to the City of Solana Beach, which moved it to its present location in La Colonia Park. (Courtesy of the Solana Beach Historical Society.)

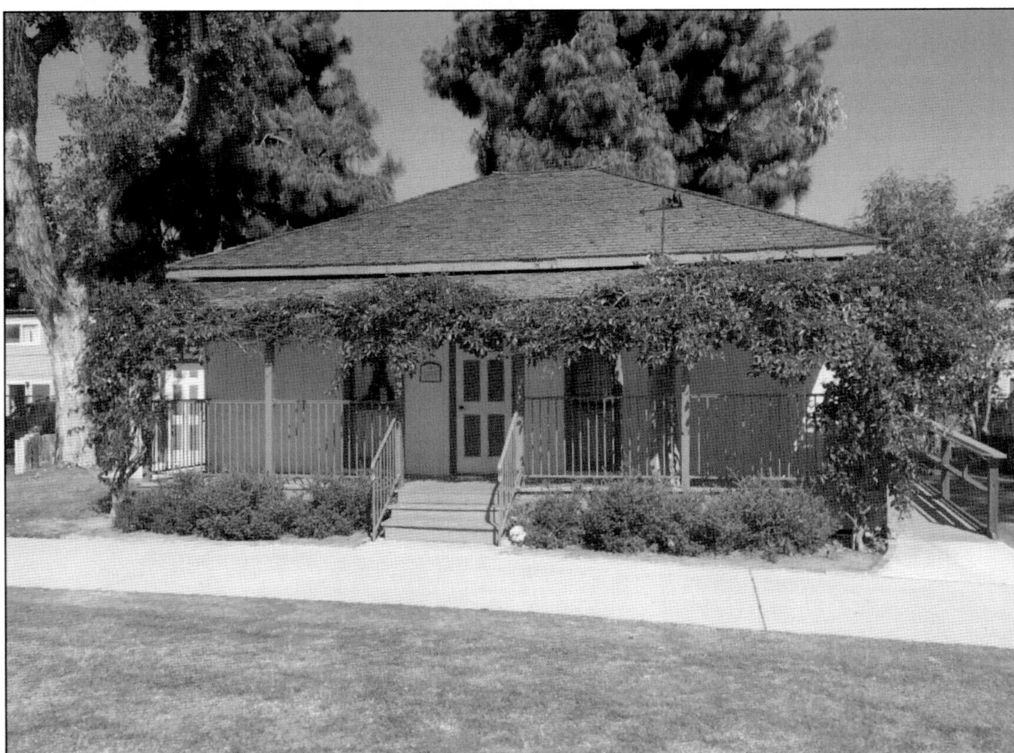

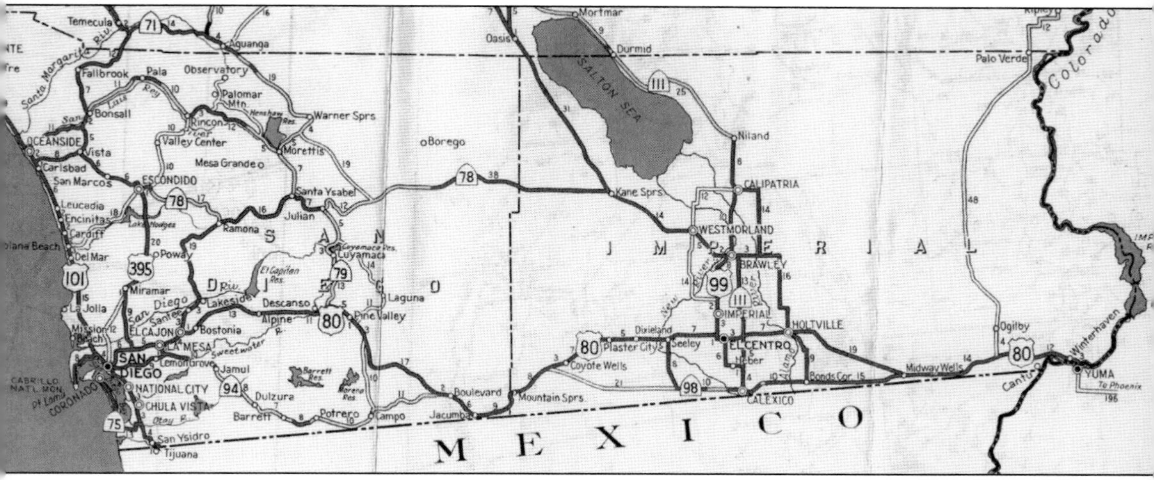

This 1944 road map literally puts Solana Beach on the map. Note that Highway 101 is the only major artery between Orange and San Diego Counties, as Interstate 5 would not be completed until the mid-1960s.

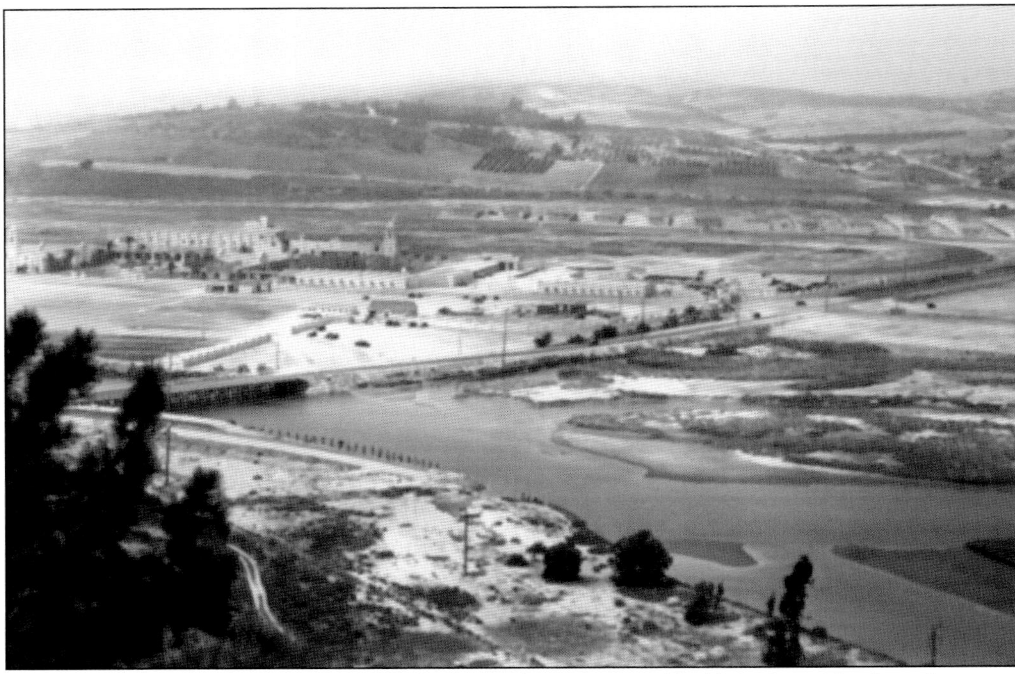

This 1930s photograph looks north, with the newly constructed Del Mar Race Track in the center left. Note the rows of planted fruit trees on the distant hilltops in the area of Solana Beach. On the right is where Interstate 5 now exists. During the Depression, progress in many areas of rural San Diego slowed, but it did not deter celebrities from coming to the racetrack and enjoying the beaches of Del Mar and Solana Beach.

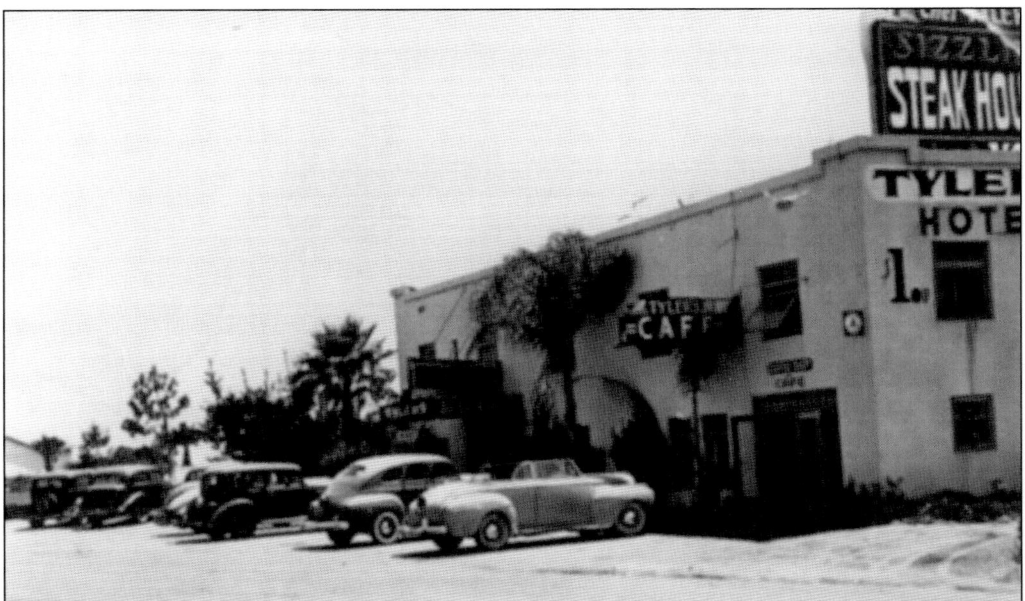

Pictured here in 1942 is Tyler's Steakhouse and Hotel, on the southwest end of what is now Encinitas on Highway 101. The property is now part of the Self-Realization Fellowship. The hotel housed military dependents during World War II. (Courtesy of the Mandeville Special Collections Library, University of California, San Diego.)

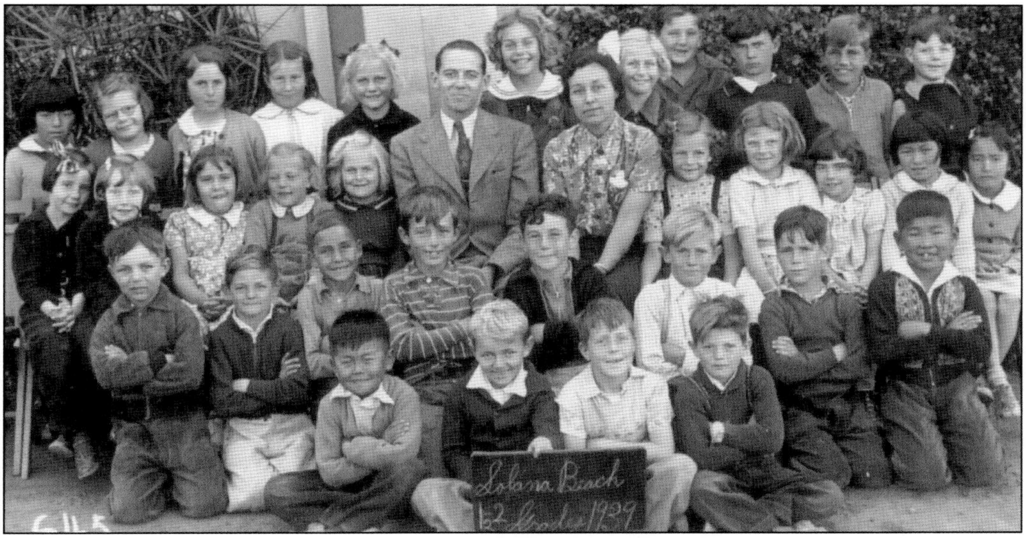

Pictured here in 1939 are the first-, second-, and third-grade classes at Solana Beach Grammar School.

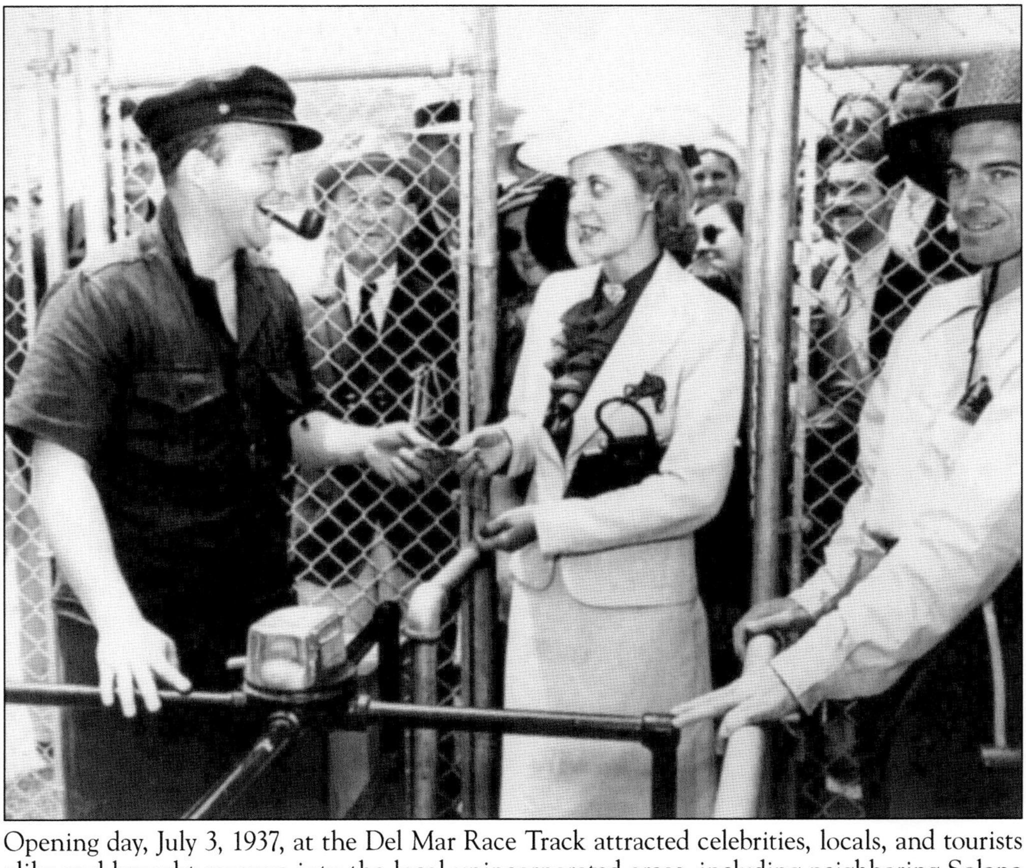

Opening day, July 3, 1937, at the Del Mar Race Track attracted celebrities, locals, and tourists alike and brought revenue into the local unincorporated areas, including neighboring Solana Beach. Rancho Santa Fe resident Bing Crosby greeted fans personally at the gate. (Courtesy of the Del Mar Historical Society.)

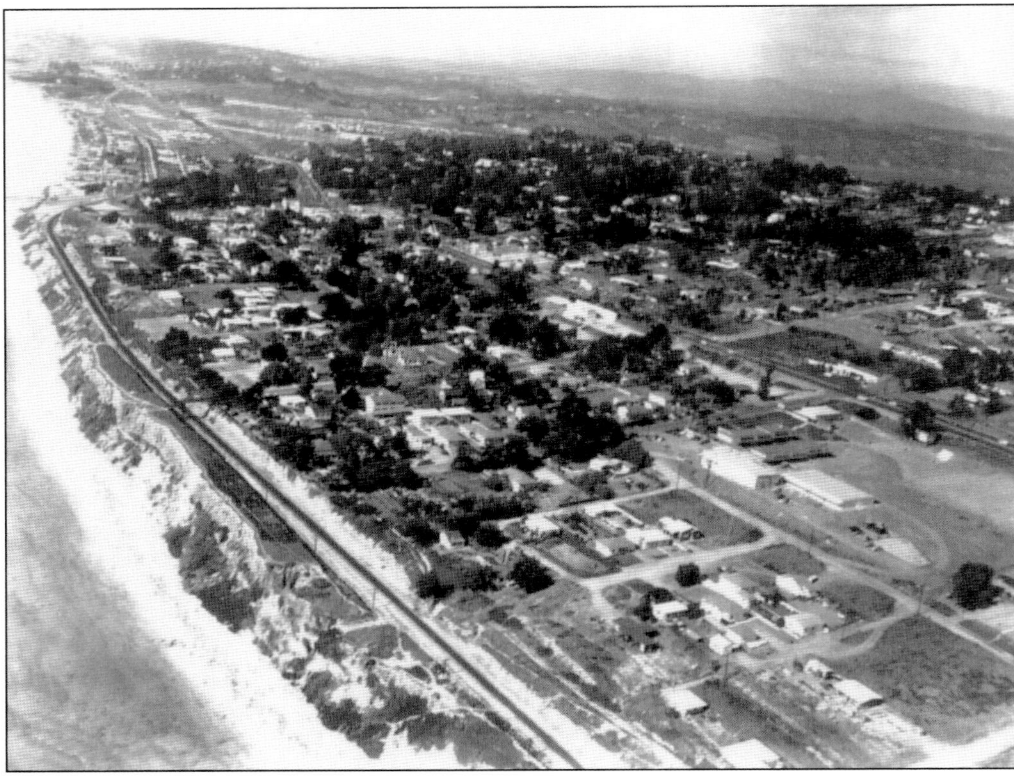

This 1930s aerial shot looks north from Del Mar into Solana Beach, off in the distance. (Courtesy of the Mandeville Special Collections Library, University of California, San Diego.)

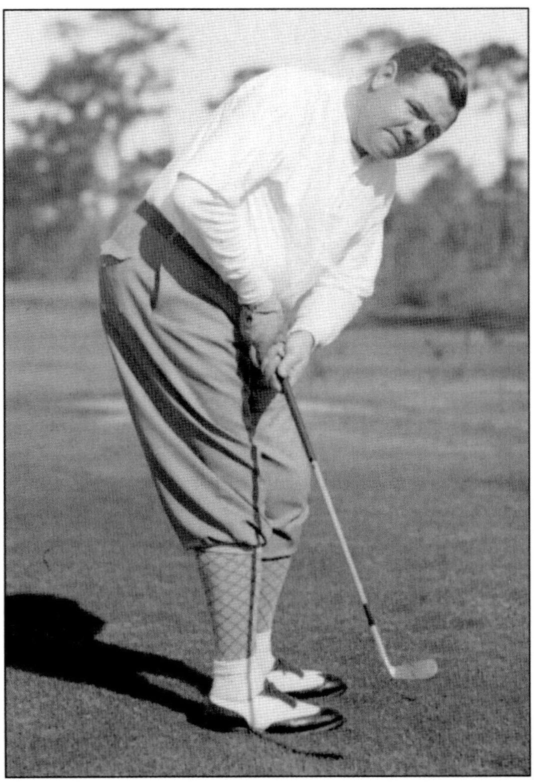

In 1937, the iconic crooner Bing Crosby hosted the first national pro-am golf championship, known as the Crosby Clambake, at Rancho Santa Fe Golf Club. Trading his baseball bat for a golf club, Babe Ruth takes a swing at the Crosby Clambake in Rancho Santa Fe. (Courtesy of the Rancho Santa Fe Historical Society.)

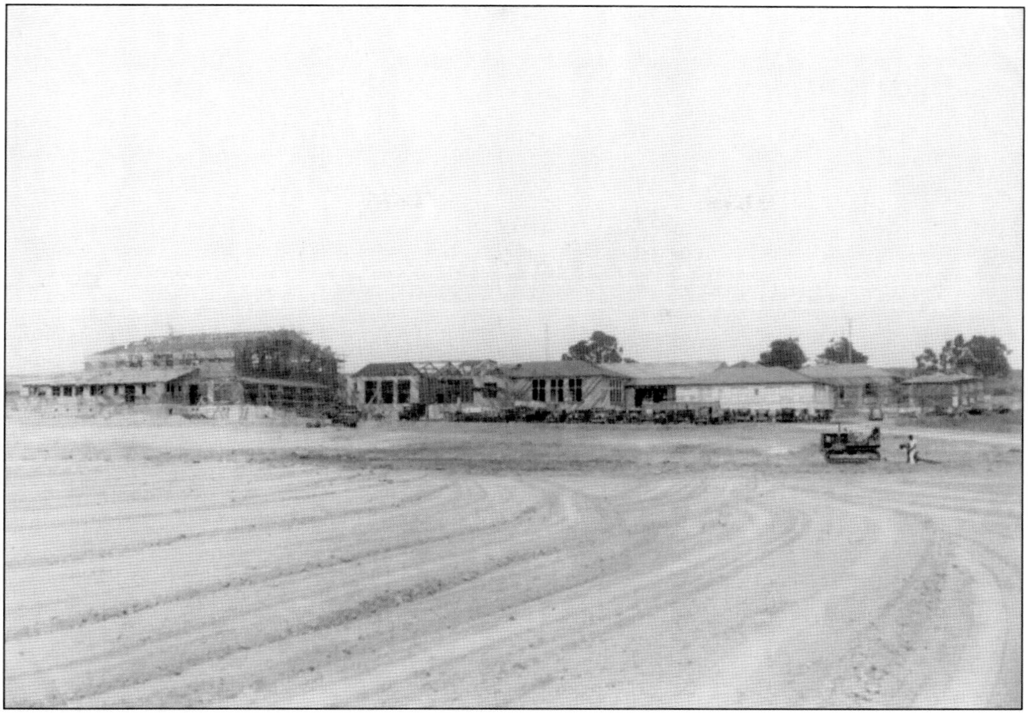

The construction of San Dieguito Union High School began in 1936. It was built to serve the needs of Solana Beach, Encinitas, Del Mar, and Carlsbad when it opened in 1937. When the school first opened, most of the North County region of San Diego County was extremely rural. Students were bused in from nearby unincorporated areas. (Courtesy of the San Diego Heritage Museum.)

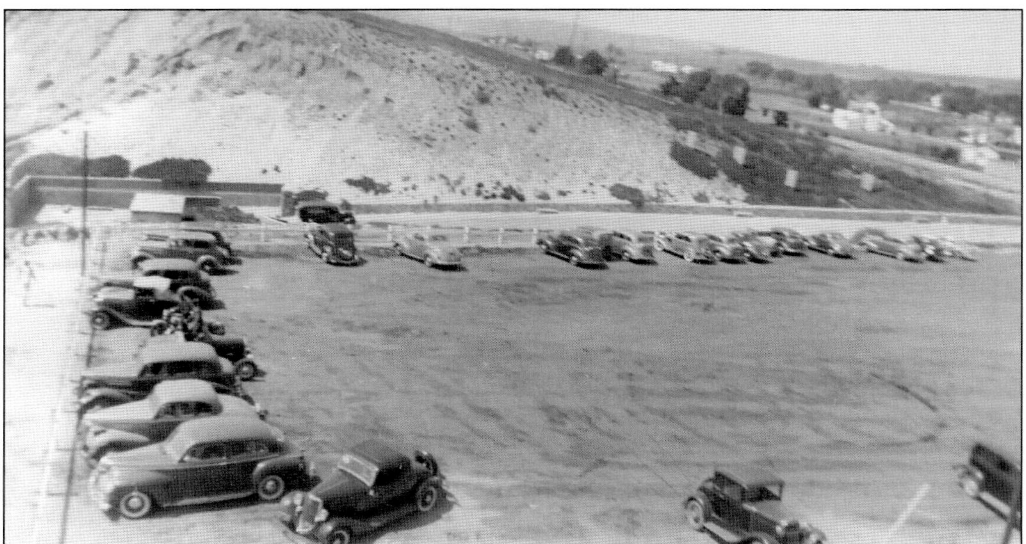

Pictured here in 1942 is the parking lot of what is now Fletcher Cove looking north. Note the undeveloped area on the bluff where the Solana Beach Community Center is located today. (Courtesy of the Solana Beach Department of Marine Safety.)

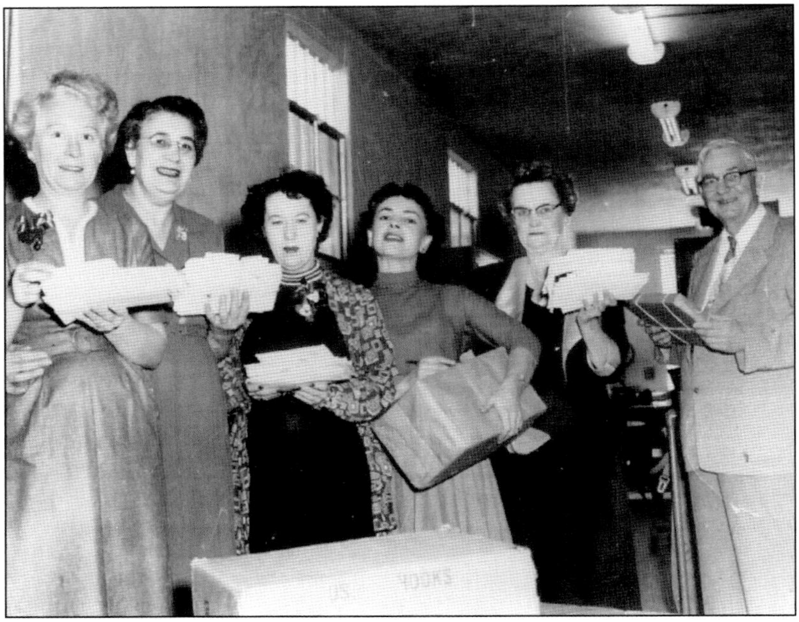

This 1940s photograph shows the first Solana Beach Post Office.

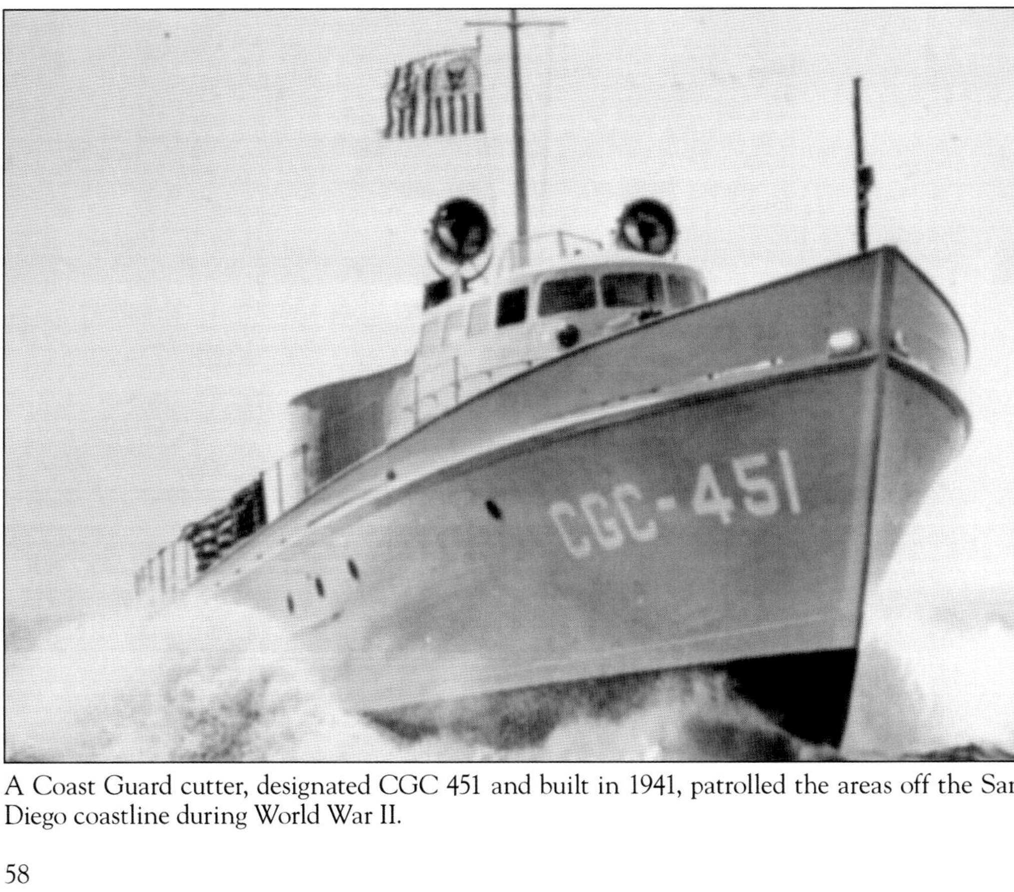

A Coast Guard cutter, designated CGC 451 and built in 1941, patrolled the areas off the San Diego coastline during World War II.

Four

Saviors of the Sea
The Lifeguards of Solana Beach

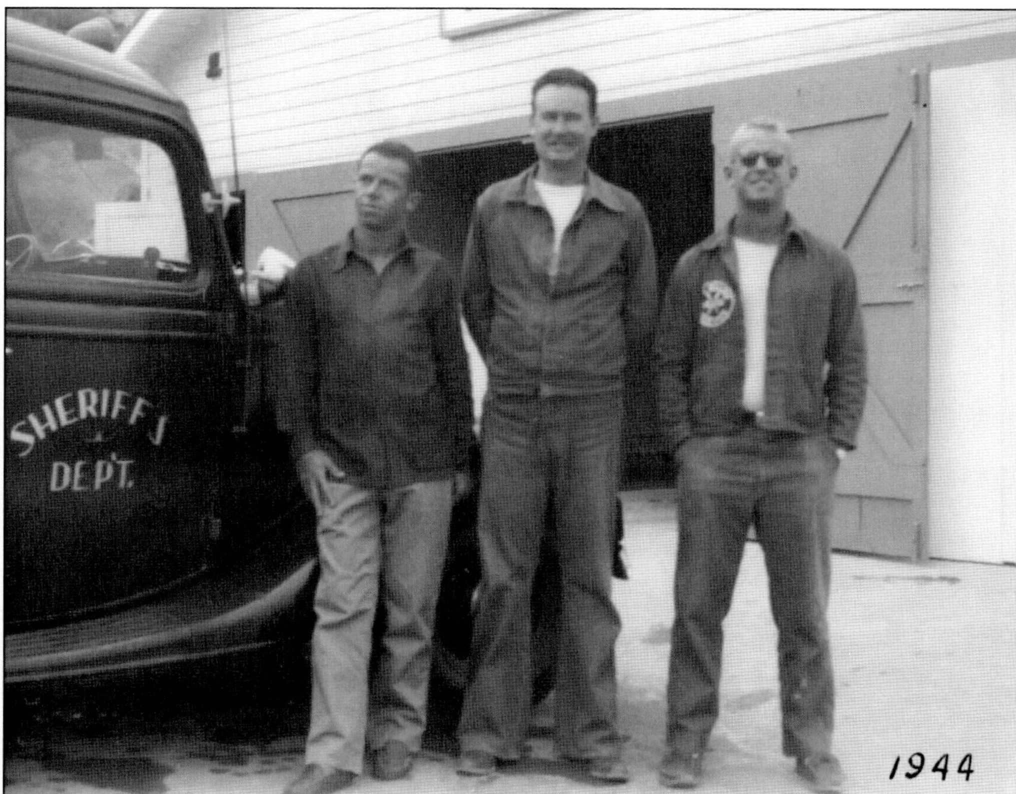

Solana Beach lifeguards were originally members of the sheriff's department. Pictured here in 1944 are John Rigon (left) and John Brennan (center) with an unidentified man. (Courtesy of the Solana Beach Department of Marine Safety.)

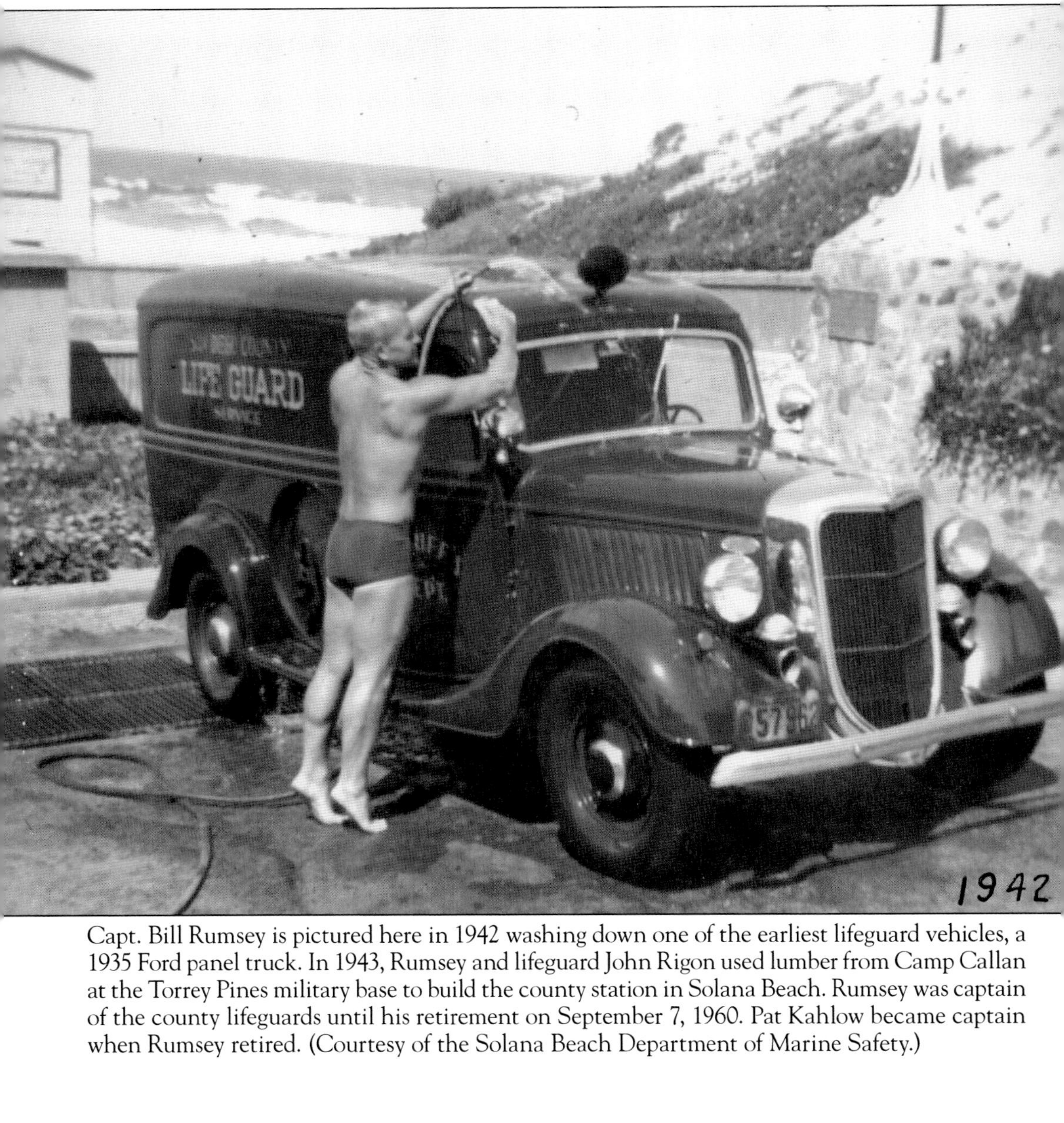

Capt. Bill Rumsey is pictured here in 1942 washing down one of the earliest lifeguard vehicles, a 1935 Ford panel truck. In 1943, Rumsey and lifeguard John Rigon used lumber from Camp Callan at the Torrey Pines military base to build the county station in Solana Beach. Rumsey was captain of the county lifeguards until his retirement on September 7, 1960. Pat Kahlow became captain when Rumsey retired. (Courtesy of the Solana Beach Department of Marine Safety.)

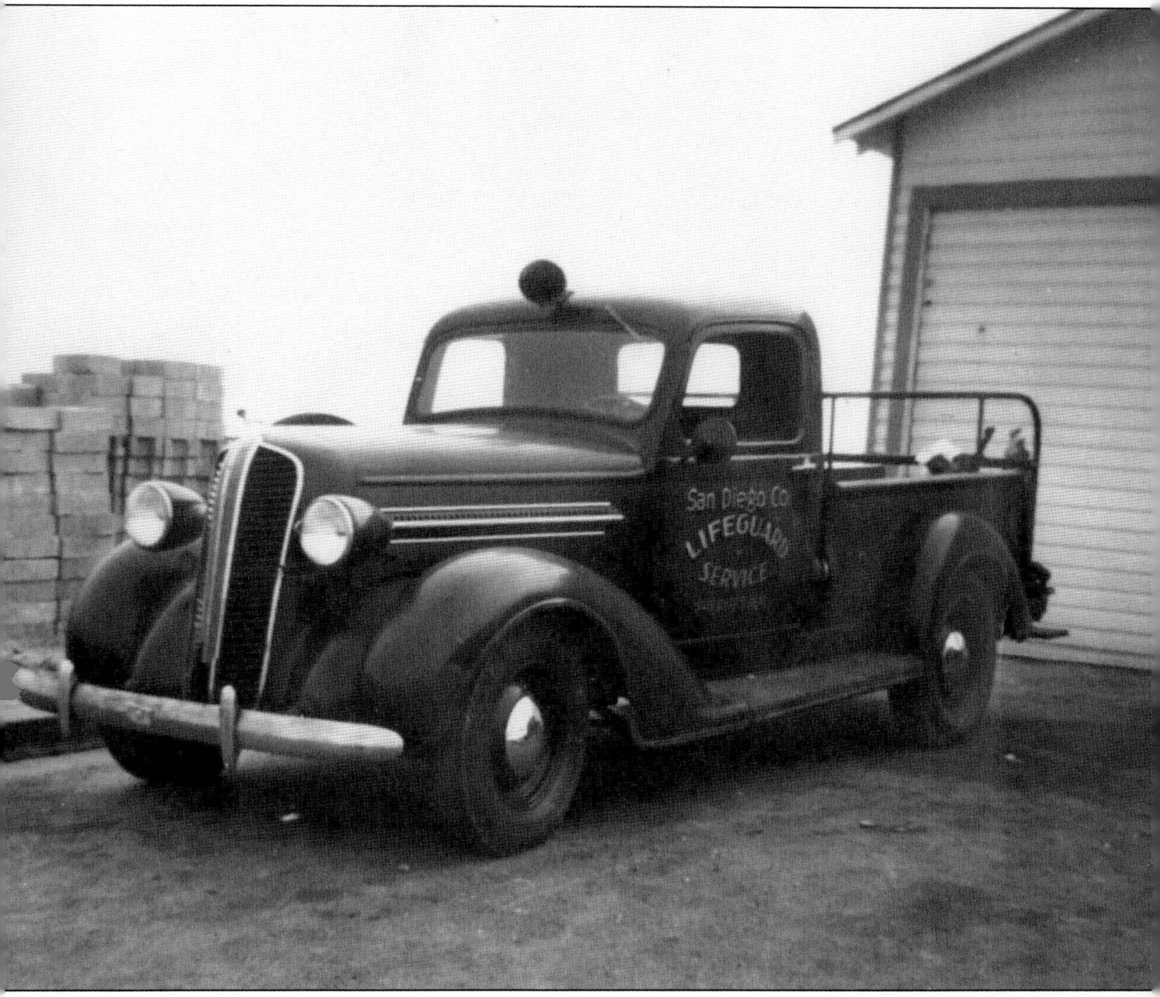

Pictured here in 1946 is another early lifeguard vehicle parked in front of the Solana Beach Lifeguard Station in Fletcher Cove. (Courtesy of the Solana Beach Department of Marine Safety.)

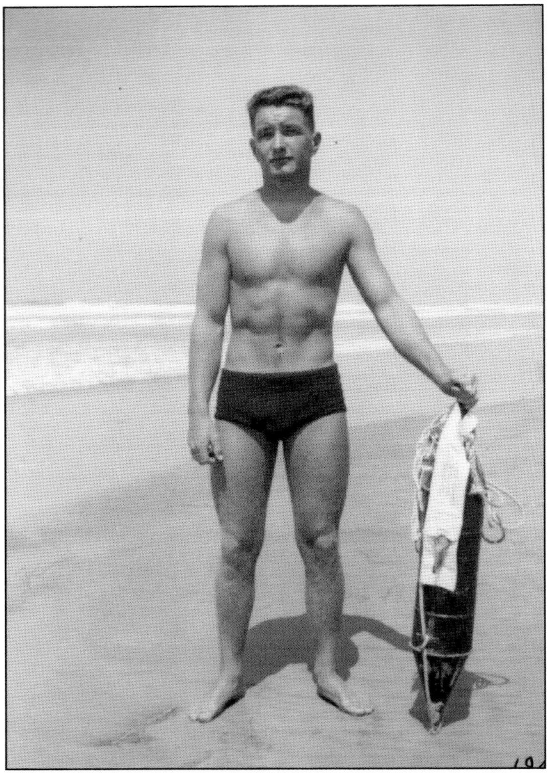

A Solana Beach lifeguard with a standard-issue rescue buoy is pictured here in 1946. The following year, the San Diego Lifeguard Service was transferred from the police department to the newly formed parks and recreation department. (Courtesy of the Solana Beach Department of Marine Safety.)

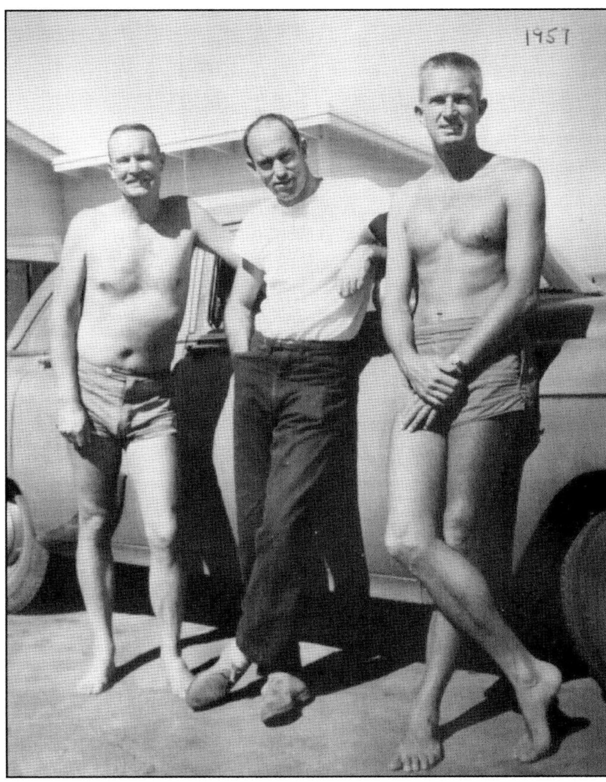

Three Solana Beach lifeguards pose in front of the lifeguard station in Fletcher Cove in 1957. Lifeguards received uniform apparel, regular performance testing for lifeguards was initiated, and a standardized hiring procedure was adopted. Equipment improvements included two-way radios in emergency vehicles and main lifeguard stations. (Courtesy of the Solana Beach Department of Marine Safety.)

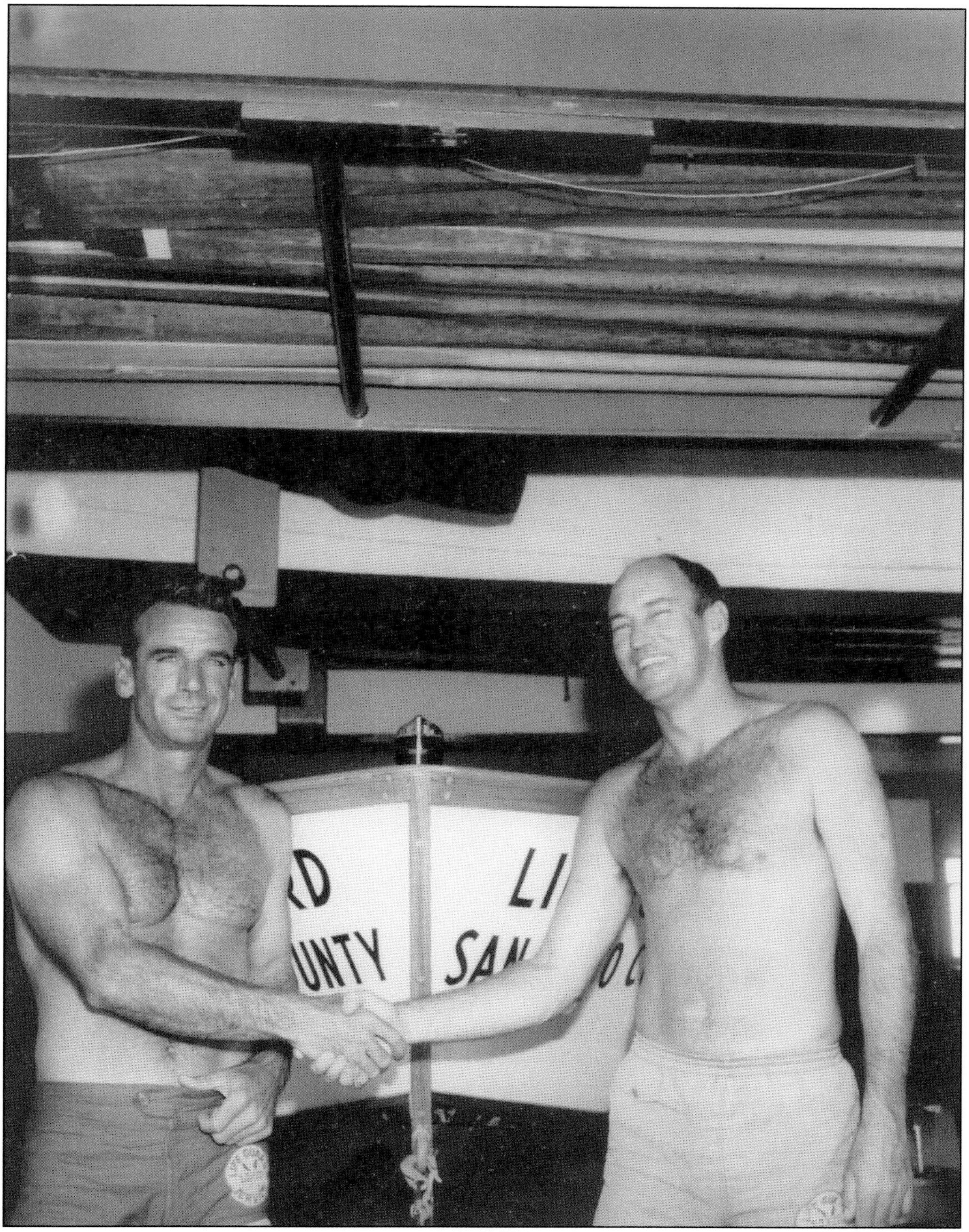

Shot during the summer of 1961, this photograph shows Lt. Bill Lathers (left) and Capt. Pat Kahlow. Lathers had been working at the county station in Imperial Beach, transferring to Solana Beach in 1956 when the city of Imperial Beach incorporated and took control of the lifeguard services. (Courtesy of the Solana Beach Department of Marine Safety.)

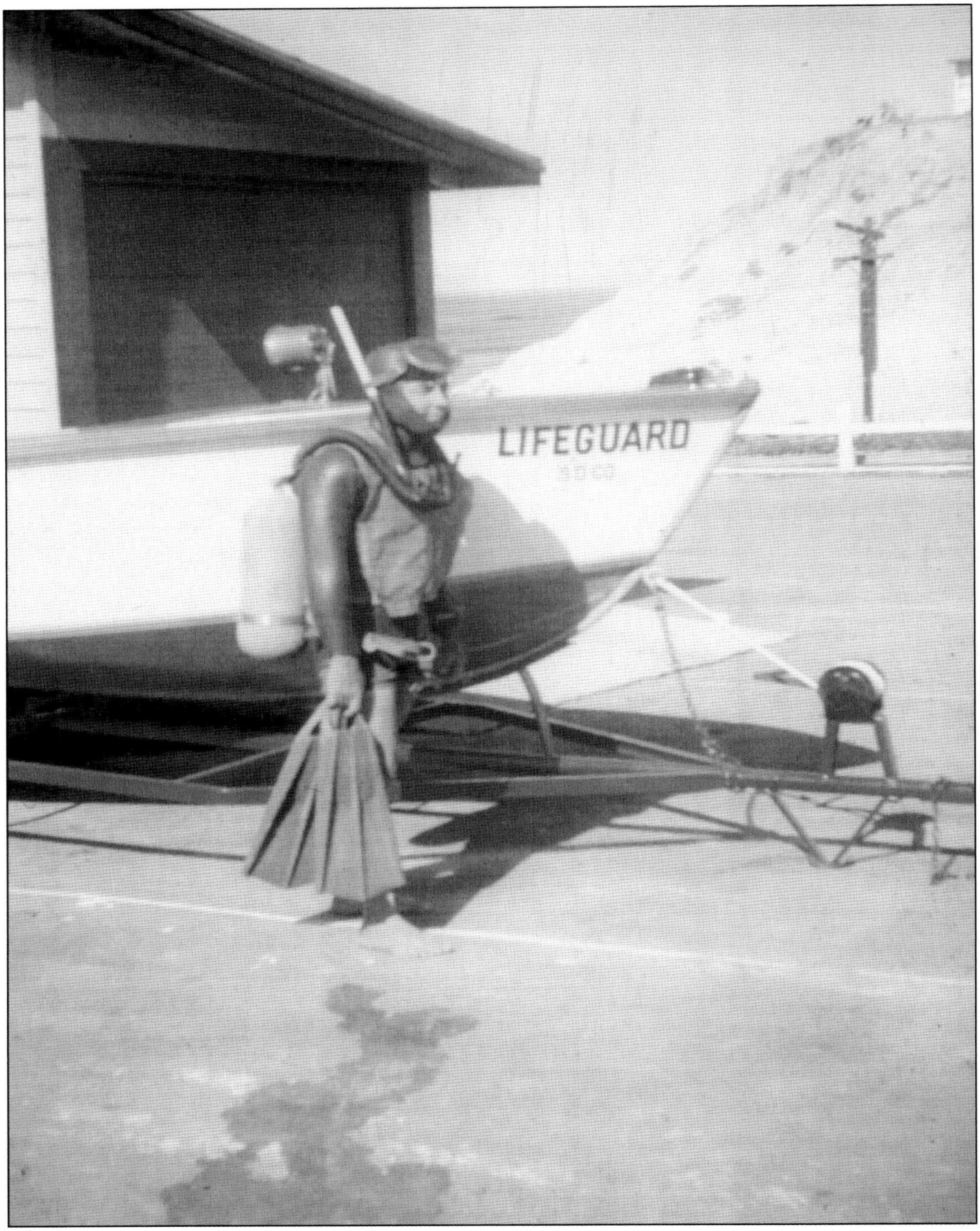

This lifeguard station in Solana Beach was photographed some time in the 1960s. In the 1950s, diving became a popular sport, which triggered a substantial increase in water activity, prompting the creation of the San Diego Lifeguard Service Dive Rescue Team. (Courtesy of the Solana Beach Department of Marine Safety.)

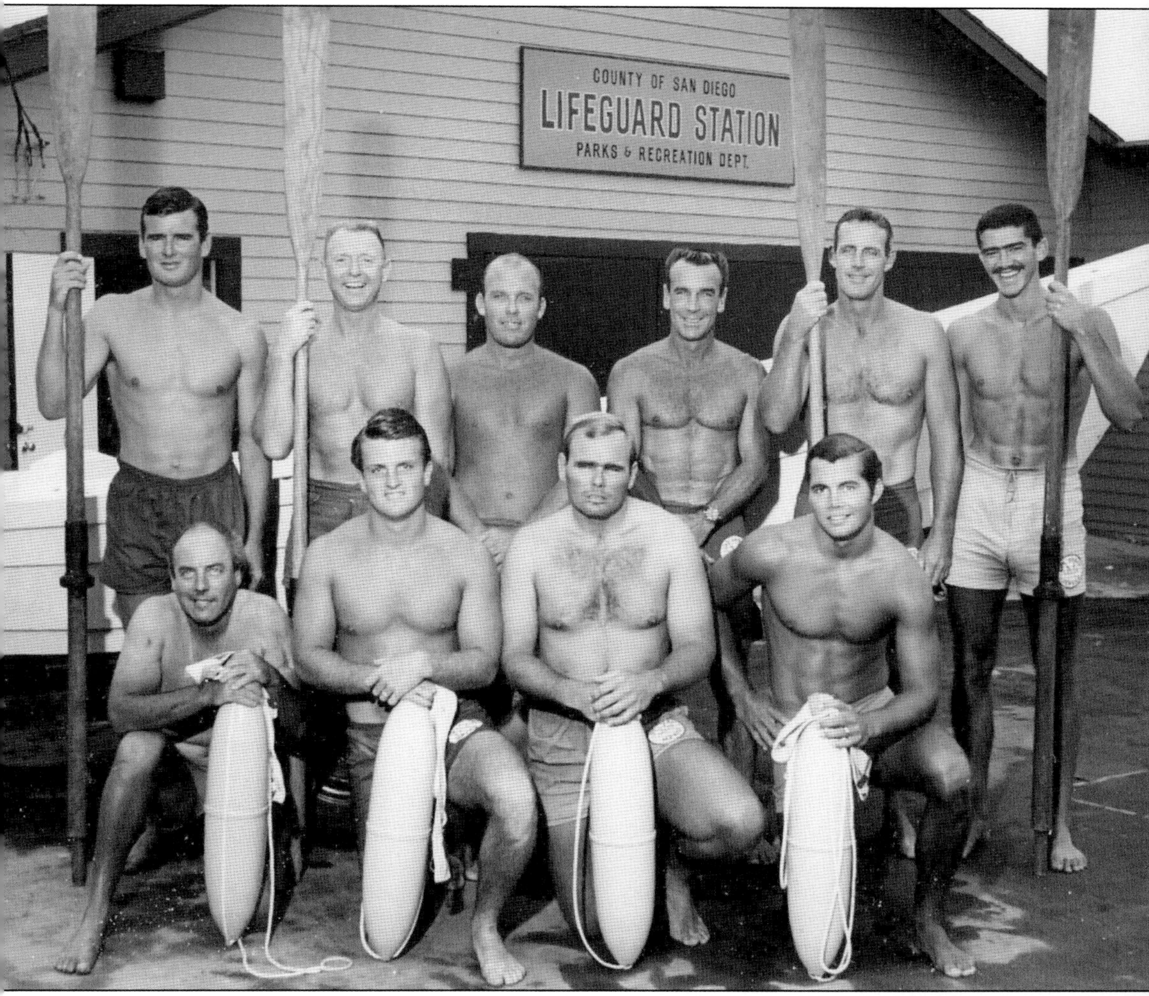

This shot of the lifeguards is from 1956. It became a tradition to take an annual group portrait of the lifeguards. (Courtesy of the Solana Beach Department of Marine Safety.)

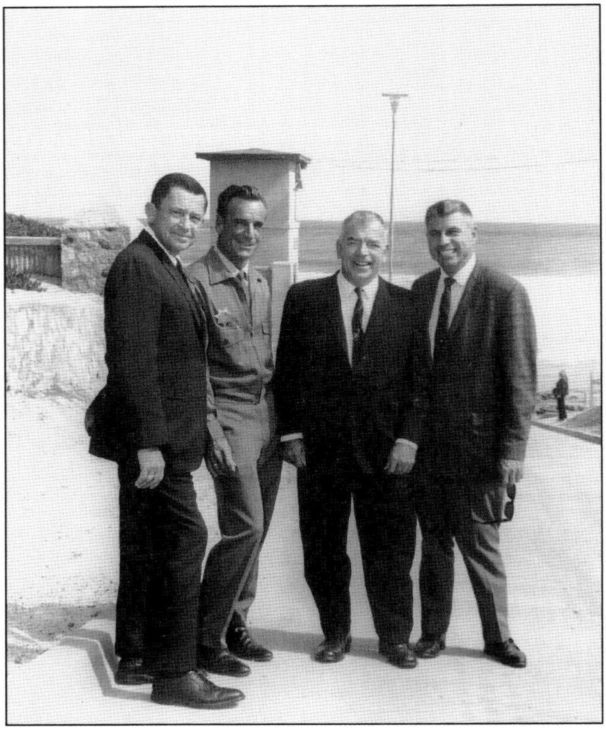

Pictured here in the 1960s are Bob Cozens (far left) and second lifeguard captain of Solana Beach Bill Lathers (second from left). (Courtesy of the Solana Beach Department of Marine Safety.)

Lieutenant Considine (left) and Captain Lathers are pictured here in January 1965. (Courtesy of the Solana Beach Department of Marine Safety.)

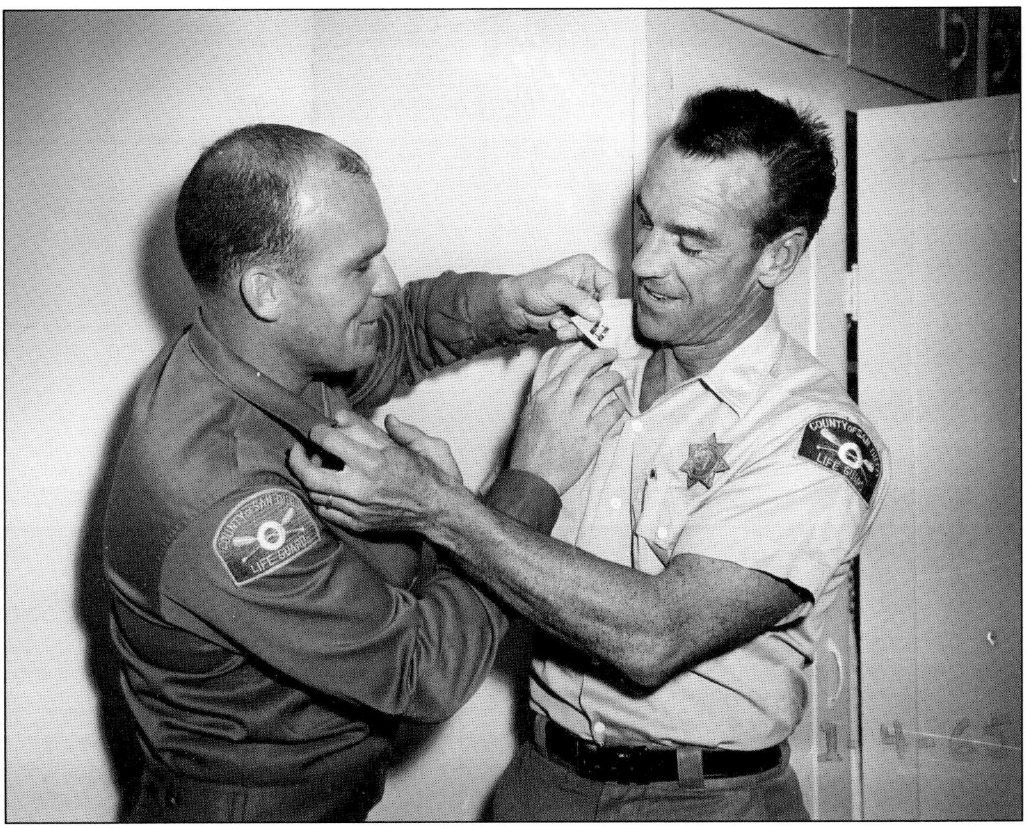

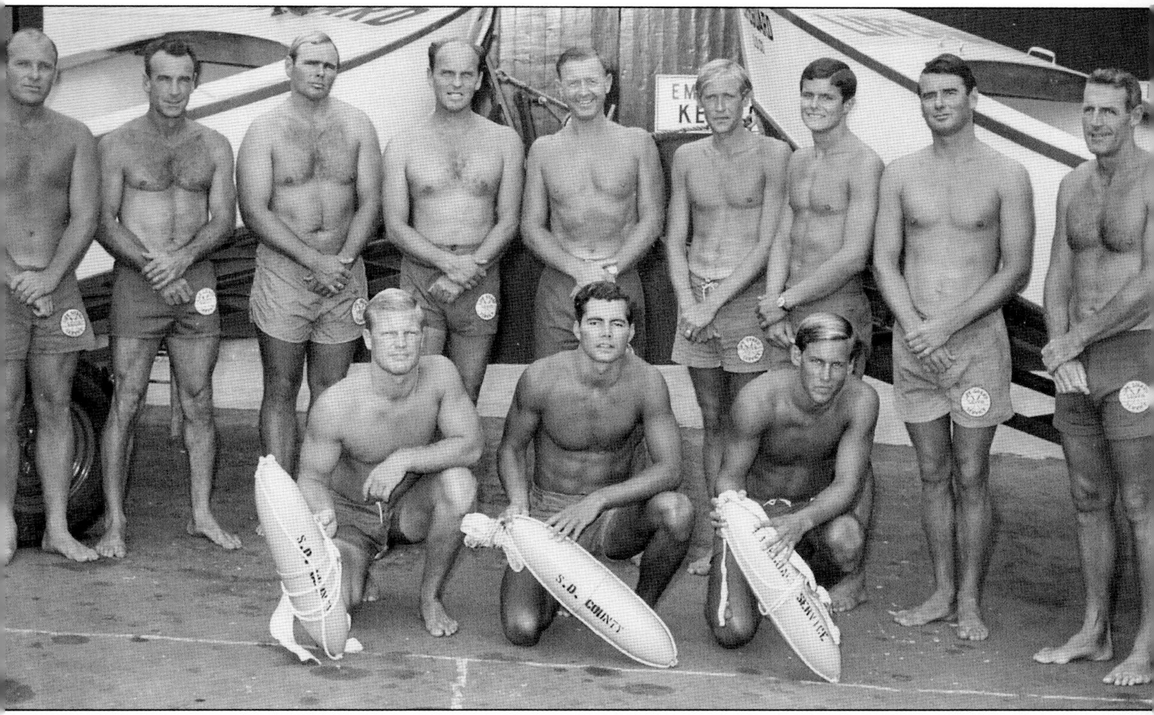

This is another 1960s photograph of the Solana Beach lifeguard crew. (Courtesy of the Solana Beach Department of Marine Safety.)

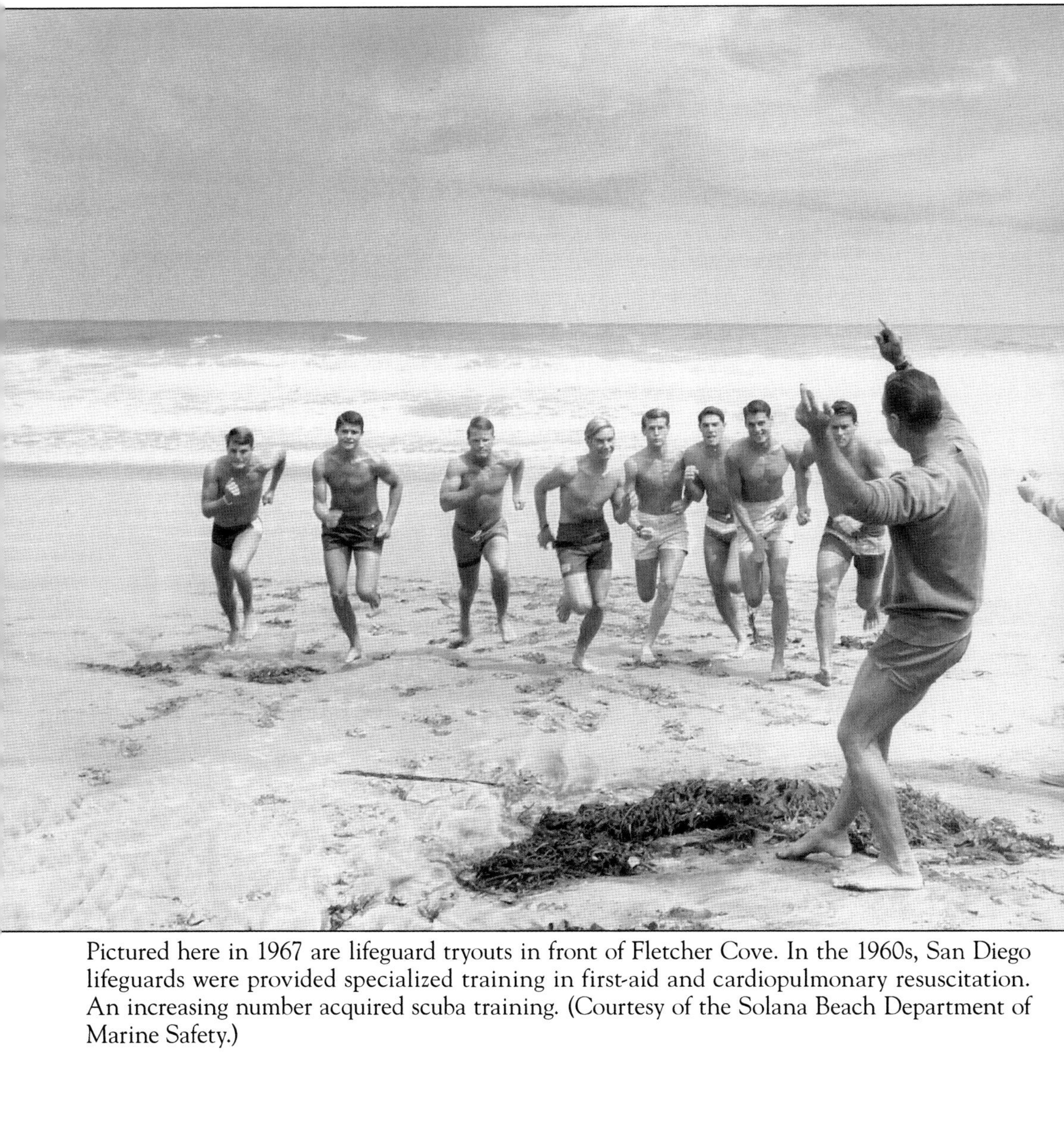

Pictured here in 1967 are lifeguard tryouts in front of Fletcher Cove. In the 1960s, San Diego lifeguards were provided specialized training in first-aid and cardiopulmonary resuscitation. An increasing number acquired scuba training. (Courtesy of the Solana Beach Department of Marine Safety.)

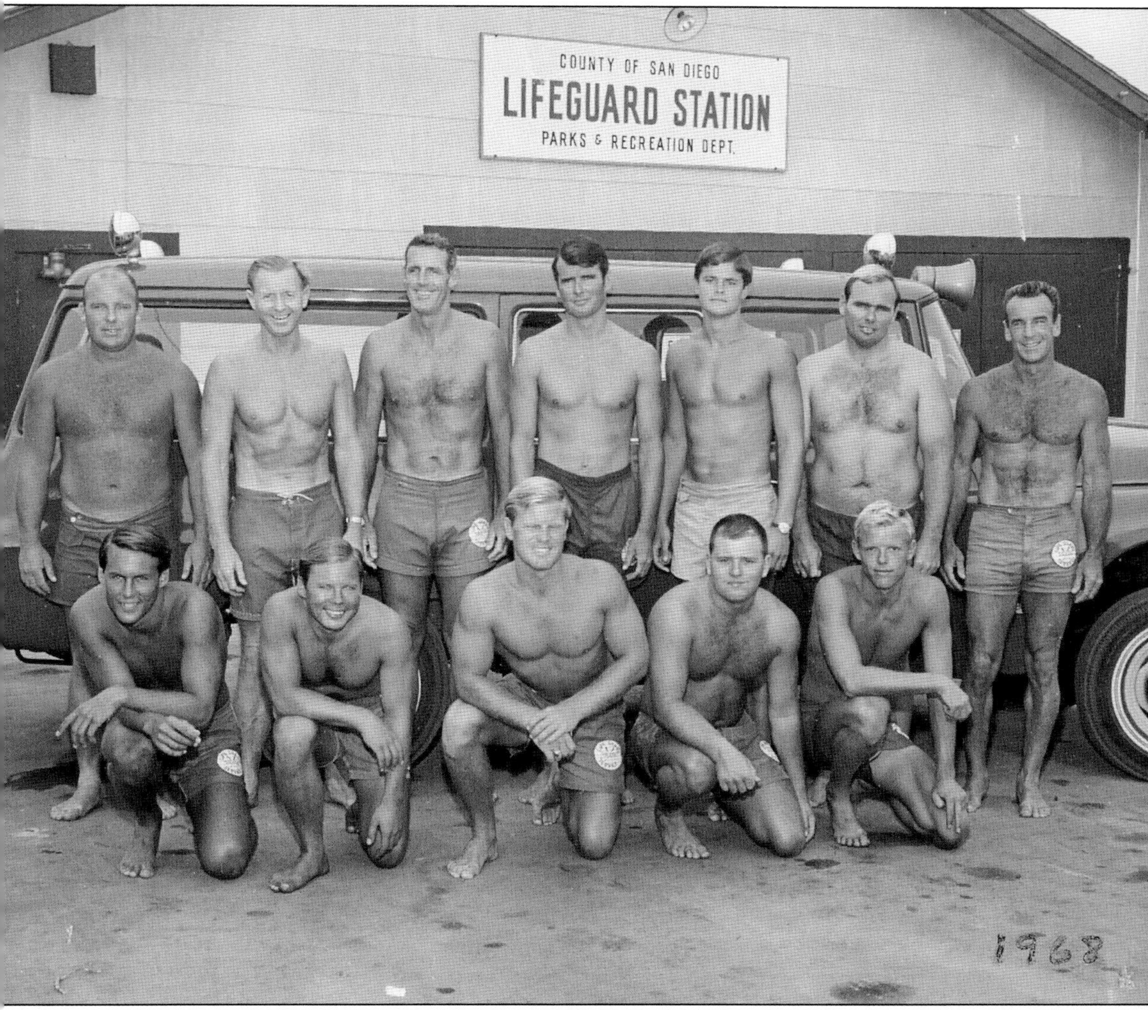

This is a group shot of the lifeguard crew in 1968. Behind the lifeguards is an International Harvester Travelall, a full-size, truck-based utility vehicle, a precursor to the modern SUV. (Courtesy of the Solana Beach Department of Marine Safety.)

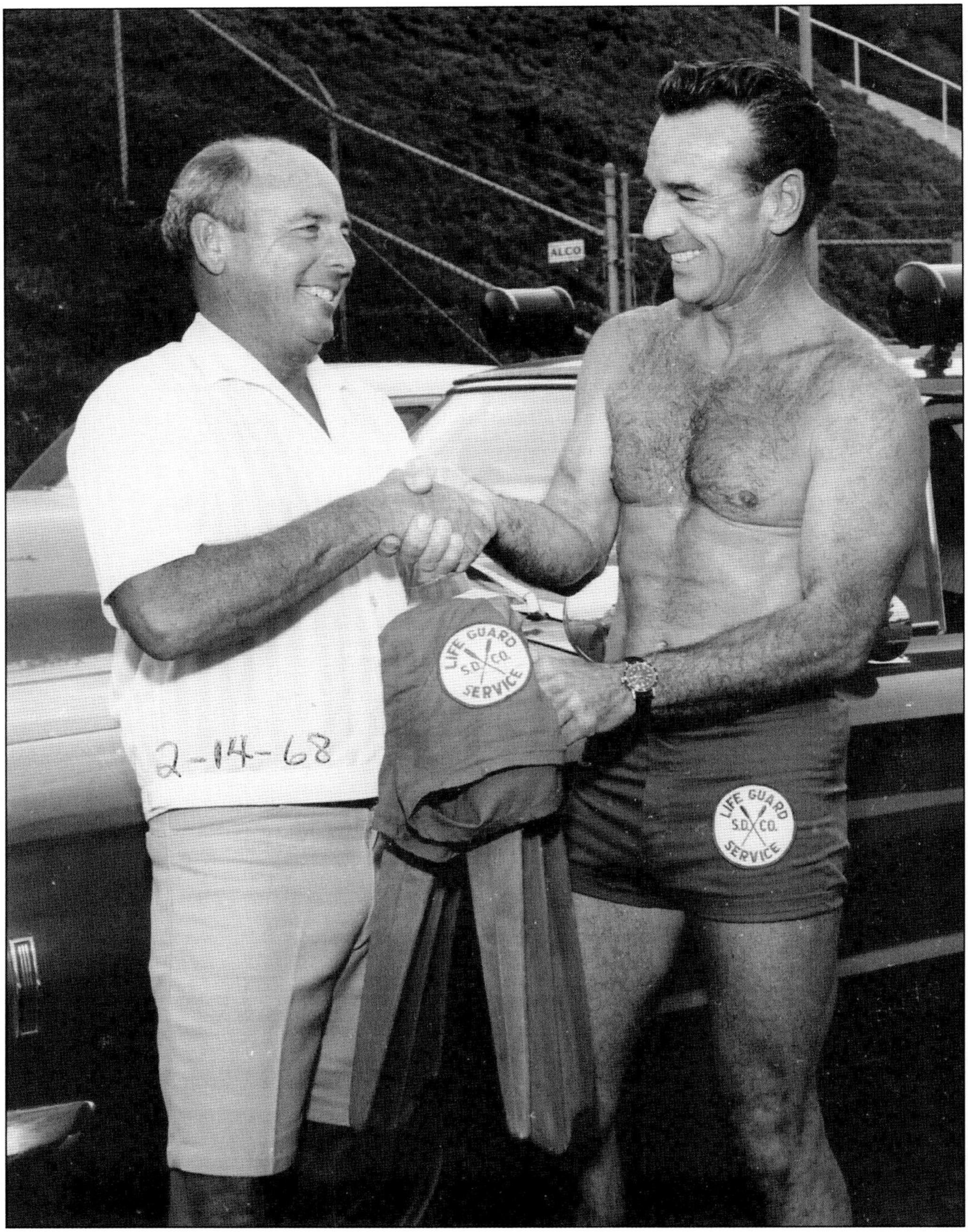

Capt. Jim Lathers (right) is pictured here congratulating lifeguard Knox Harris on his 27-year career in the lifeguard services. Harris began his career in 1941 and was forced to retire in 1968 due to an injury to his Achilles tendon during a rescue. (Courtesy of the Solana Beach Department of Marine Safety.)

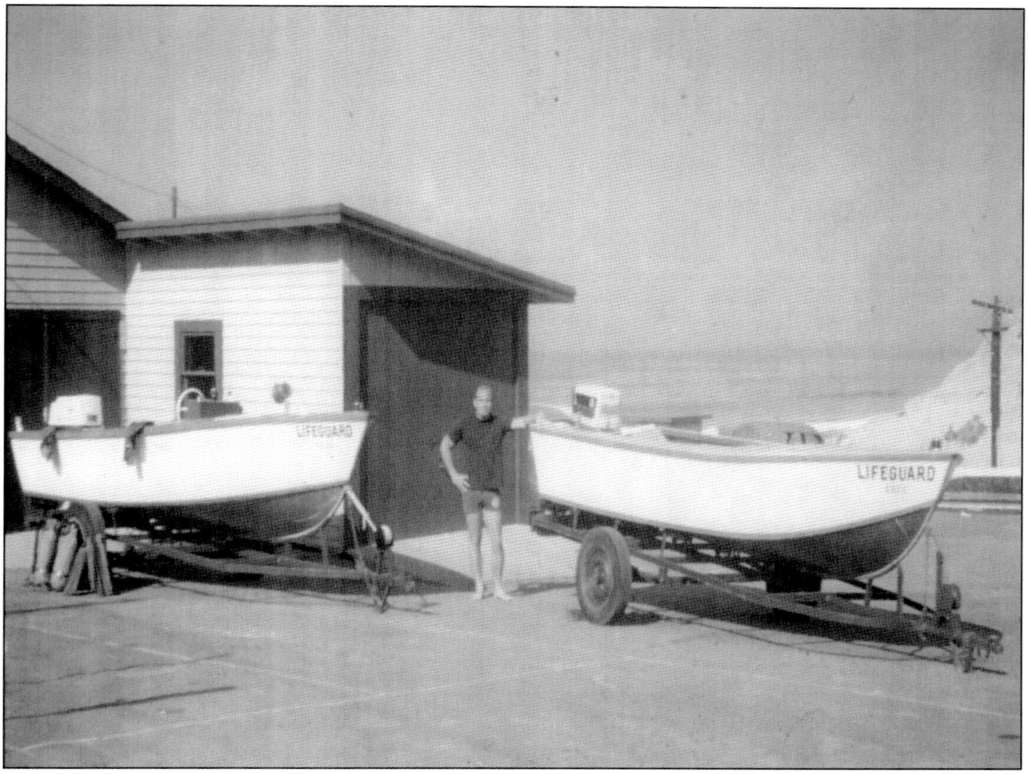

By the late 1960s, San Diego County began to appropriate more funds to the parks and recreation department, which managed the lifeguards of Solana Beach. Here, the county delivers two fairly new lifeboats, which were able to rescue surfers, swimmers, divers, and small recreational vehicles when needed. (Courtesy of the Solana Beach Department of Marine Safety.)

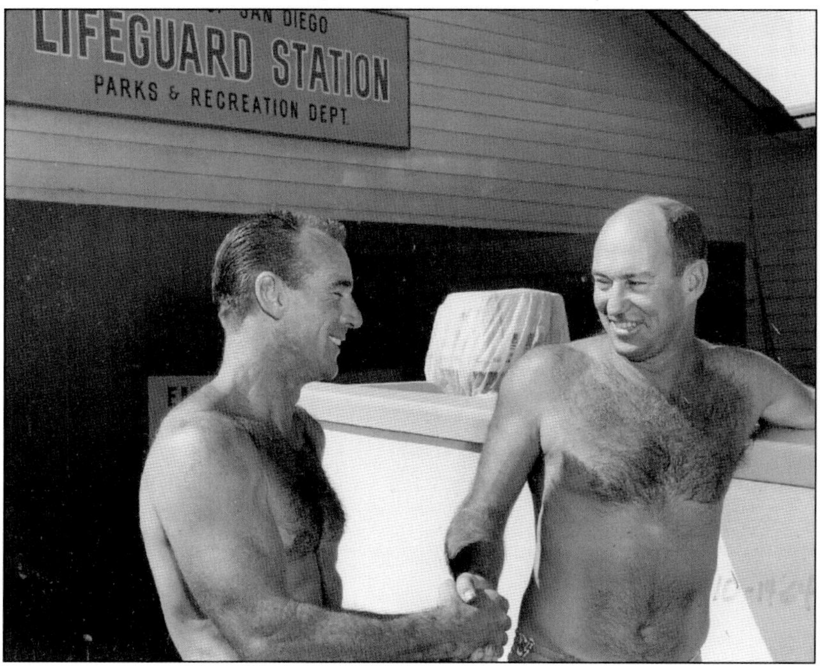

Bill Lathers (left) and Knox Harris are pictured here in 1964. (Courtesy of the Solana Beach Department of Marine Safety.)

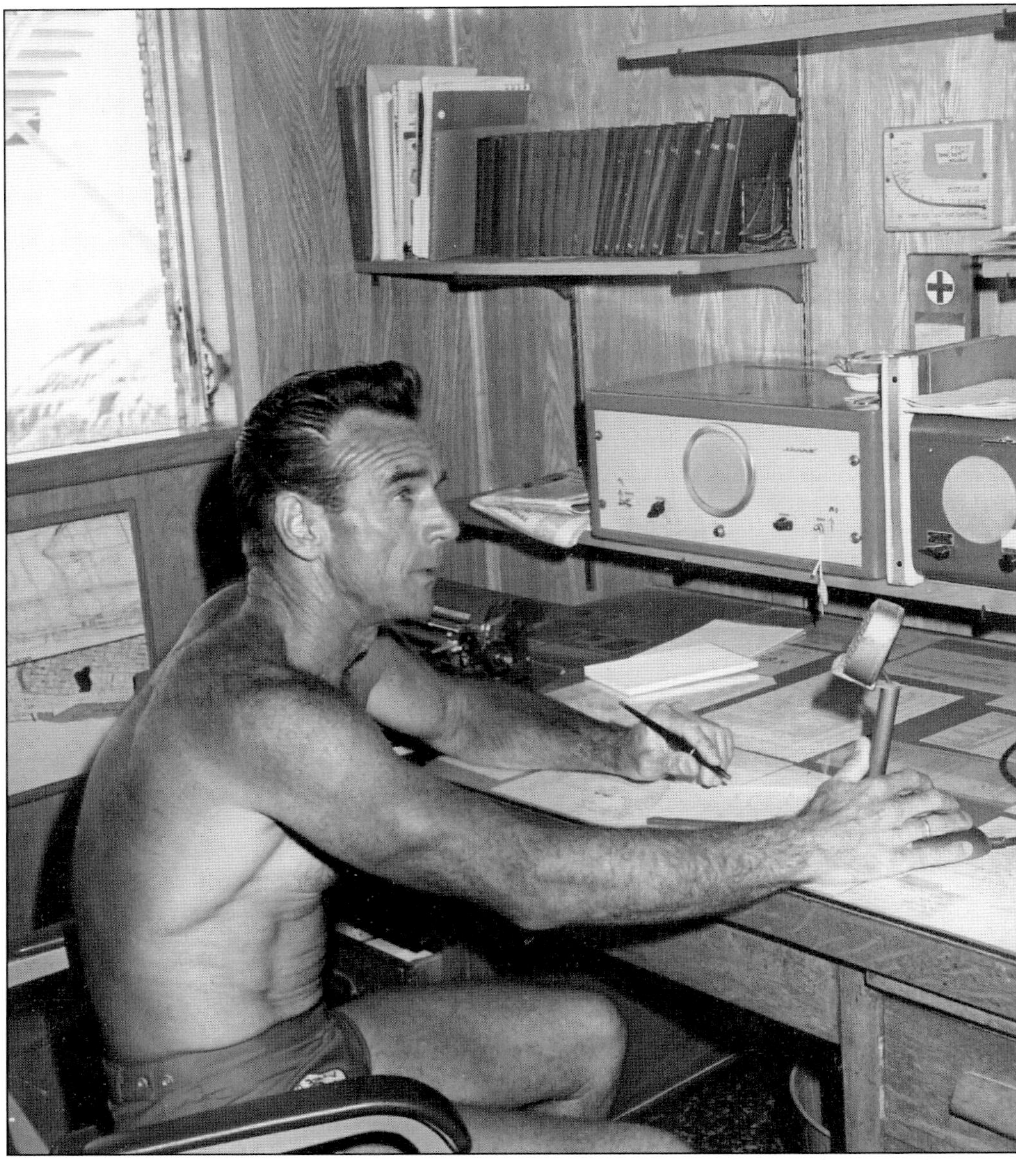

Bill Lathers is pictured here in 1971 at his desk at the Solana Beach lifeguard station. (Courtesy of the Solana Beach Department of Marine Safety.)

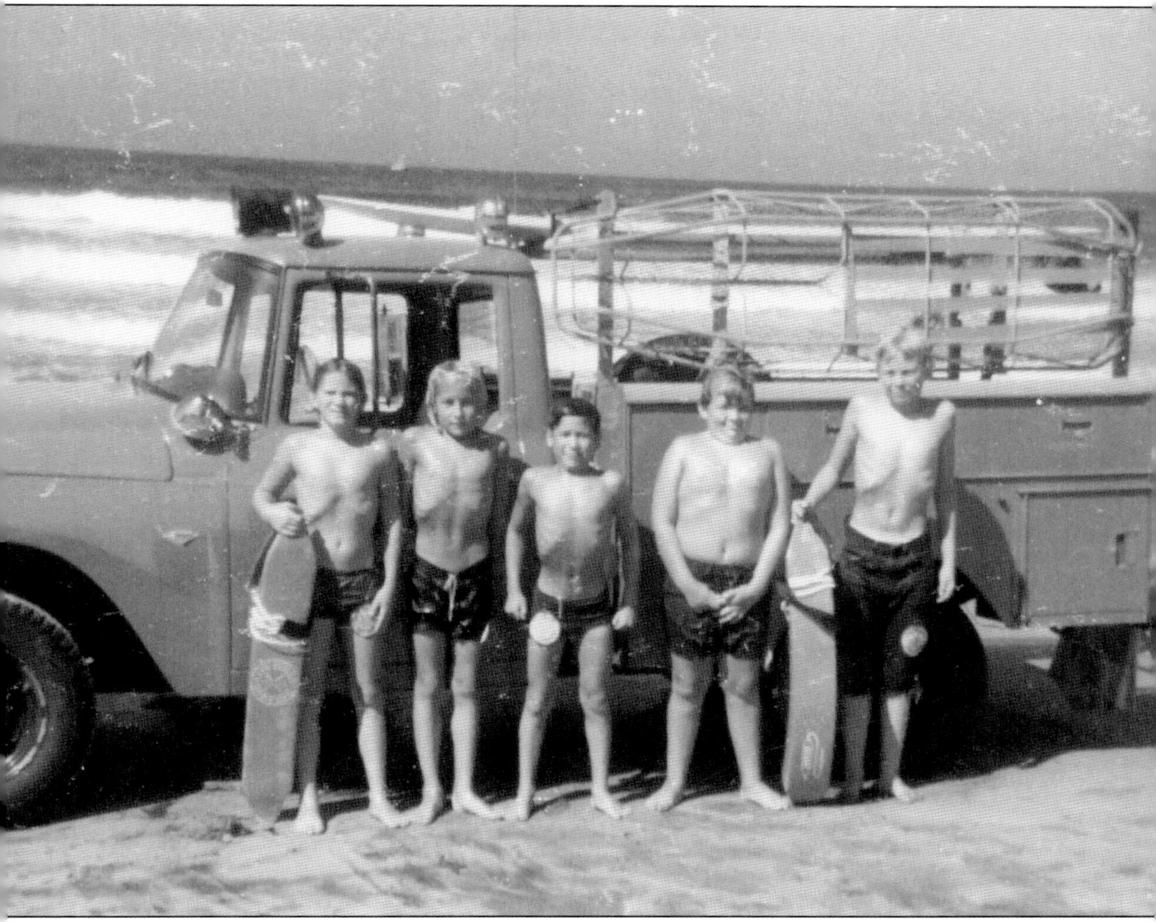

These junior lifeguards, from left to right Mike Gilkey, Blake Urwell, Miguel Urwell, John Miller, and David Miller, are posing for the camera in 1971. (Courtesy of the Solana Beach Department of Marine Safety.)

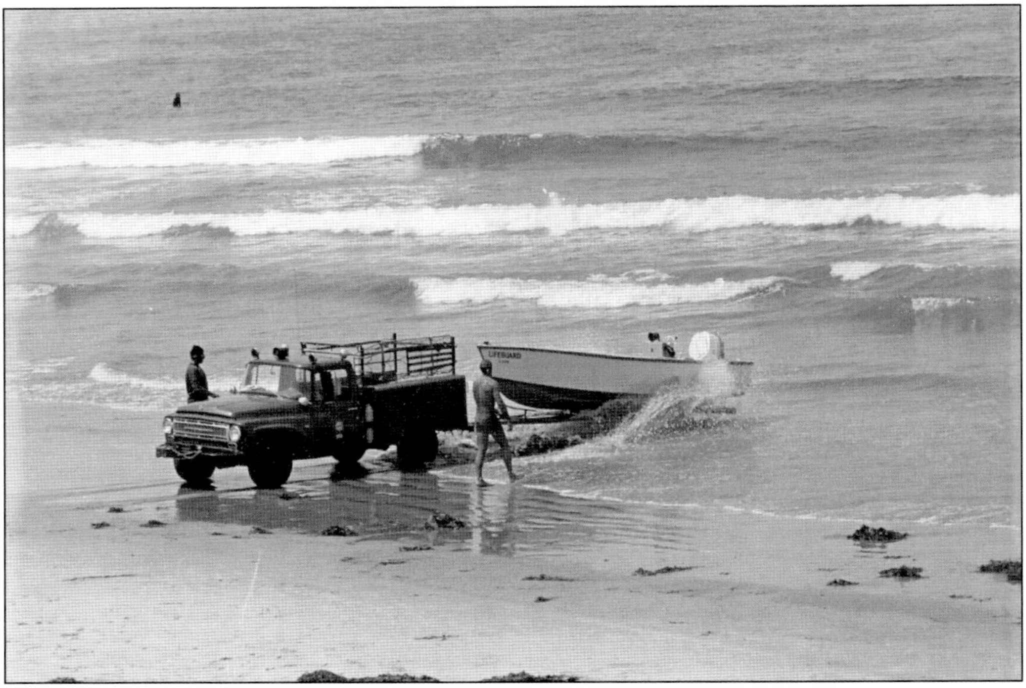

This 1971 photograph captures a rescue boat being launched on Solana Beach. In an era before inflatable and personalized watercraft, deep-water rescues required cumbersome, slow boat launches. (Courtesy of the Solana Beach Department of Marine Safety.)

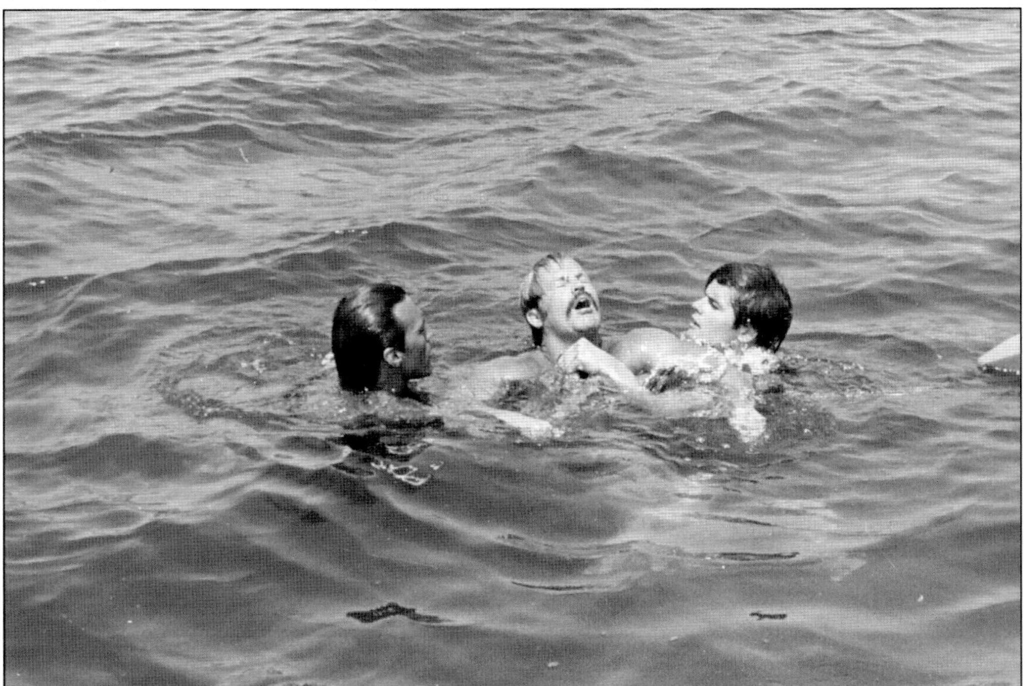

Pictured here in 1971 is a water-rescue test off Fletcher Cove. (Courtesy of the Solana Beach Department of Marine Safety.)

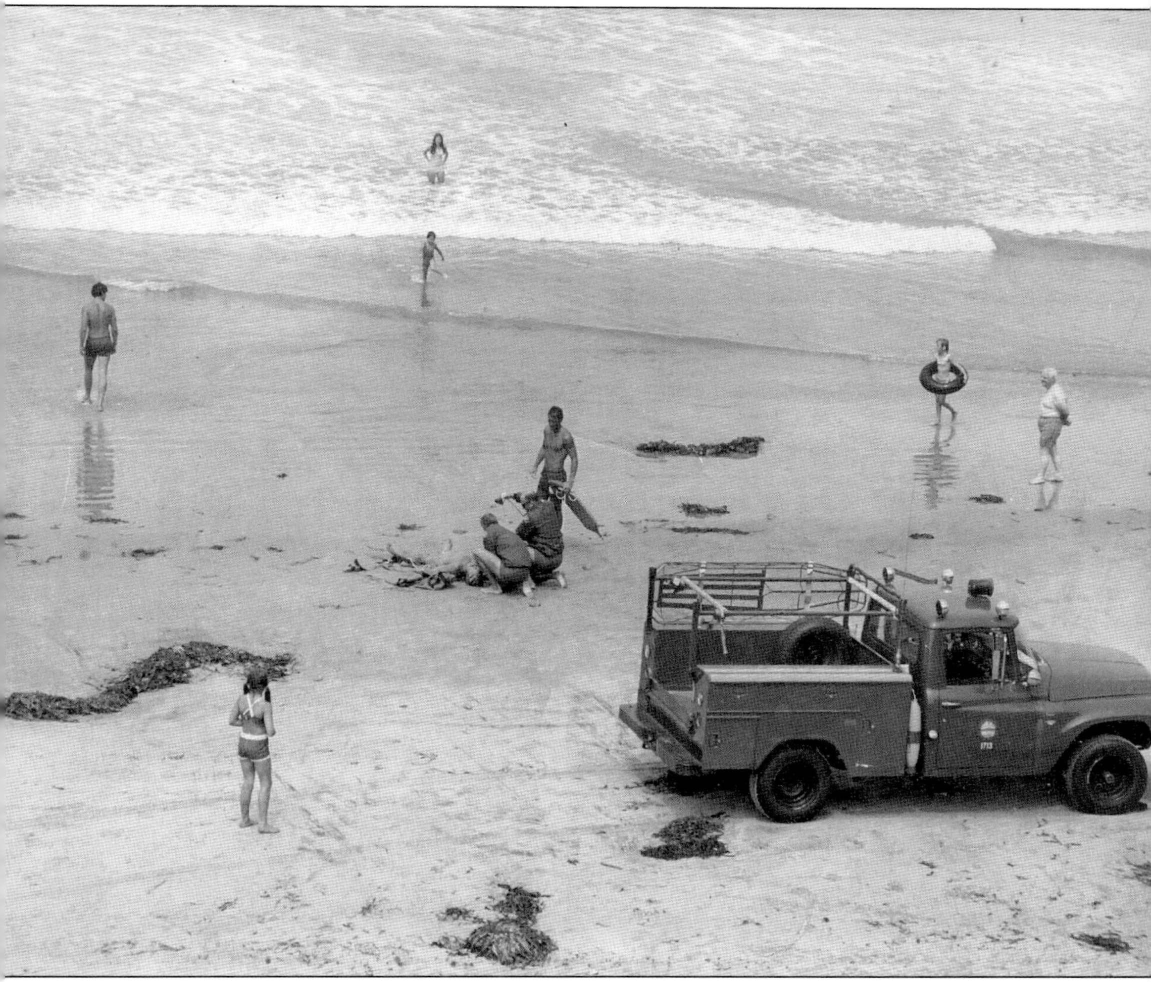

This is an actual beach rescue in progress in 1971. (Courtesy of the Solana Beach Department of Marine Safety.)

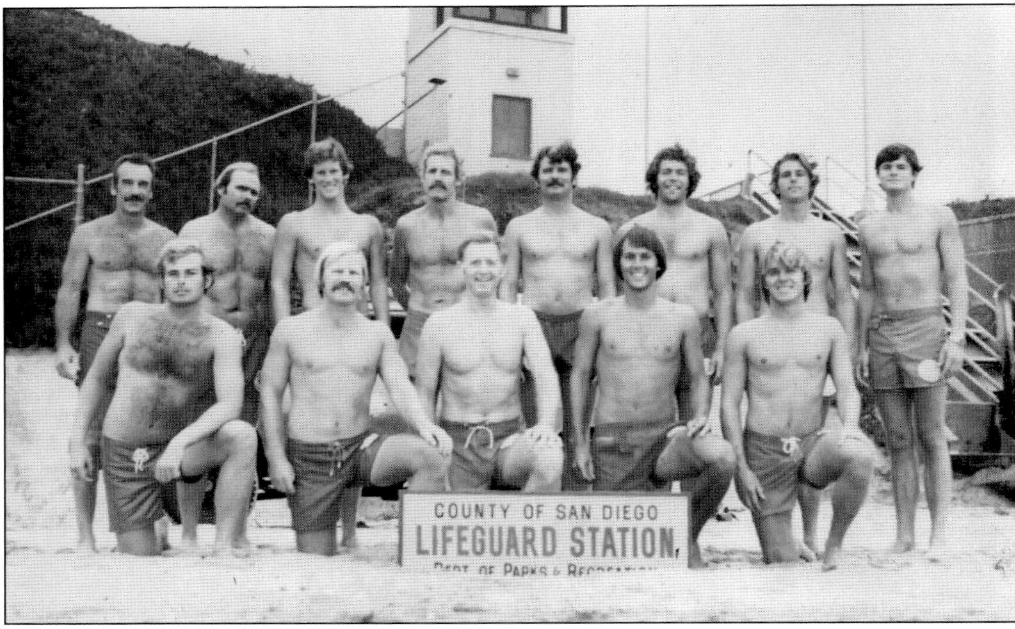

The 1973 lifeguard crew is pictured here for the annual portrait. (Courtesy of the Solana Beach Department of Marine Safety.)

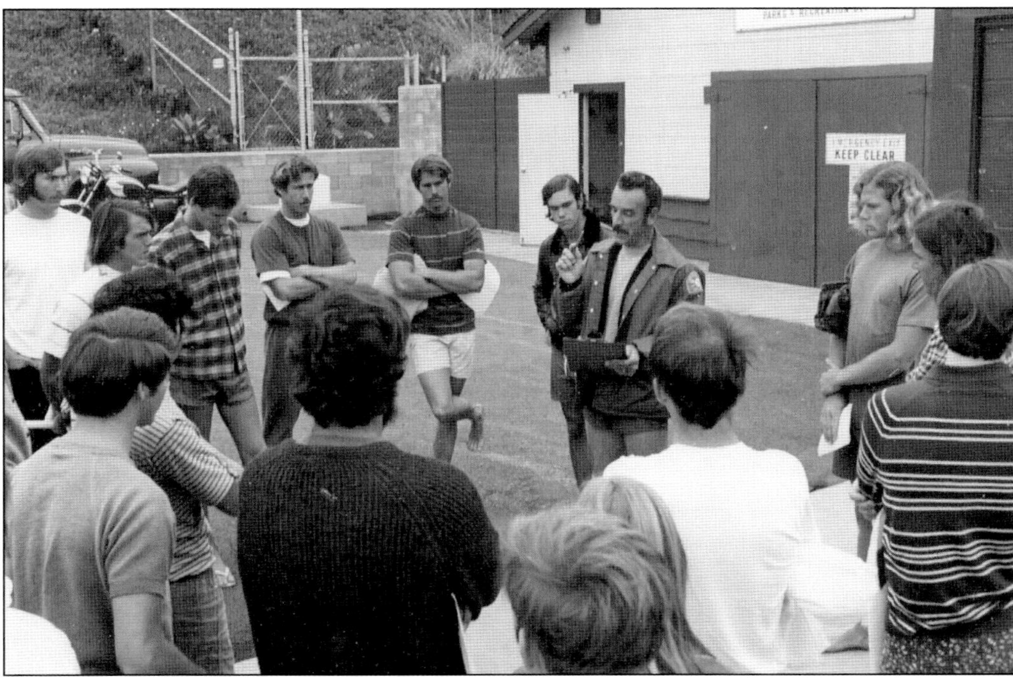

Bill Lathers is pictured here administering the seasonal lifeguard test in the late spring of 1973. Lifeguard tryouts took place in Fletcher Cove each year. (Courtesy of the Solana Beach Department of Marine Safety.)

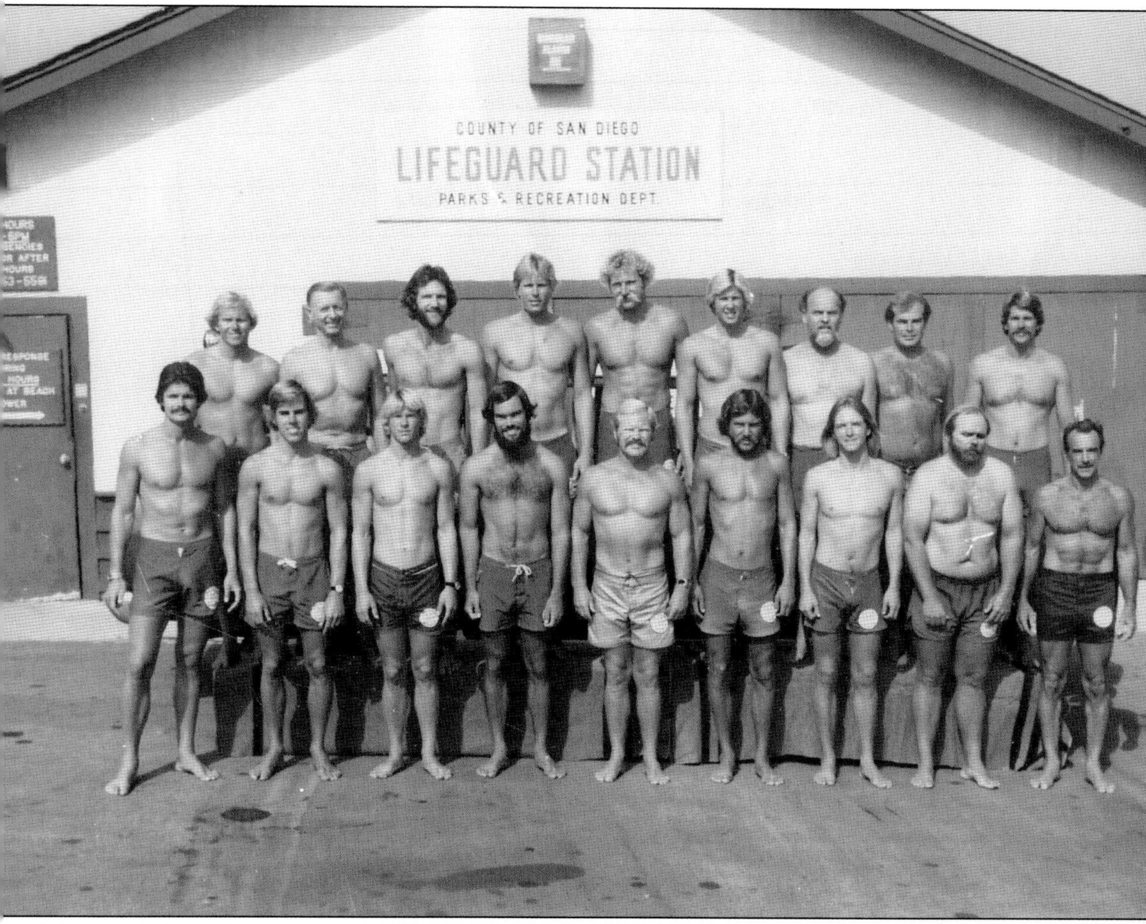

The 1978 lifeguard crew is pictured here just outside of the station. (Courtesy of the Solana Beach Department of Marine Safety.)

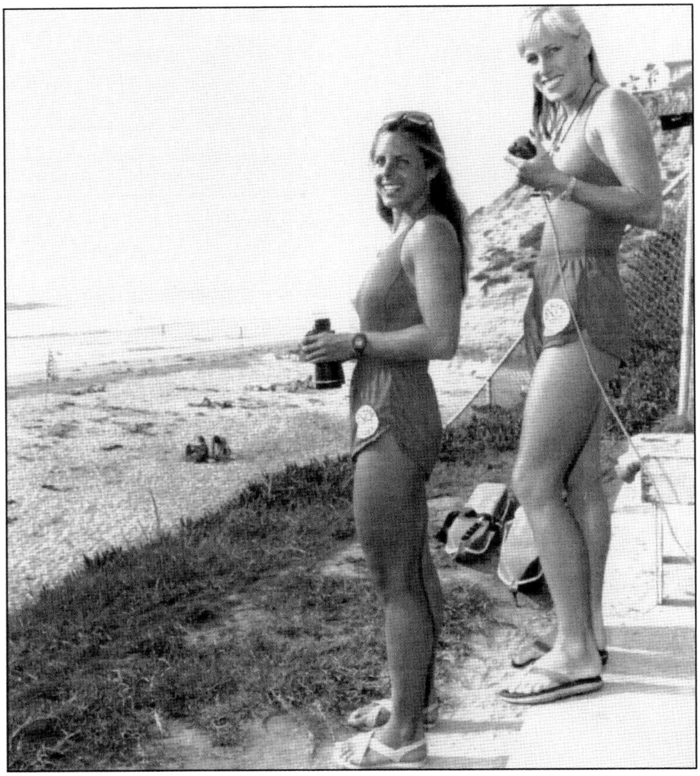

The first two female Solana Beach lifeguards washed ashore in 1980. Pictured on the left is Linda Kimora. (Courtesy of the Solana Beach Department of Marine Safety.)

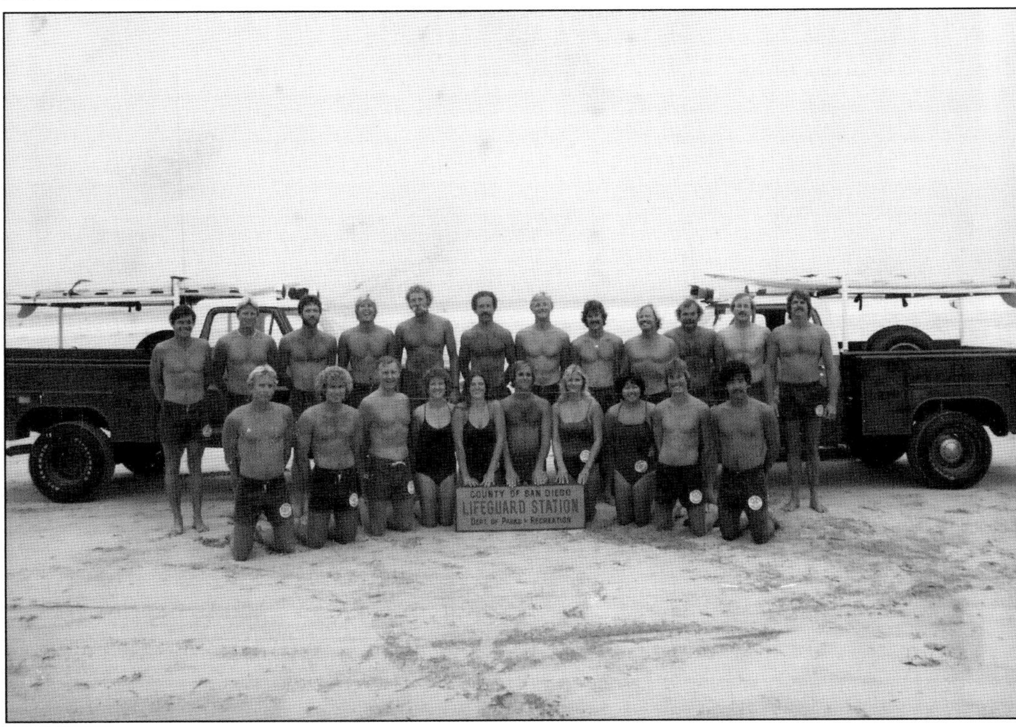

This 1980s photograph of the Solana Beach crew demonstrates that more and more women were becoming lifeguards. (Courtesy of the Solana Beach Department of Marine Safety.)

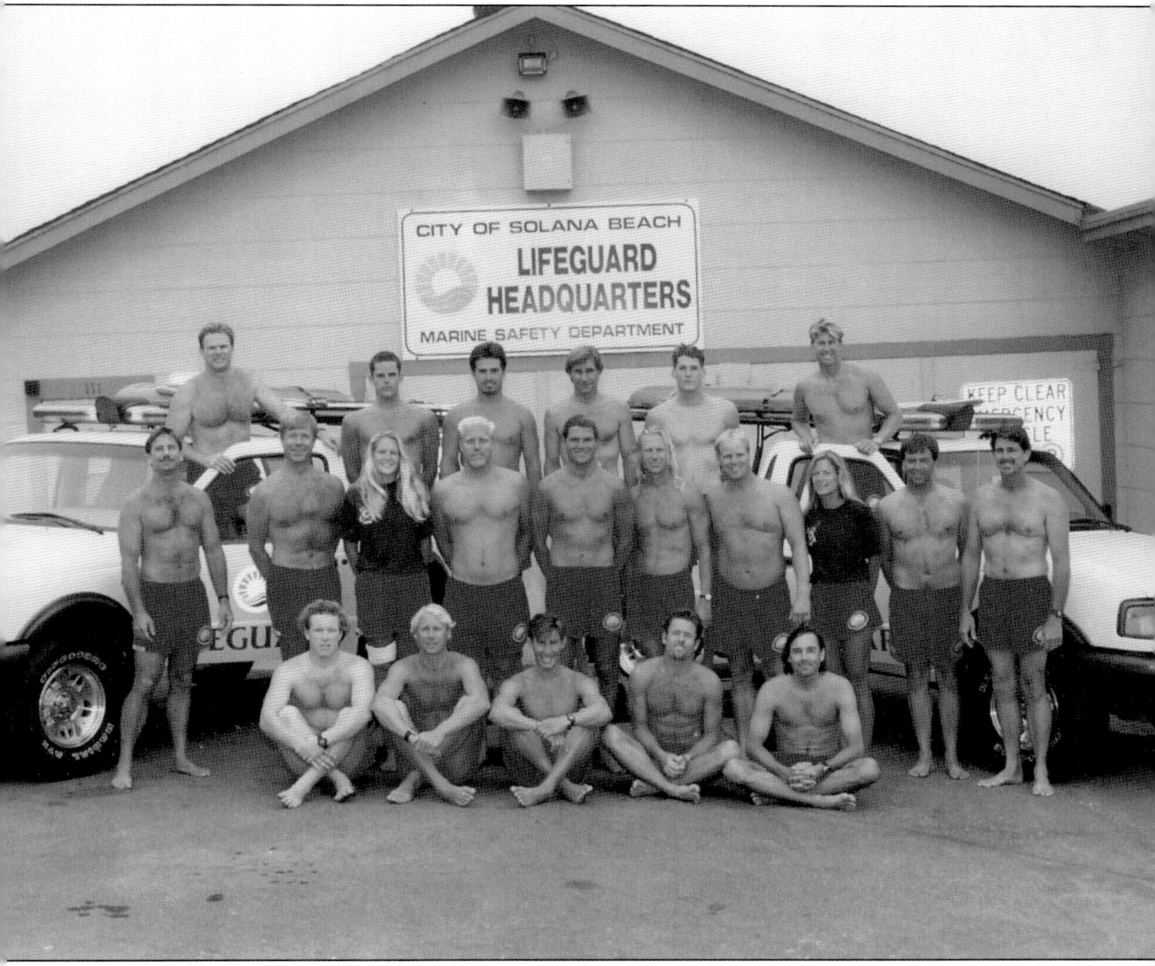

The 1995 crew is pictured here in front of the lifeguard headquarters. Note the official city logo, as Solana Beach had achieved cityhood in 1986. (Courtesy of the Solana Beach Department of Marine Safety.)

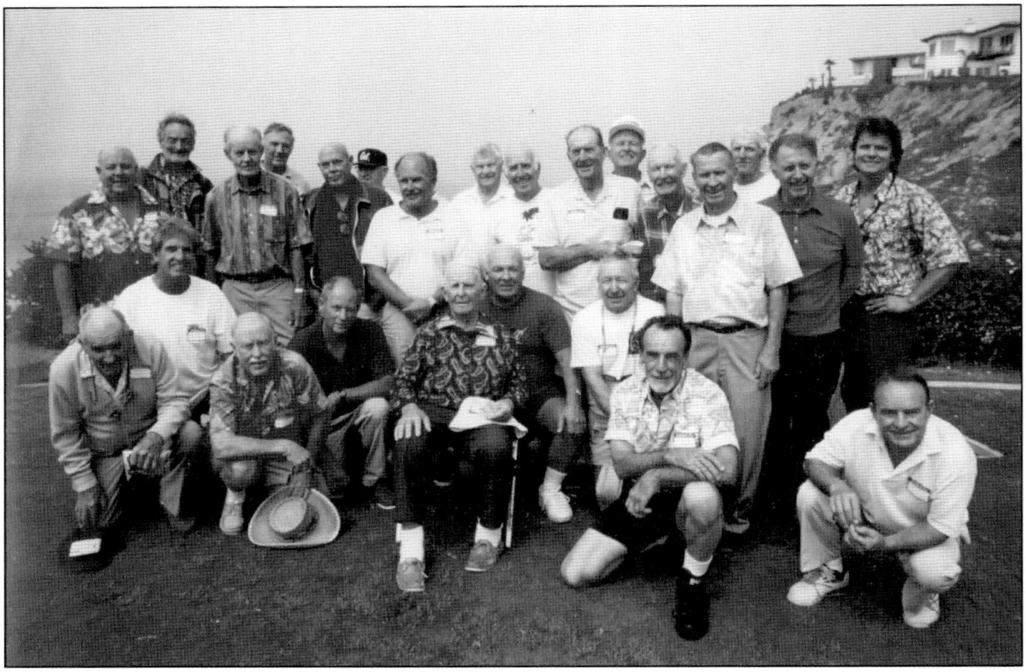

Seen here in the 1990s is a reunion of several Solana Beach lifeguards. Some in attendance had served the area since the 1940s. (Courtesy of the Solana Beach Department of Marine Safety.)

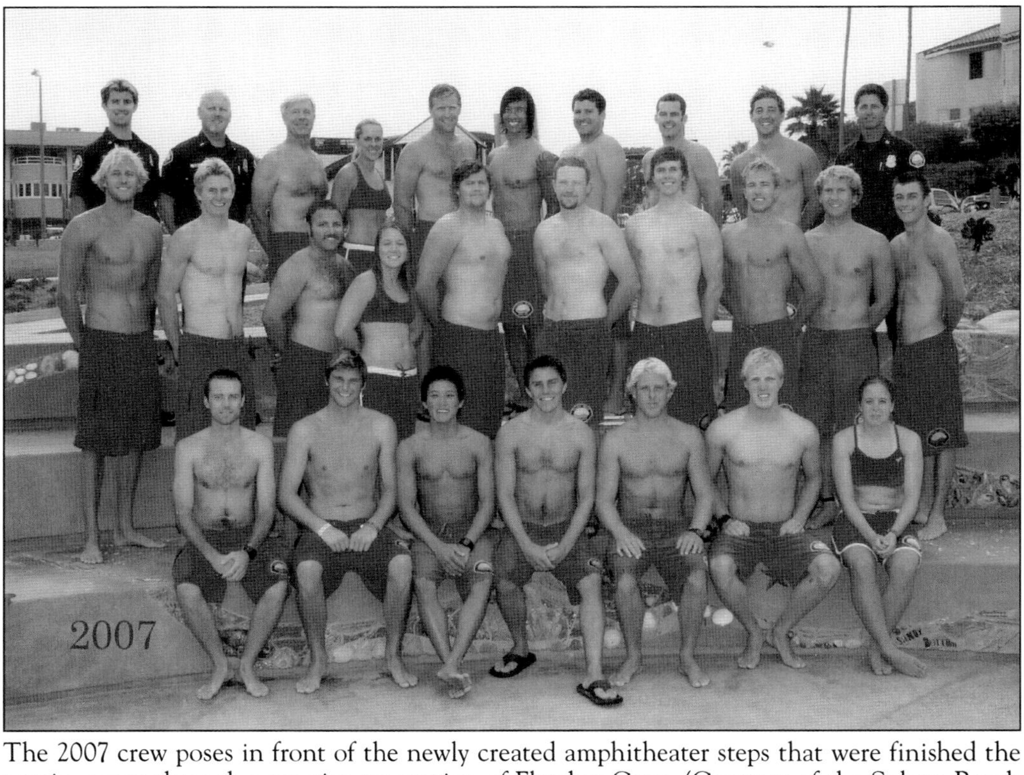

The 2007 crew poses in front of the newly created amphitheater steps that were finished the previous year through a massive renovation of Fletcher Cove. (Courtesy of the Solana Beach Department of Marine Safety.)

Five

Postwar Progress
The 1950s and 1960s

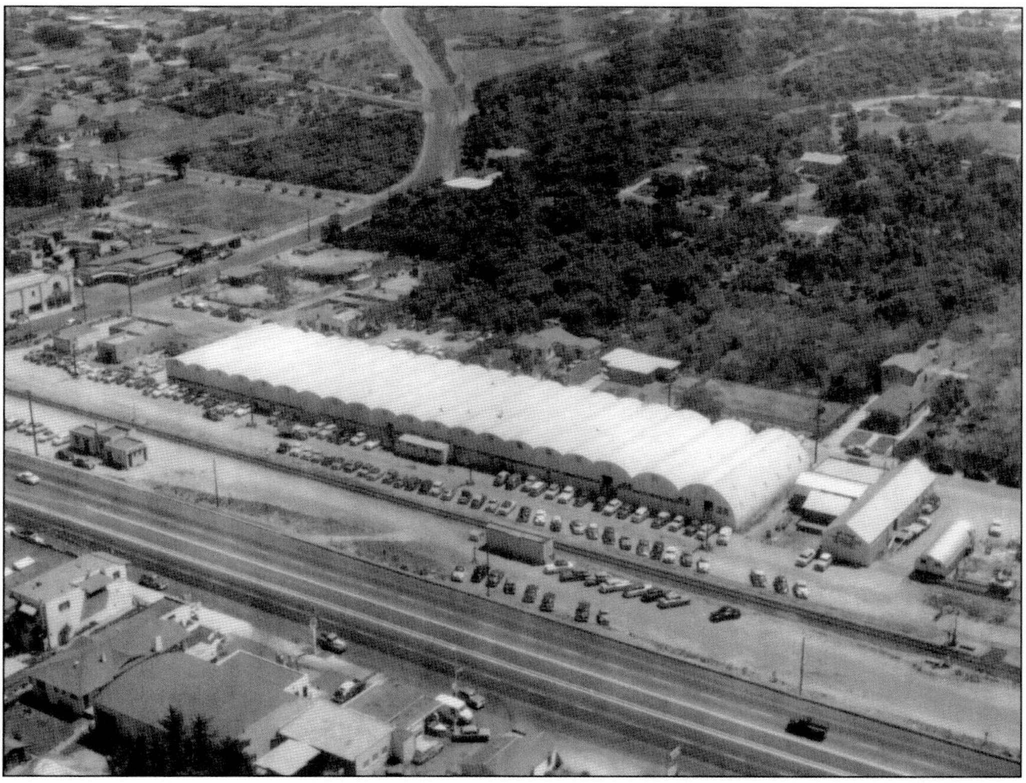

This 1950s shot looks east over Highway 101 to the Bill Jack Scientific Instrument Company. Businessman Bill Jack established his company in the late 1940s in a row of Quonset huts he had built along North Cedros Avenue. The gently sloping rooflines later became one of the landmarks of Solana Beach, which was reconfigured to house restaurants and shops and influenced the design of the train station.

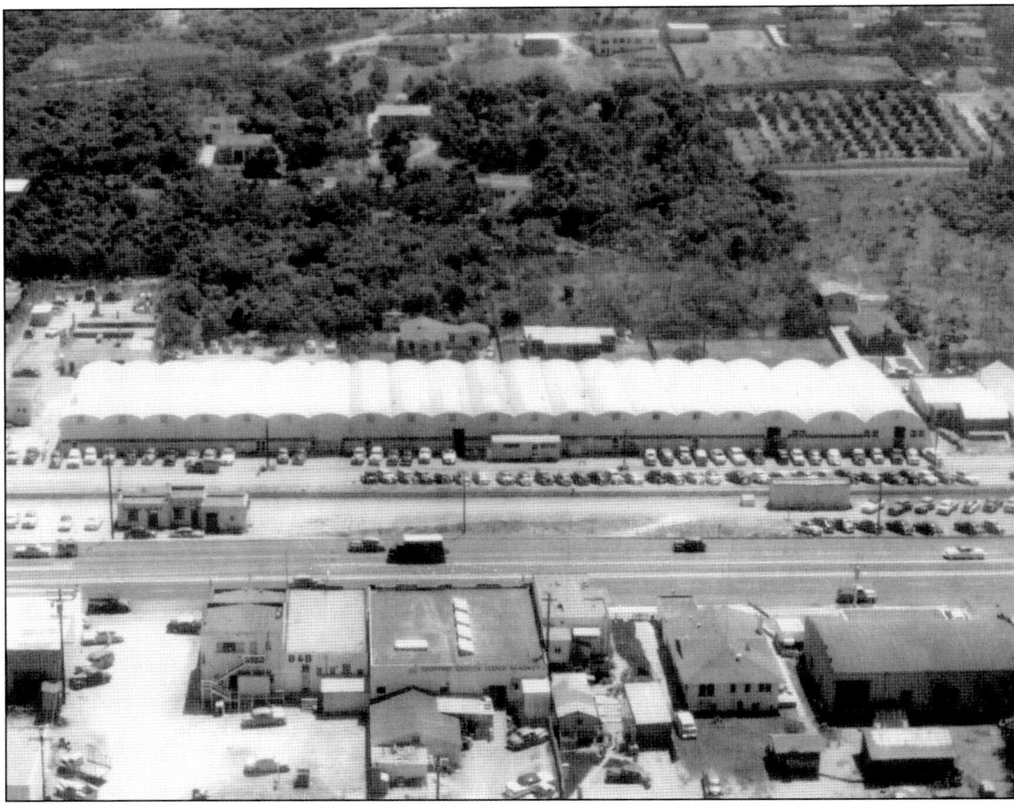

Jack's company built a variety of equipment, including reconnaissance photographic apparatus, motors, tachometers, and police and test-pilot helmets.

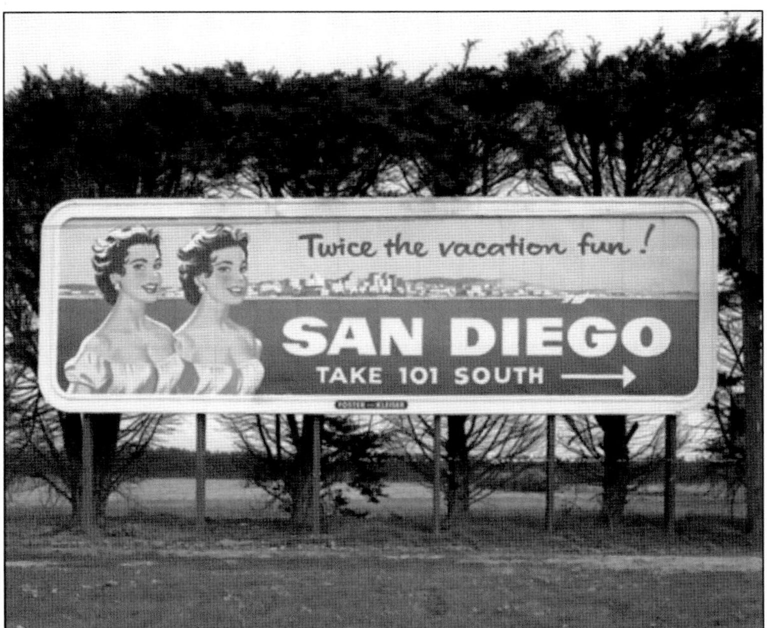

This mid-century tourism sign beckoned to travelers along Highway 101. The 1950s brought with it economic growth throughout the county, affording families from neighboring counties looking for fun and adventure the opportunity to enjoy the ideal climate in San Diego. Highway 101 was still the major artery into San Diego County from the north.

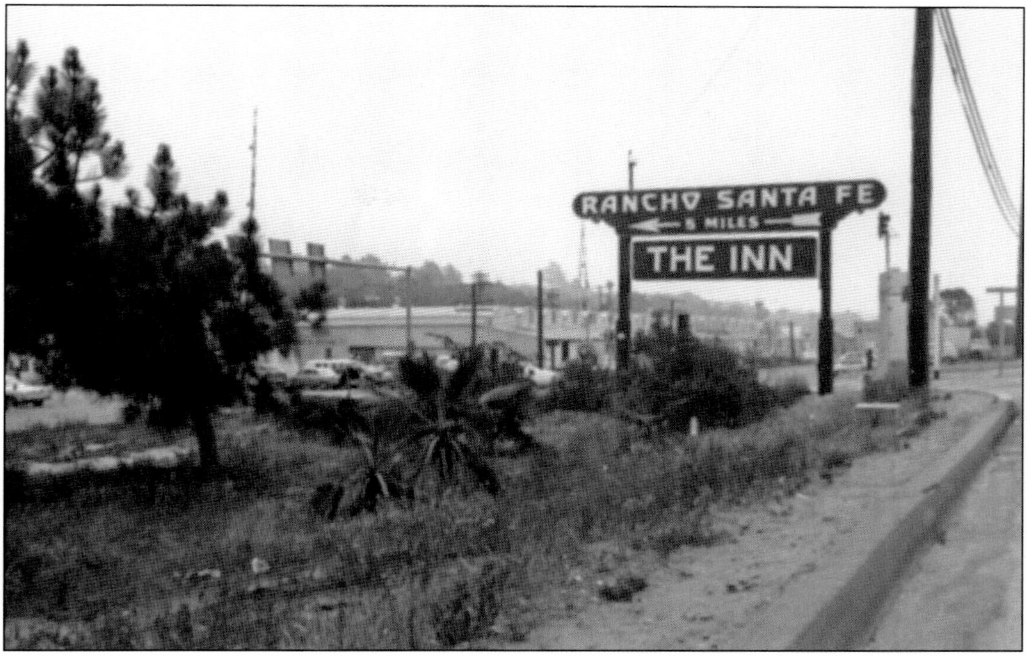

This 1960s shot along Highway 101 looking south points the way to Rancho Santa Fe along Lomas Santa Fe Drive. Situated just left of the sign are the Quonset huts that would later become the Cedros Design Center.

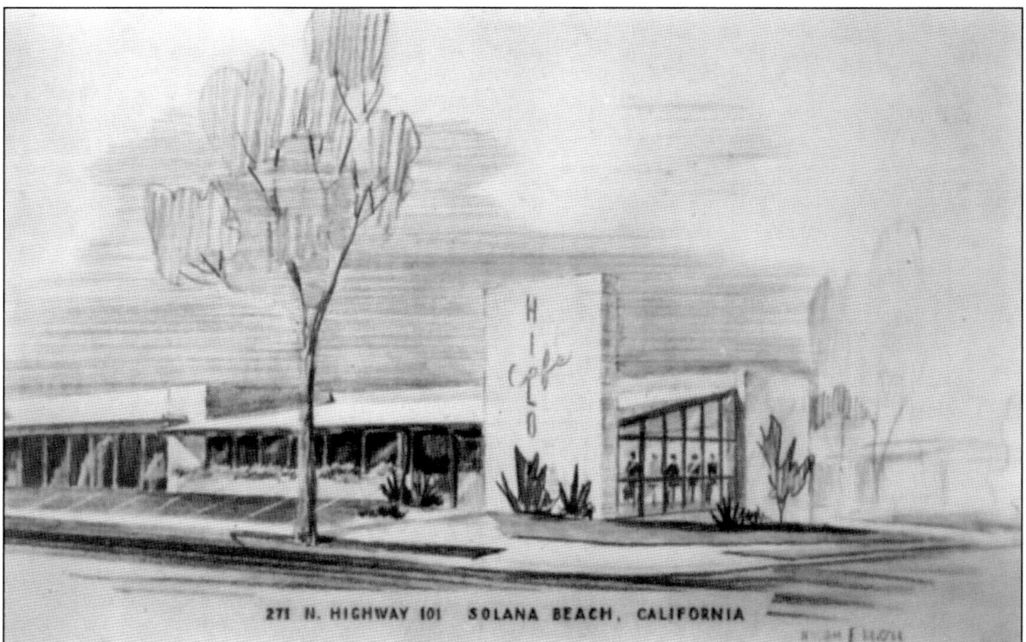

This is a postcard advertising the Hi Lo Café, located at the corner of Highway 101 and Estrella Street. Businesses attempted to attract vacationers heading into San Diego looking for a place to stop for a quick bite to eat. The Hi Lo Café beckoned travelers looking for a family-friendly atmosphere for breakfast, lunch, or dinner.

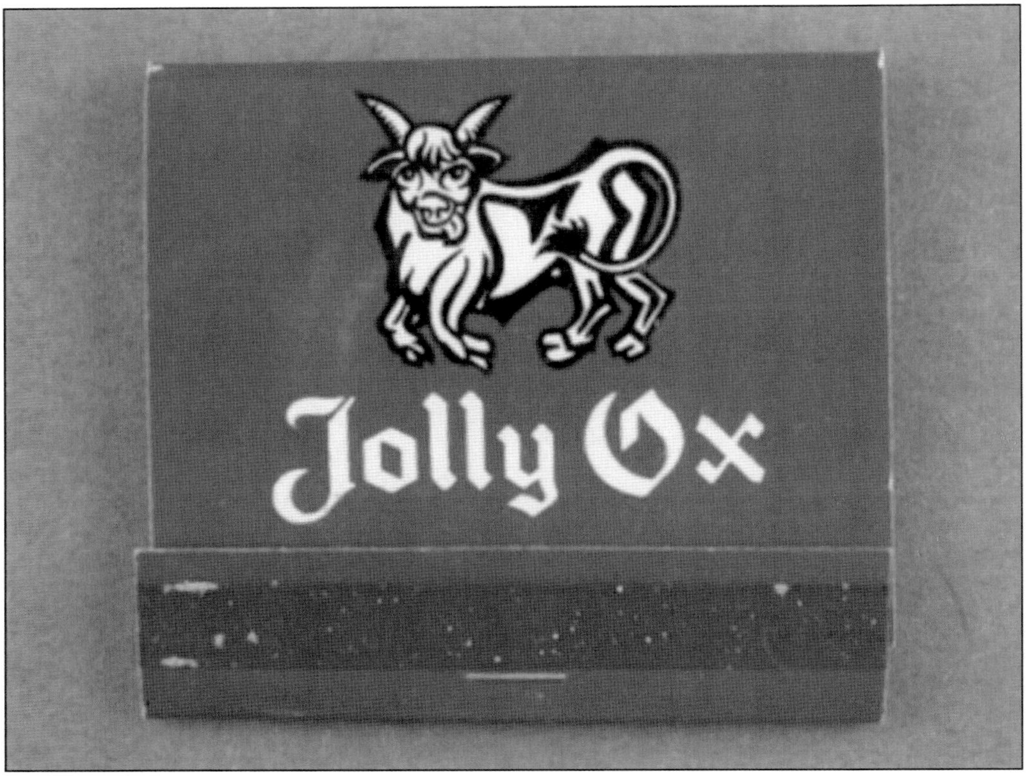

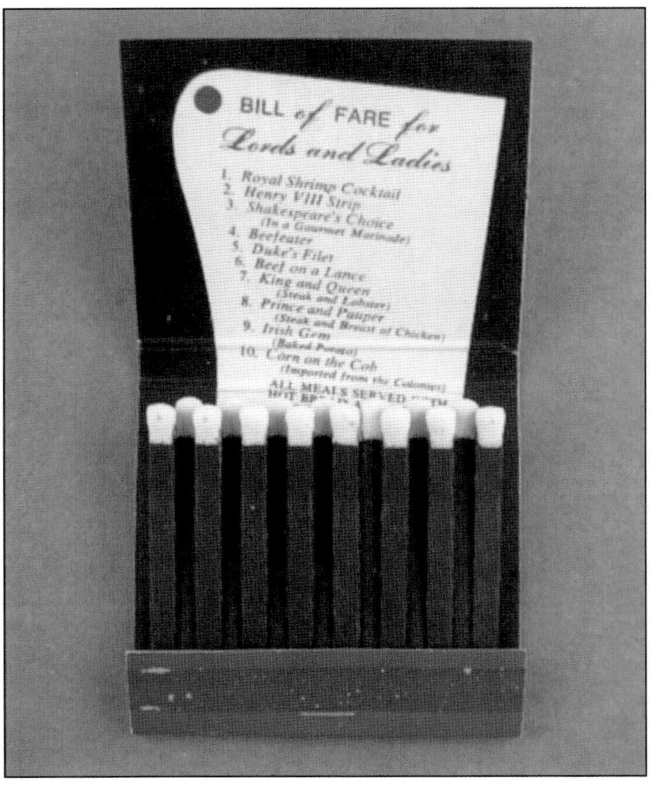

This matchbook from the Jolly Ox restaurant in Solana Beach is likely from the 1960s. The Jolly Ox was part of a chain run by Steak & Ale.

The Jolly Ox featured English pub–style food. Offerings included "Henry VIII Strip," and "Shakespeare's Choice."

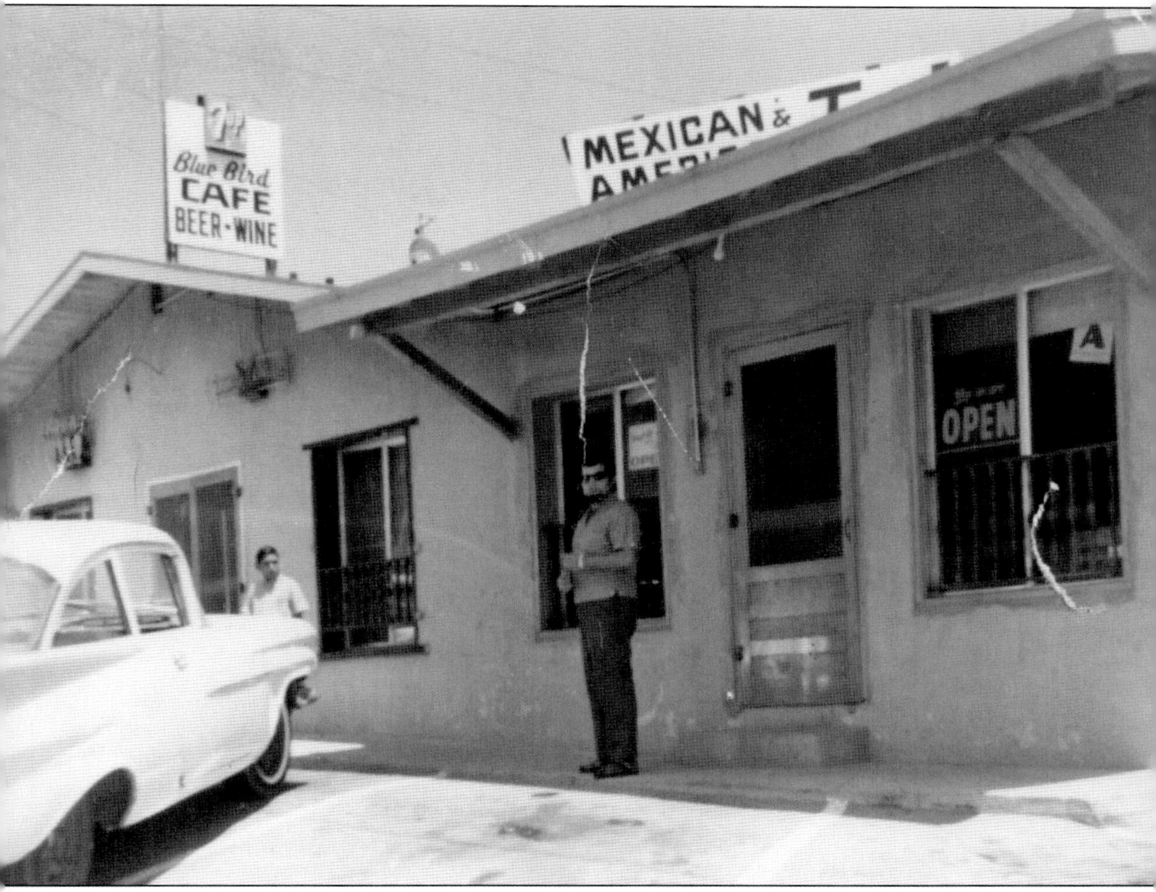

The Blue Bird Café is pictured here in the early 1960s. Formerly located at 646 Valley Avenue in the heart of Eden Gardens, the café was also known as El Pajaro Azul and had a blue parrot as its mascot.

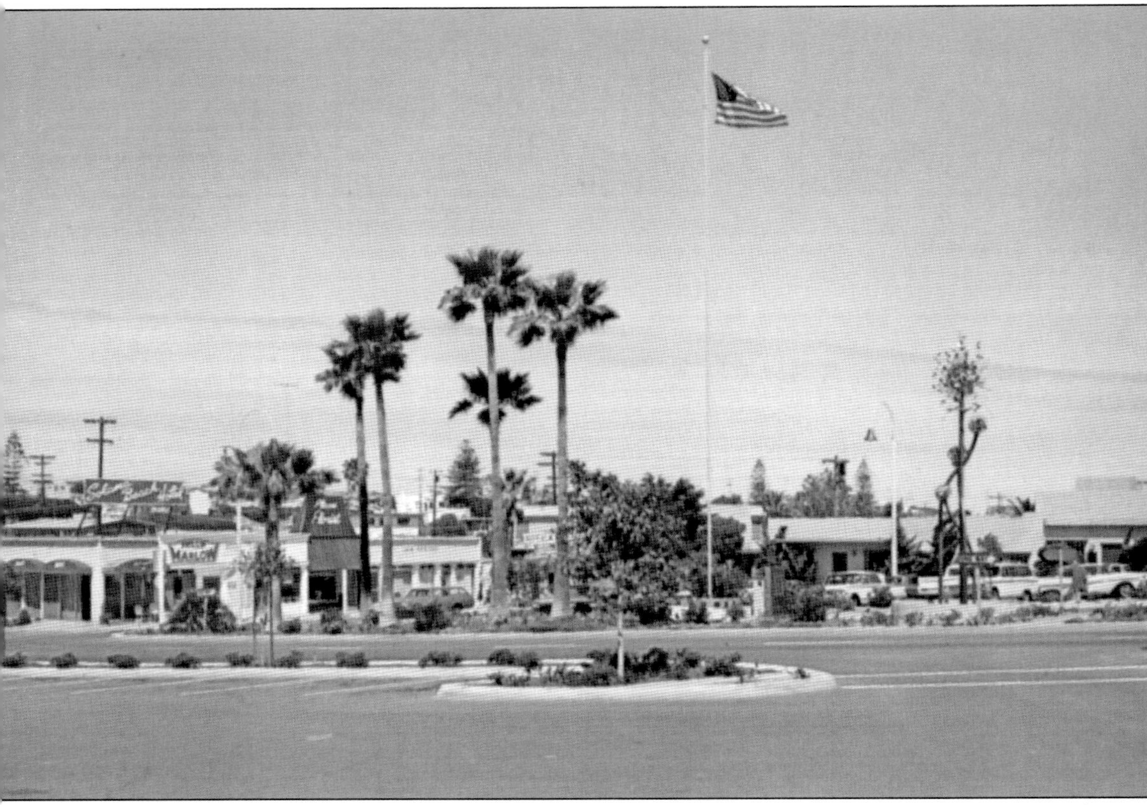

This shot form the late 1960s or early 1970s looks northwest off of Lomas Santa Fe Drive in the Plaza. Note on the left the Solana Beach Hotel, which has been a mainstay since the 1920s.

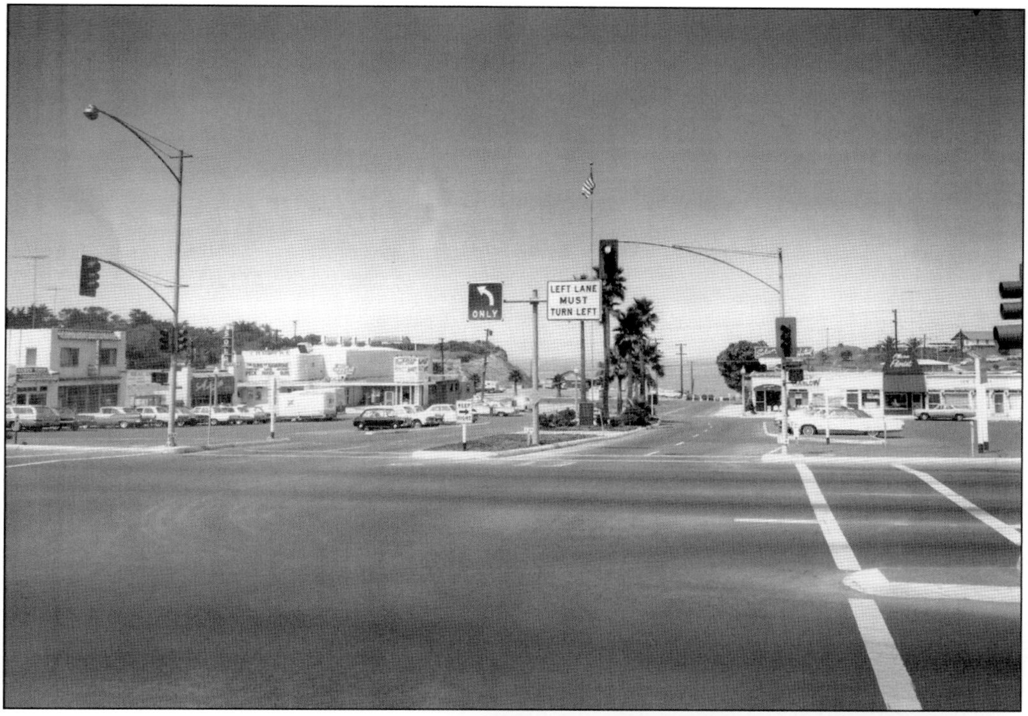

This view looking west down Lomas Santa Fe Drive toward Fletcher Cove was taken sometime in the 1970s.

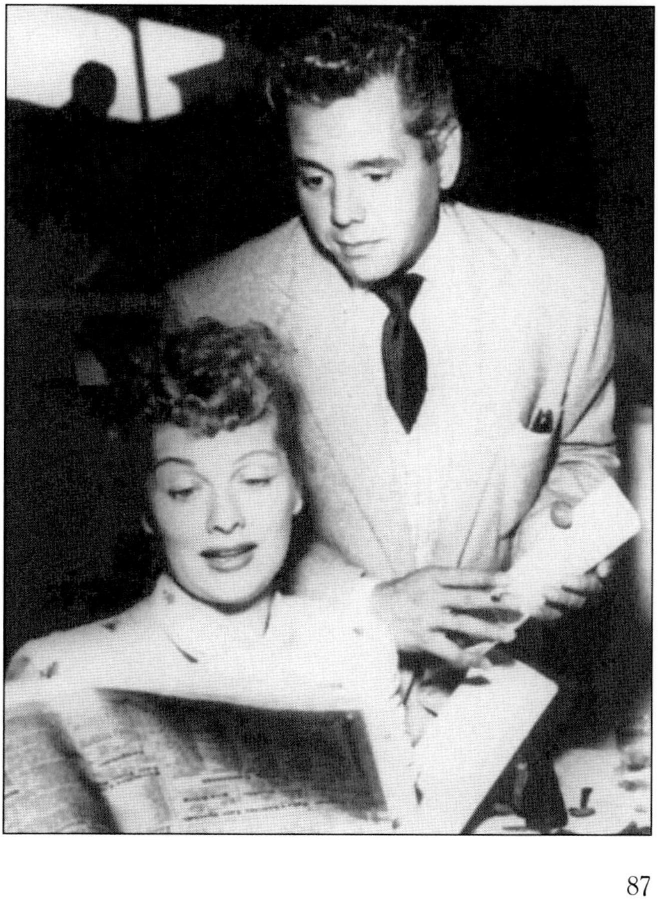

Celebrities, including Desi and Lucy, continued to hit Solana Beach's adjacent Del Mar Racetrack during the 1950s and 1960s. Arnaz lived in Del Mar at 1920 Ocean Front Drive and could be seen in surrounding Solana Beach until his death in 1986. (Courtesy of the Del Mar Historical Society.)

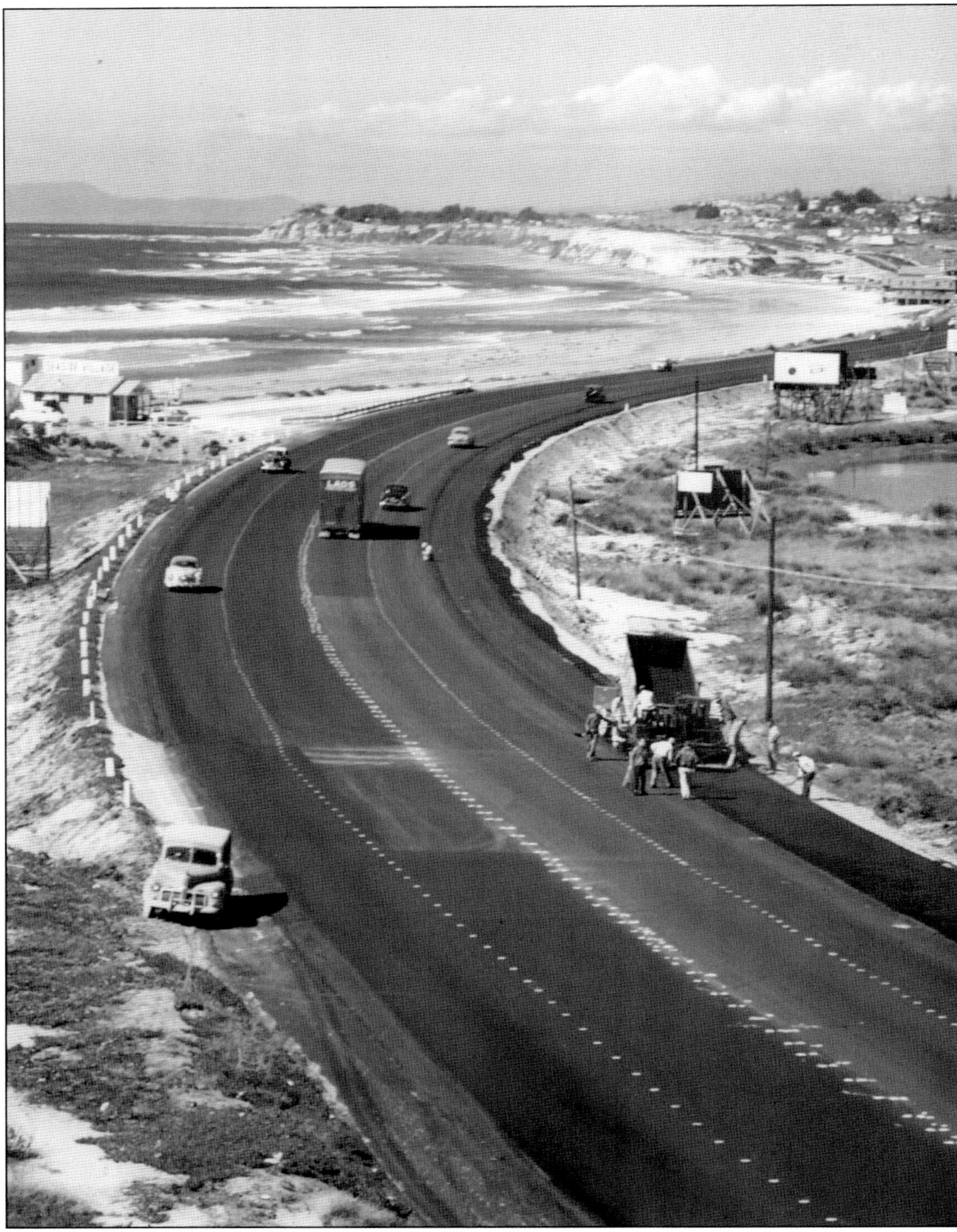

This late 1950s shot taken from what is now the northern edge of Solana Beach city limits looks north along Highway 101 into what is now Cardiff and Encinitas. (Courtesy of the Solana Beach Historical Society.)

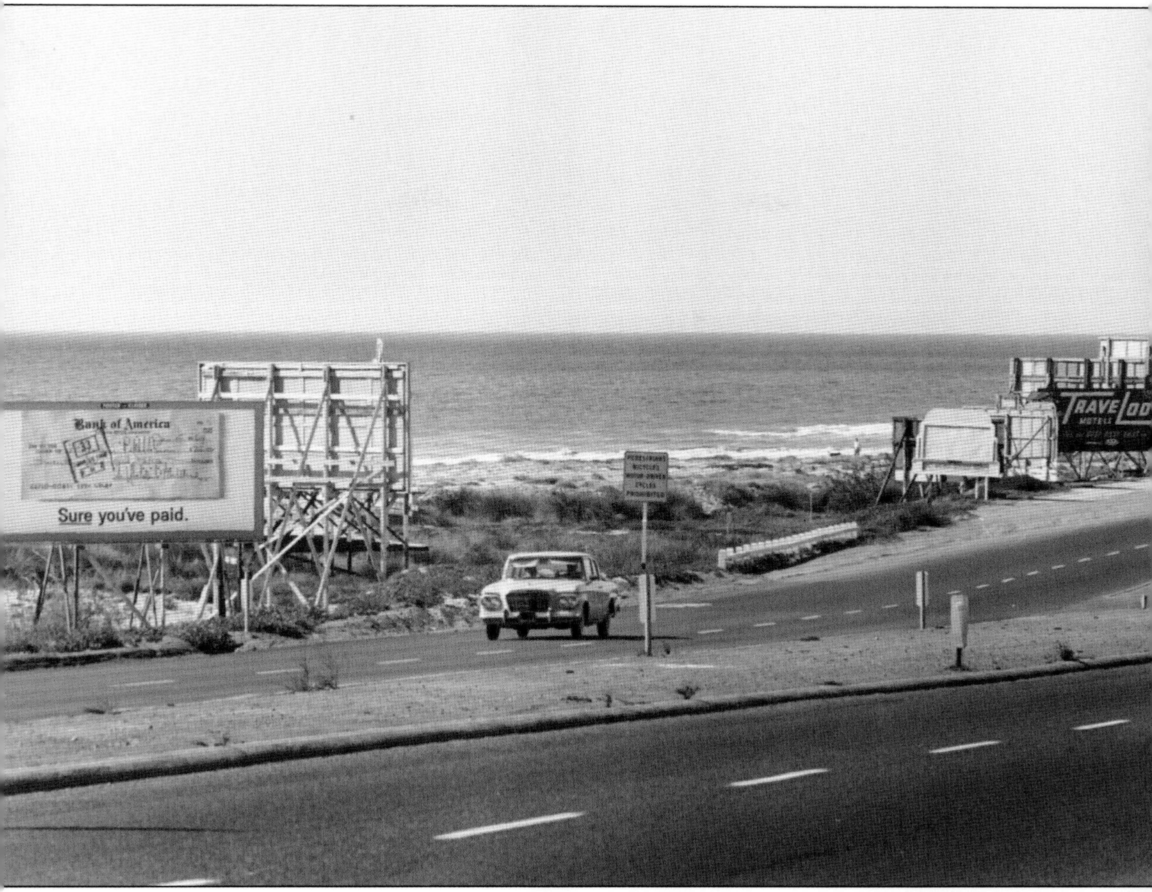

This photograph looks northwest down Highway 101 in 1964 just prior to the opening of Interstate 5.

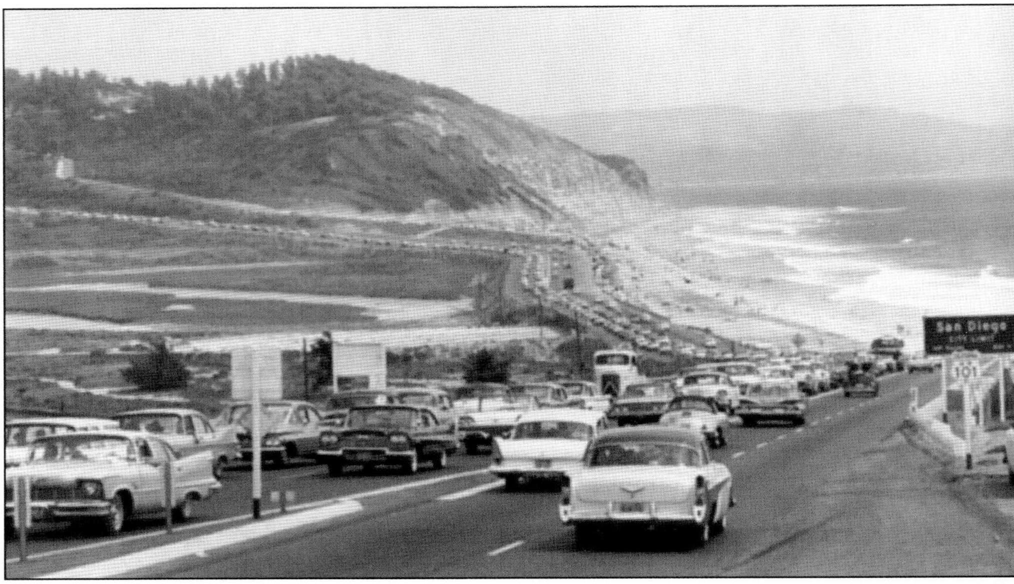

Highway 101 is pictured here in 1961 looking south into Torrey Pines. Note the traffic and the need for an interstate highway system that would cut through Solana Beach. The stretch seen, along with the North Torrey Pines Road Bridge, received a seismic retrofit in 2014. This section of road is popular with commuters, tourists, and cyclists, as it offers one of the most picturesque views in the county.

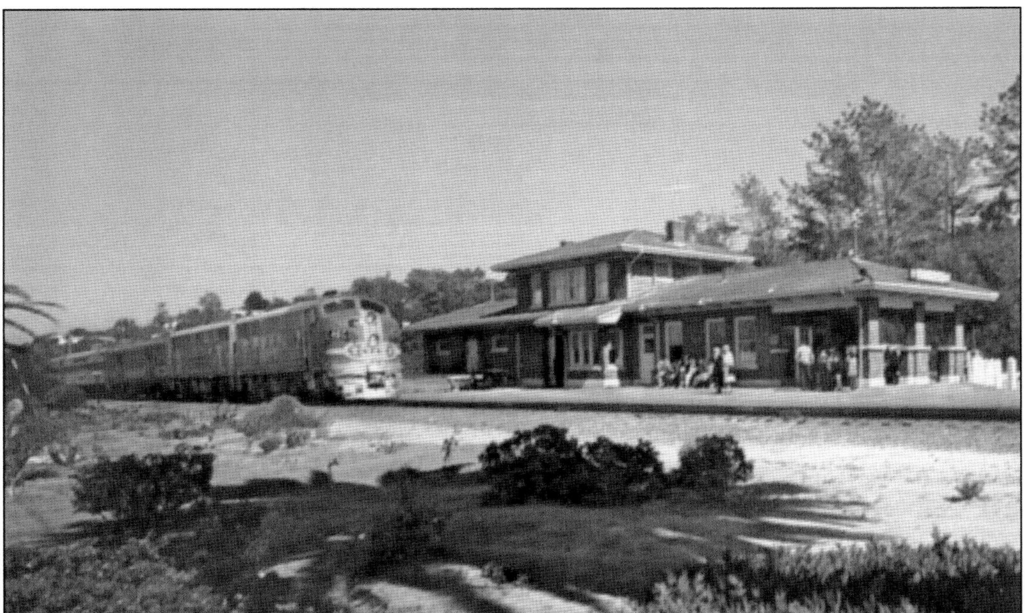

This 1960s photograph shows the Del Mar Train Station soon after Del Mar gained cityhood in 1959. The old Solana Beach Train Station from the 1920s had been demolished, so other than the Oceanside Station, the Del Mar Station was the only passenger rail service in the area. (Courtesy of the Del Mar Historical Society.)

Six

Solana Celebrates
Theatre, Music, Art, and Design

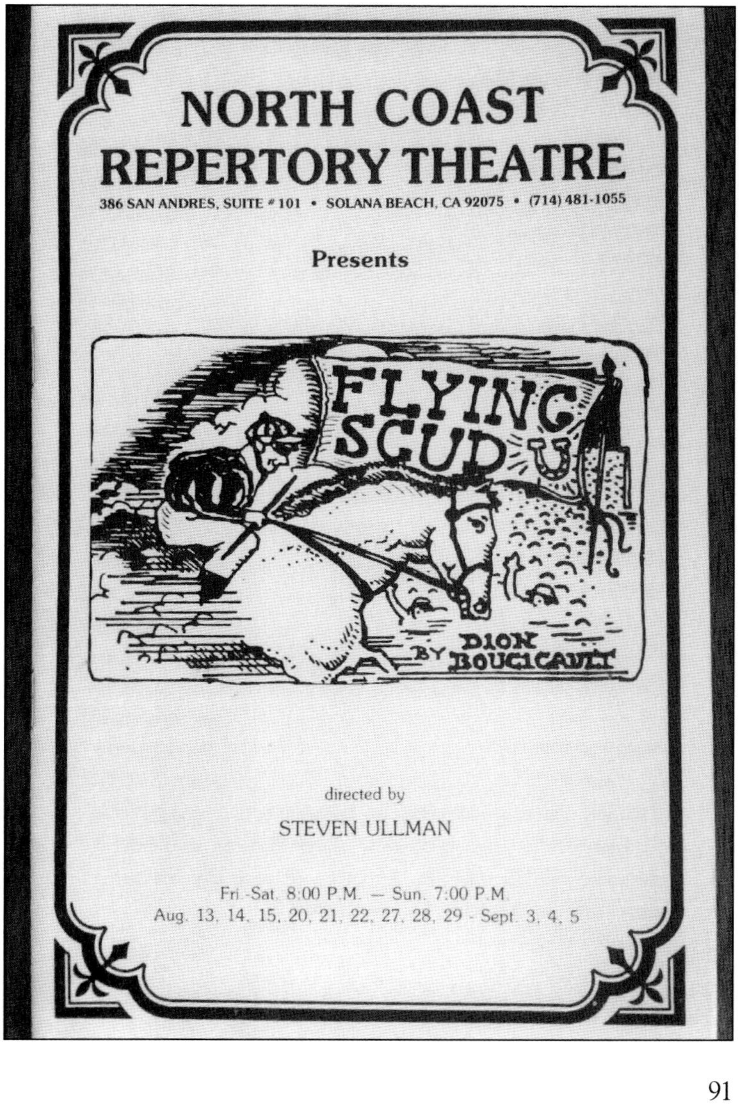

North Coast Repertory Theatre opened in 1982 in the Lomas Santa Fe Shopping Center. The original location was just across the parking lot from where the theater stands today. It was founded by Tom Blakistone, an engineer and small-business entrepreneur, and his wife, Olive. Initially an all-volunteer community theater, North Coast Rep now operates as a small professional theater. (Courtesy of North Coast Repertory Theatre.)

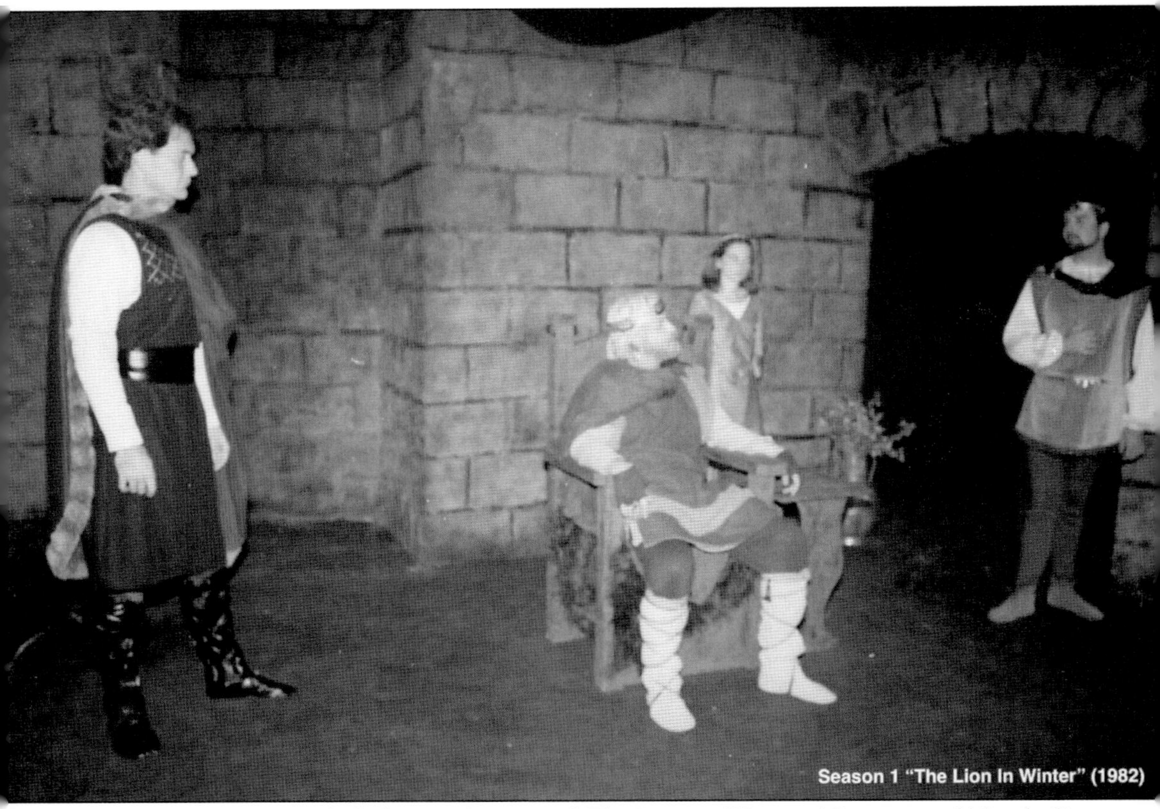

The first season included a production of *The Lion in Winter.* (Courtesy of North Coast Repertory Theatre.)

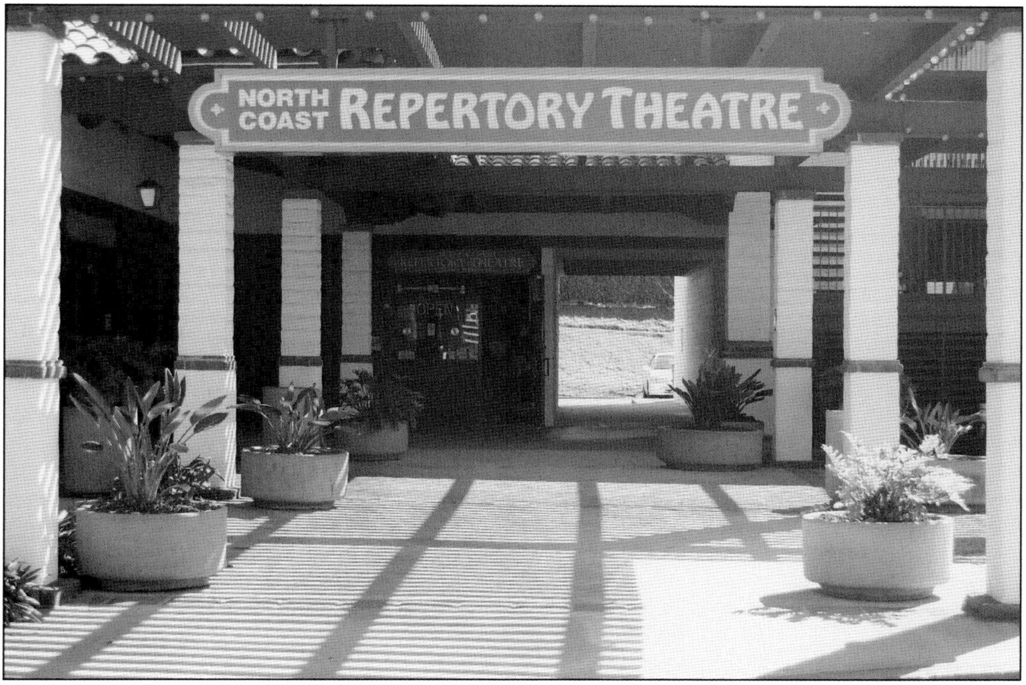

Just before the start of the third season in 1984, the theater moved across the parking lot to its current location. A new theater was built with 194 seats. It remained a community theater for several years. (Courtesy of North Coast Repertory Theatre.)

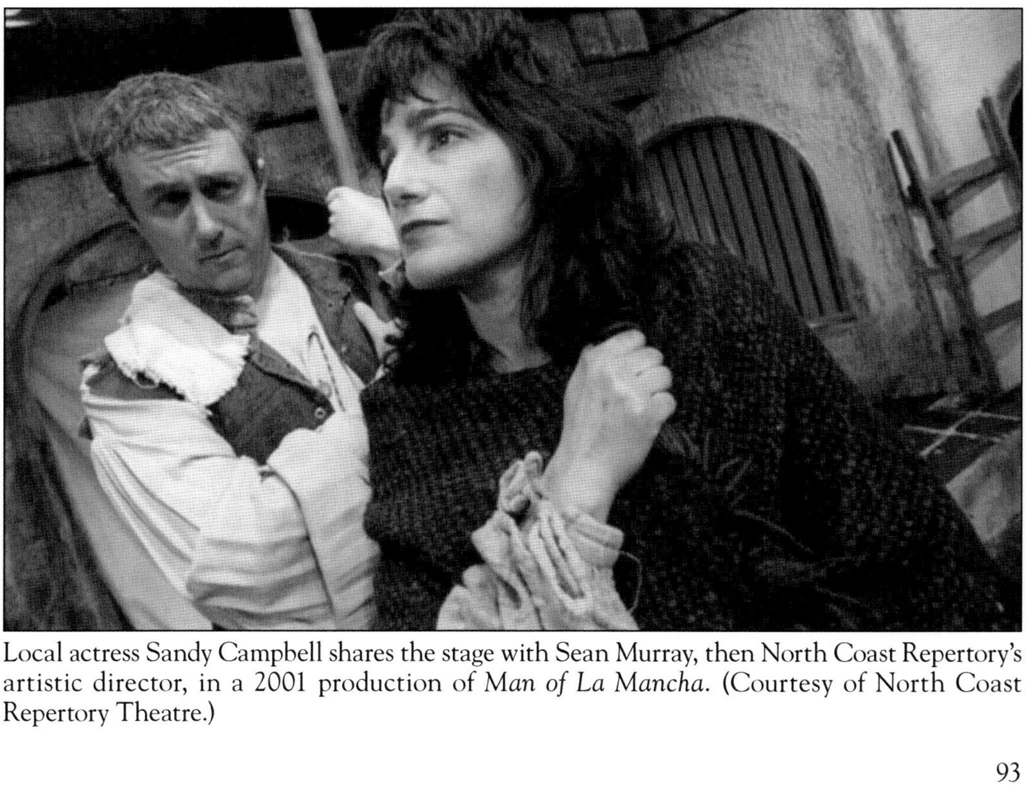

Local actress Sandy Campbell shares the stage with Sean Murray, then North Coast Repertory's artistic director, in a 2001 production of *Man of La Mancha*. (Courtesy of North Coast Repertory Theatre.)

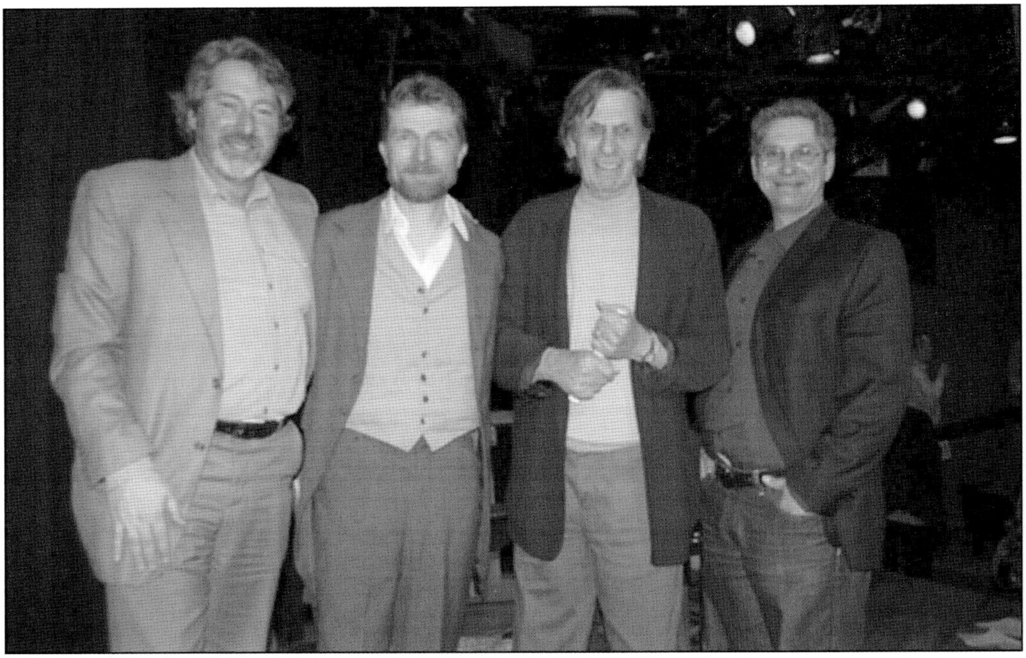

From left to right, David Ellenstein, actor Jean-Michel Richaud, actor and playwright Leonard Nimoy, and director Paul Stein pose after Nimoy's play *Vincent* in 2013. Paul Stein would also assist with another one-person show, *Ted Williams: A Tip of the Cap*. Ellenstein was named artistic director in 2003. (Courtesy of North Coast Repertory Theatre.)

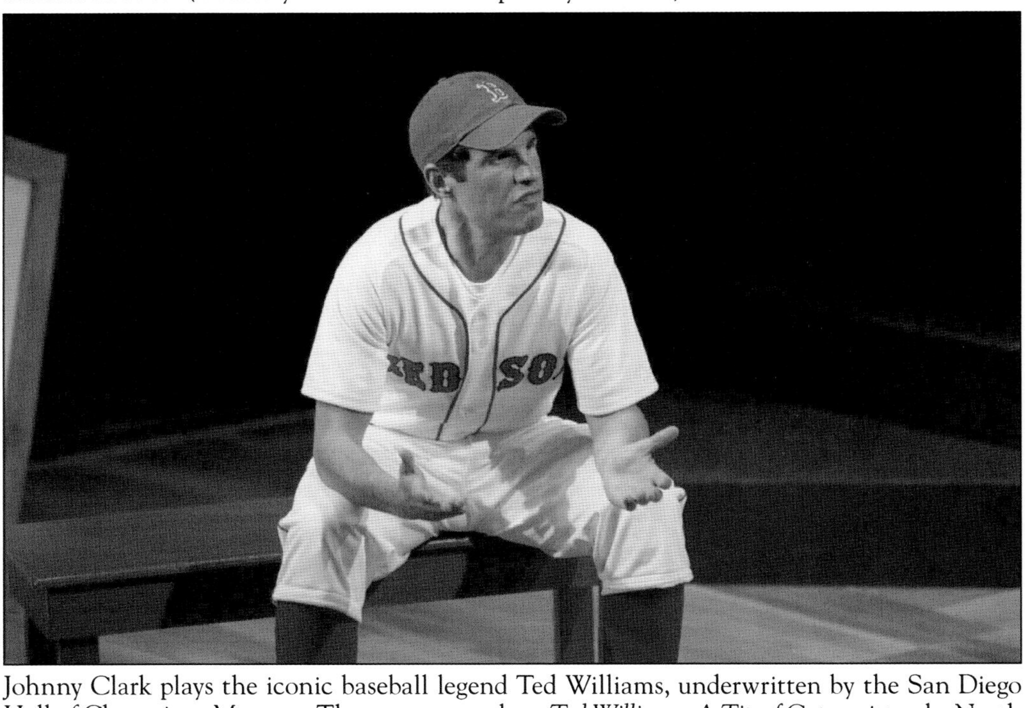

Johnny Clark plays the iconic baseball legend Ted Williams, underwritten by the San Diego Hall of Champions Museum. The one-person show *Ted Williams: A Tip of Cap*, written by North Coast Repertory's artistic associate Matt Thompson, played to sold-out crowds in 2011. (Courtesy of Aaron Rumley.)

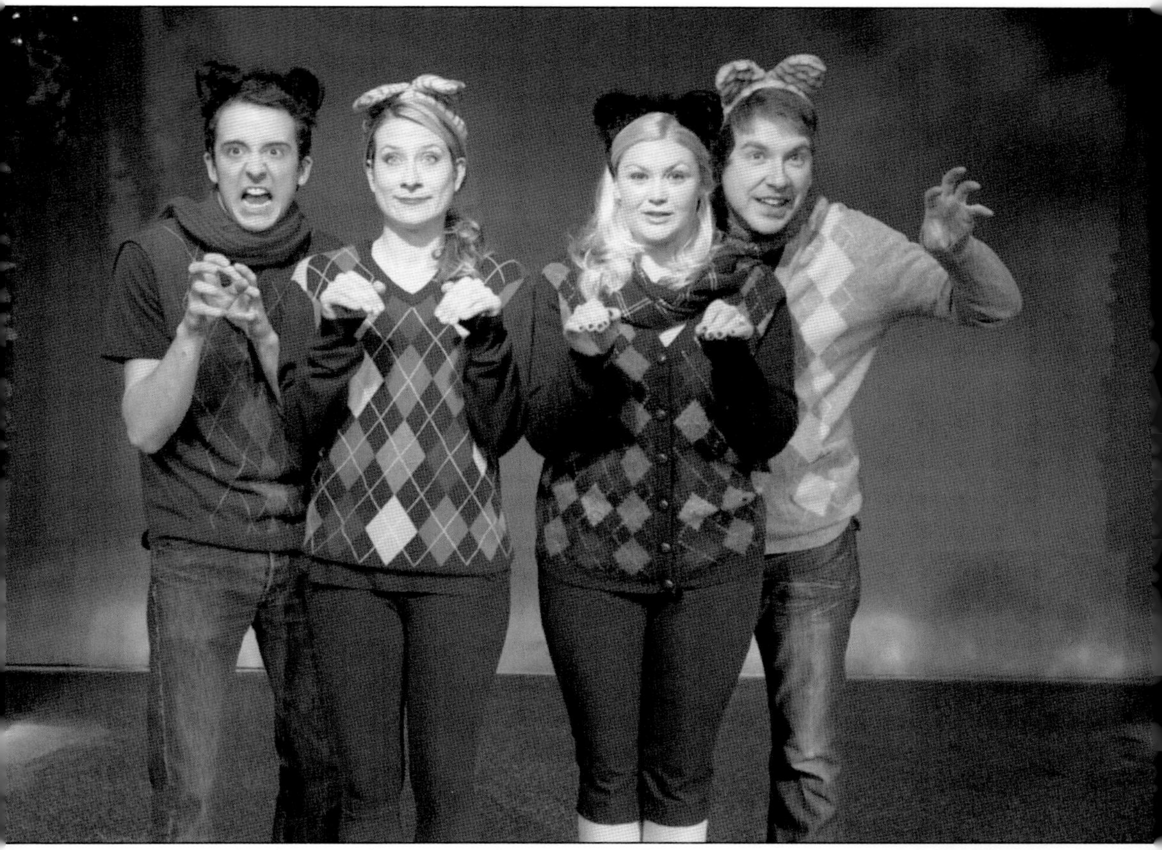

The theater was also dedicated to new works. In 2010, Ellenstein commissioned a jaunty holiday musical, *Mistletoe, Music and Mayhem*, written by Phil Johnson, Rayme Sciaroni, and Matt Thompson. The show became an instant hit and has been produced at several notable theaters. (Courtesy of Aaron Rumley.)

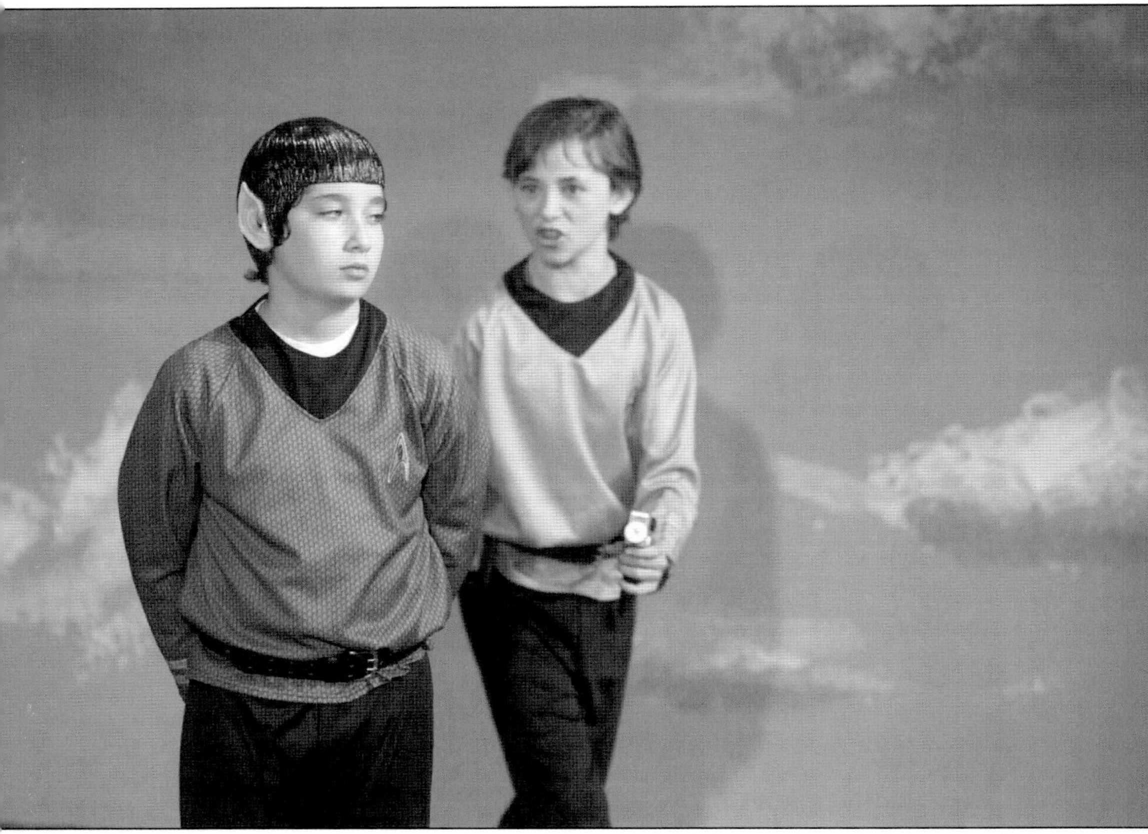

Jacob Surovsky (left) and Andrew Moore share the stage in Mike McCafferty and Matt Thompson's play *Who's on Alpha?*. The parody piece on the classic Abbott and Costello routine, "Who's on First," was produced through the Theatre School at North Coast Rep in 2009. (Courtesy of Aaron Rumley.)

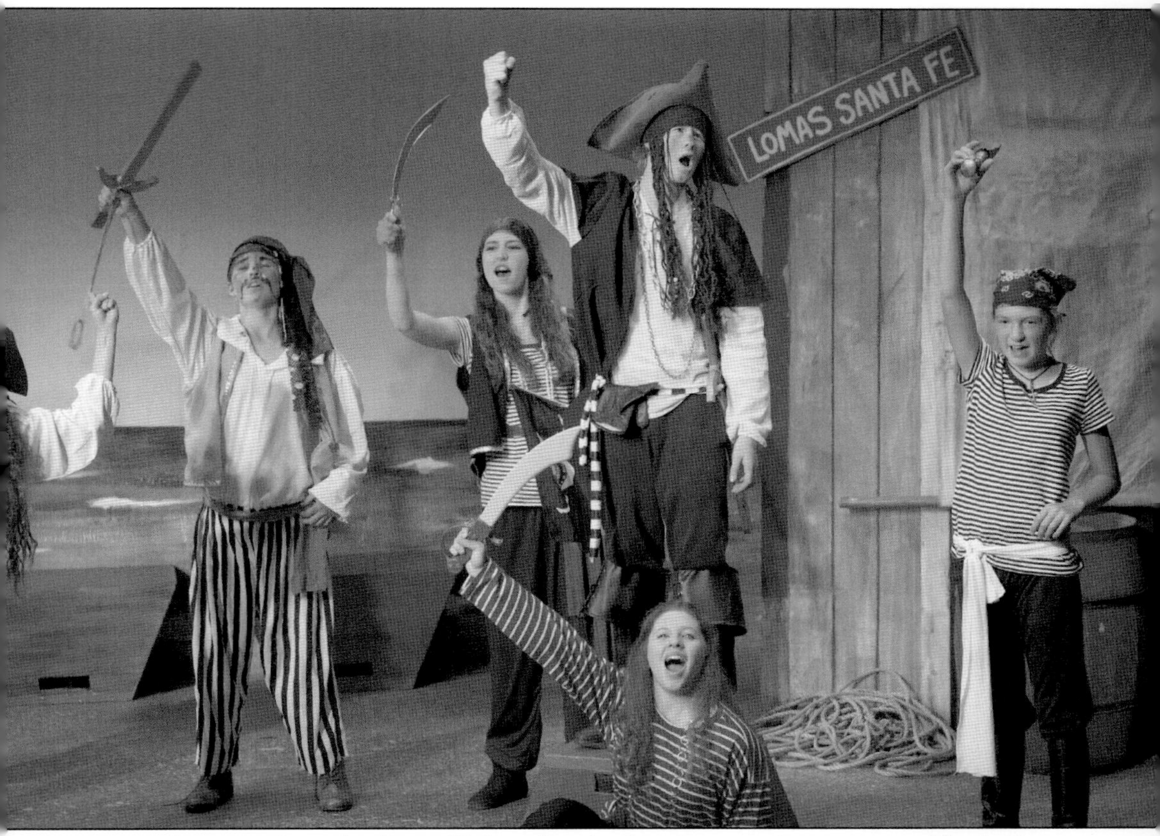

In 2010, with a grant from the City of Solana Beach, the education department at North Coast Repertory Theatre commissioned playwright Matt Thompson to write *The Perfectly Preposterous Pirate Adventure of Solana Beach*. The play chronicles the history of the city of Solana Beach. (Courtesy of Aaron Rumley.)

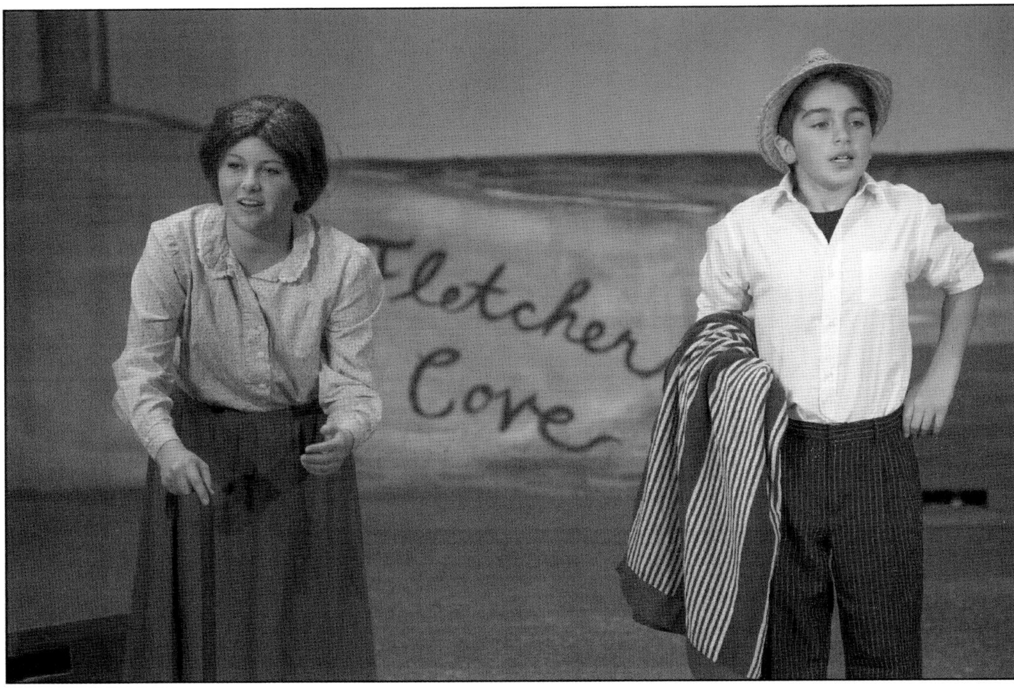

The young actors in *The Perfectly Preposterous Pirate Adventure of Solana Beach* portrayed various historical figures, including Grandma Stevens on the left and Ed Fletcher on the right. (Courtesy of Aaron Rumley.)

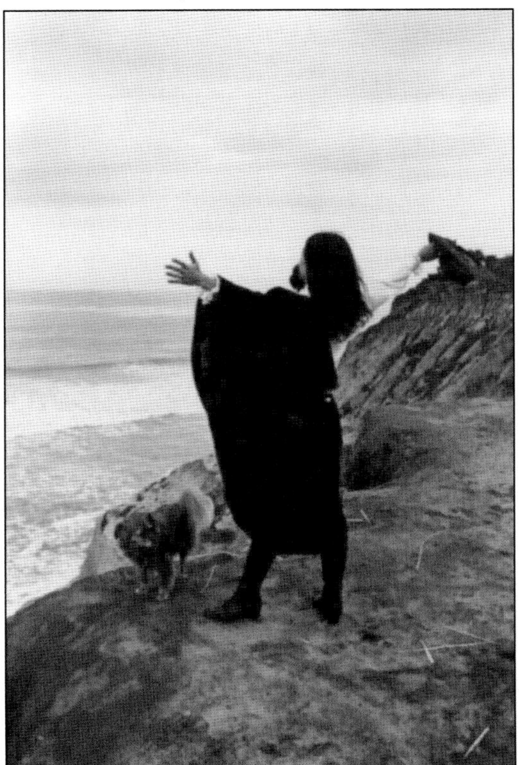

Performance artist Eleanor Antin used Solana Beach as the backdrop for her performance art. Wearing a fake beard and donning a cape and wide-brimmed hat, Antin made the rounds of San Diego as the "King of Solana Beach."

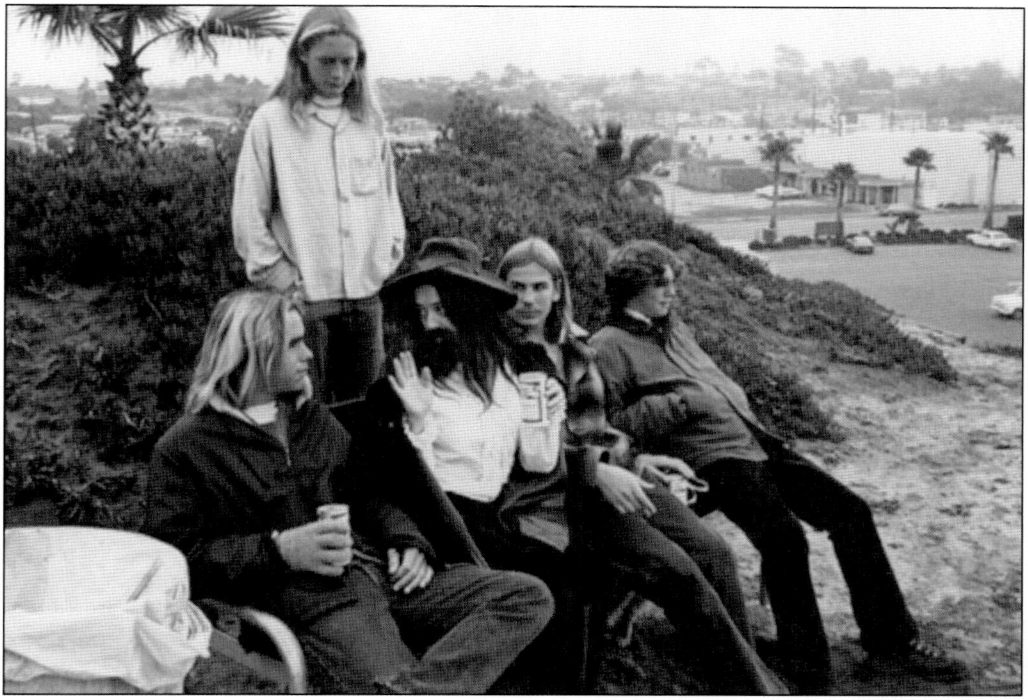

Antin is pictured here at Fletcher Cove conversing with some local admirers. Antin saw conceptual art in the 1970s as a male-dominated field and sought to infuse the art form with elements of biography and fantasy.

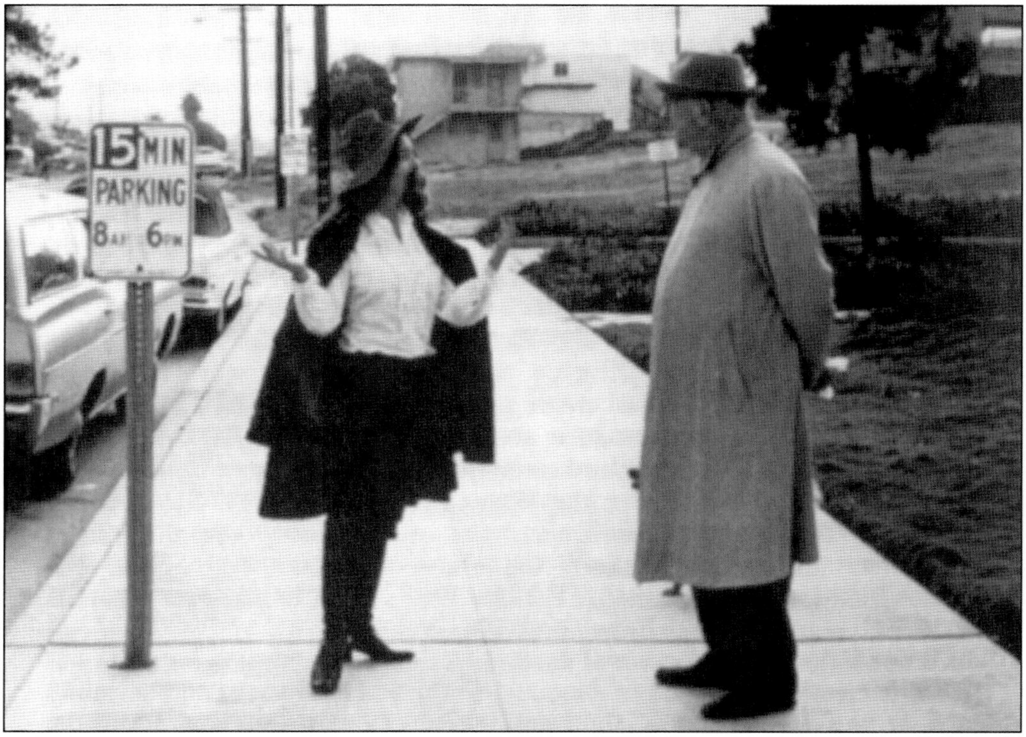

Antin is pictured here in character as the King of Solana Beach in the 1970s.

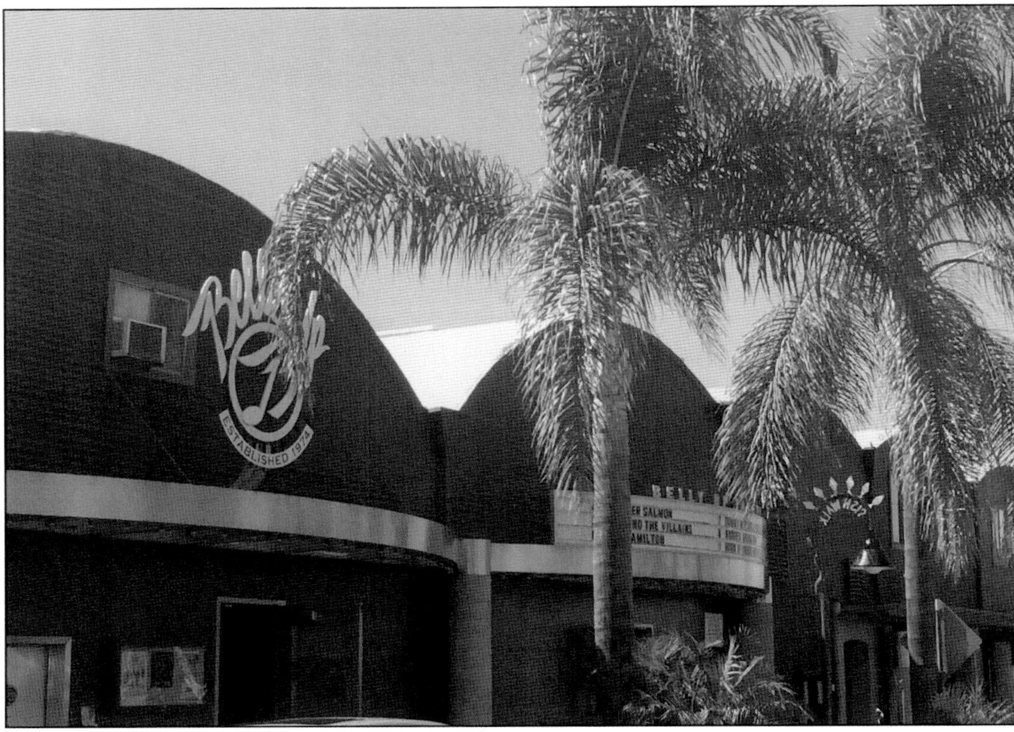

The Belly Up live-music venue, established in 1974, is pictured here in 2013.

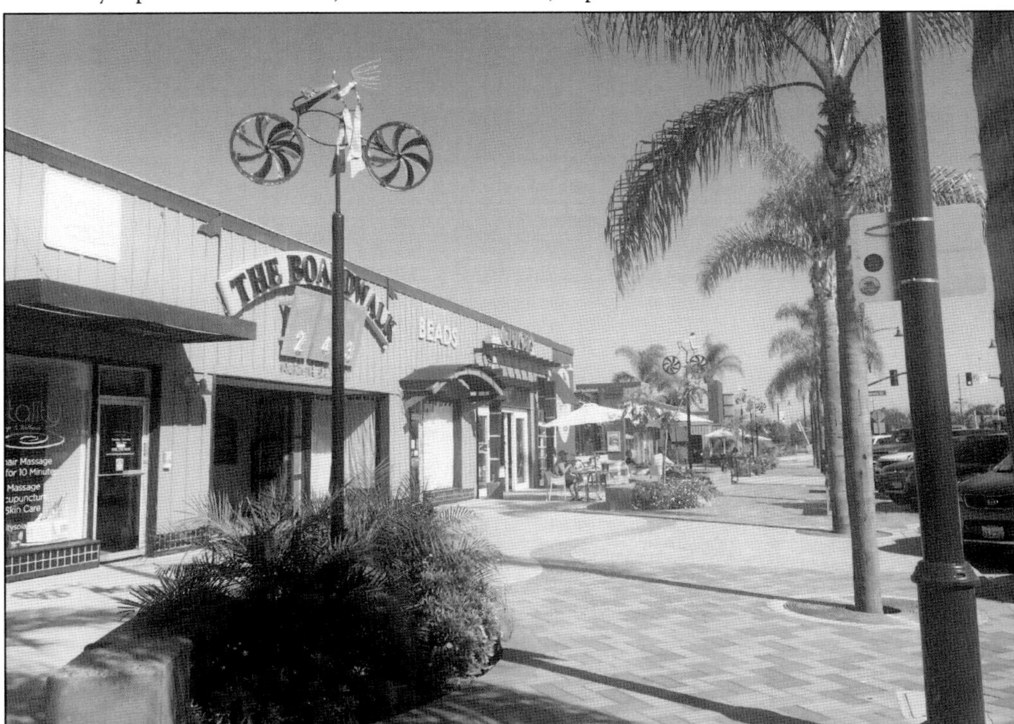

During the 2013–2014 renovation of Highway 101 throughout Solana Beach, public artwork was prominently displayed, like these fanciful bicycles.

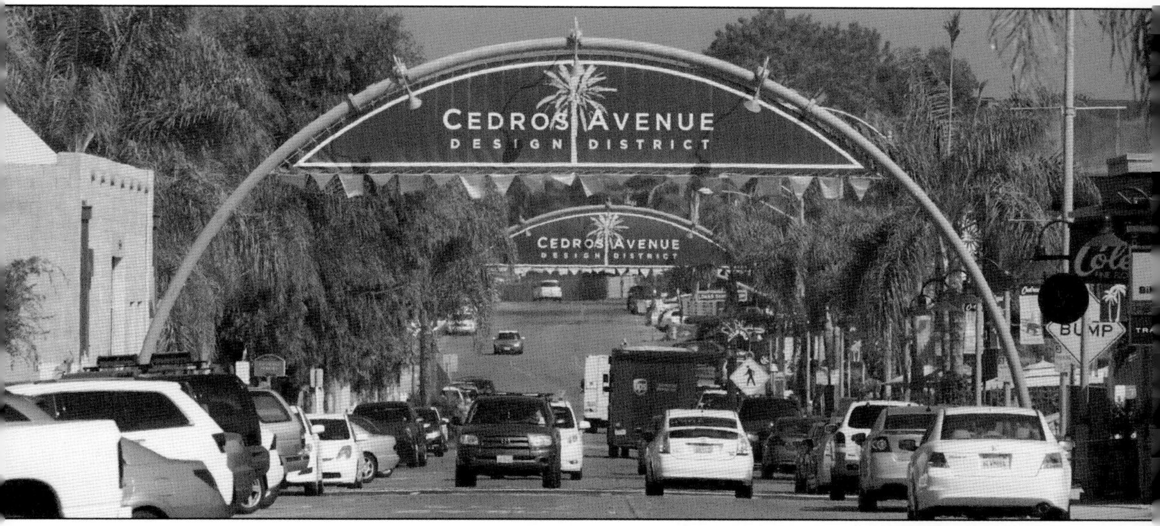

In 1997, street arches were installed, designed to echo the curved silhouette of the Quonset huts that give the avenue its signature look. In 1992, the Cedros Design Center was established in the Quonset huts that house a variety of boutiques, shops, and the Belly Up.

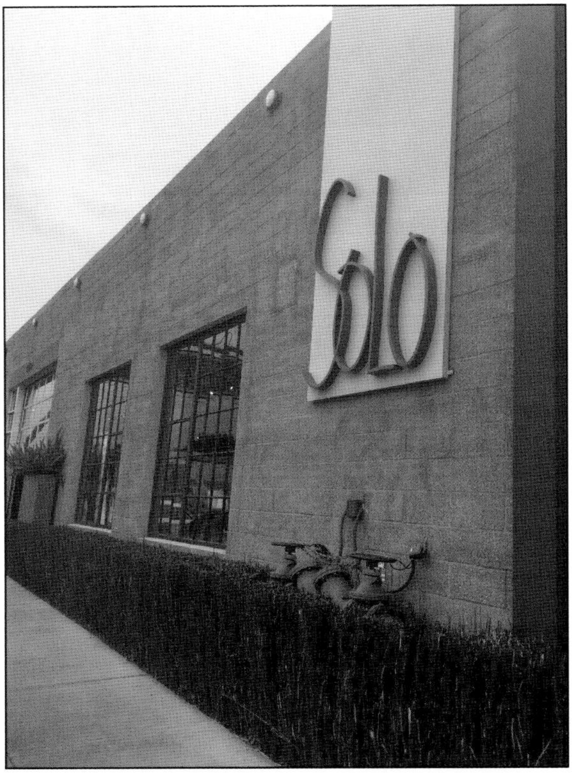

SoLo, established in the Cedros Design District in July 2001, is a 4,000-square-foot retail store containing more than a dozen distinctive boutiques. Carrying an eclectic line of products, SoLo is San Diego's largest outlet for handpicked architectural, design, and lifestyle books.

The entrance to the award-winning Coastal Rail Trail is marked by two beautifully crafted mosaic arches created by artist Betsy Schultz. The Coastal Rail Trail and the Gateway Arches were honored for outstanding design and land use.

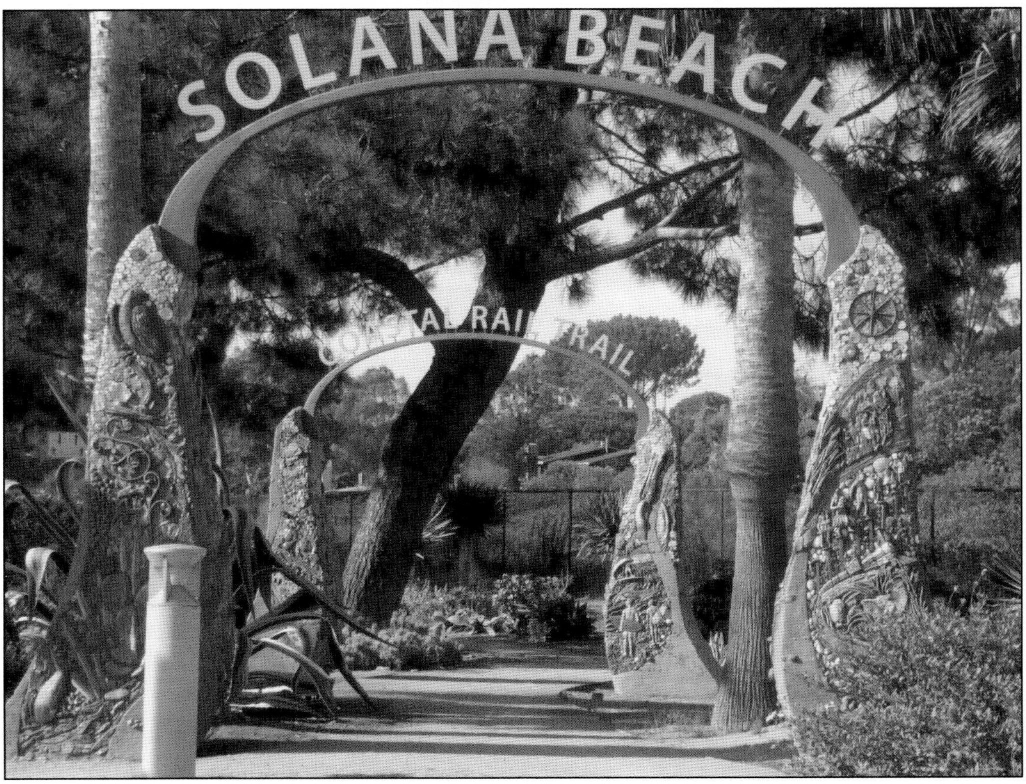

Seven

The Birth of a City
The 1980s and Beyond

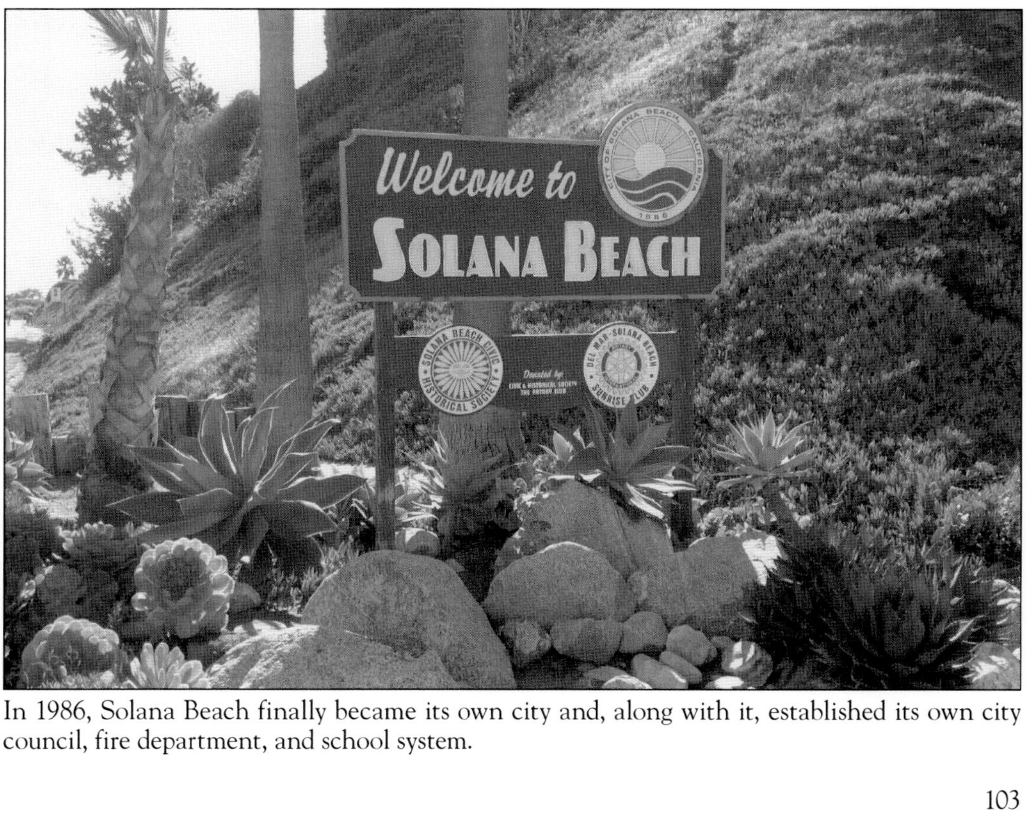

In 1986, Solana Beach finally became its own city and, along with it, established its own city council, fire department, and school system.

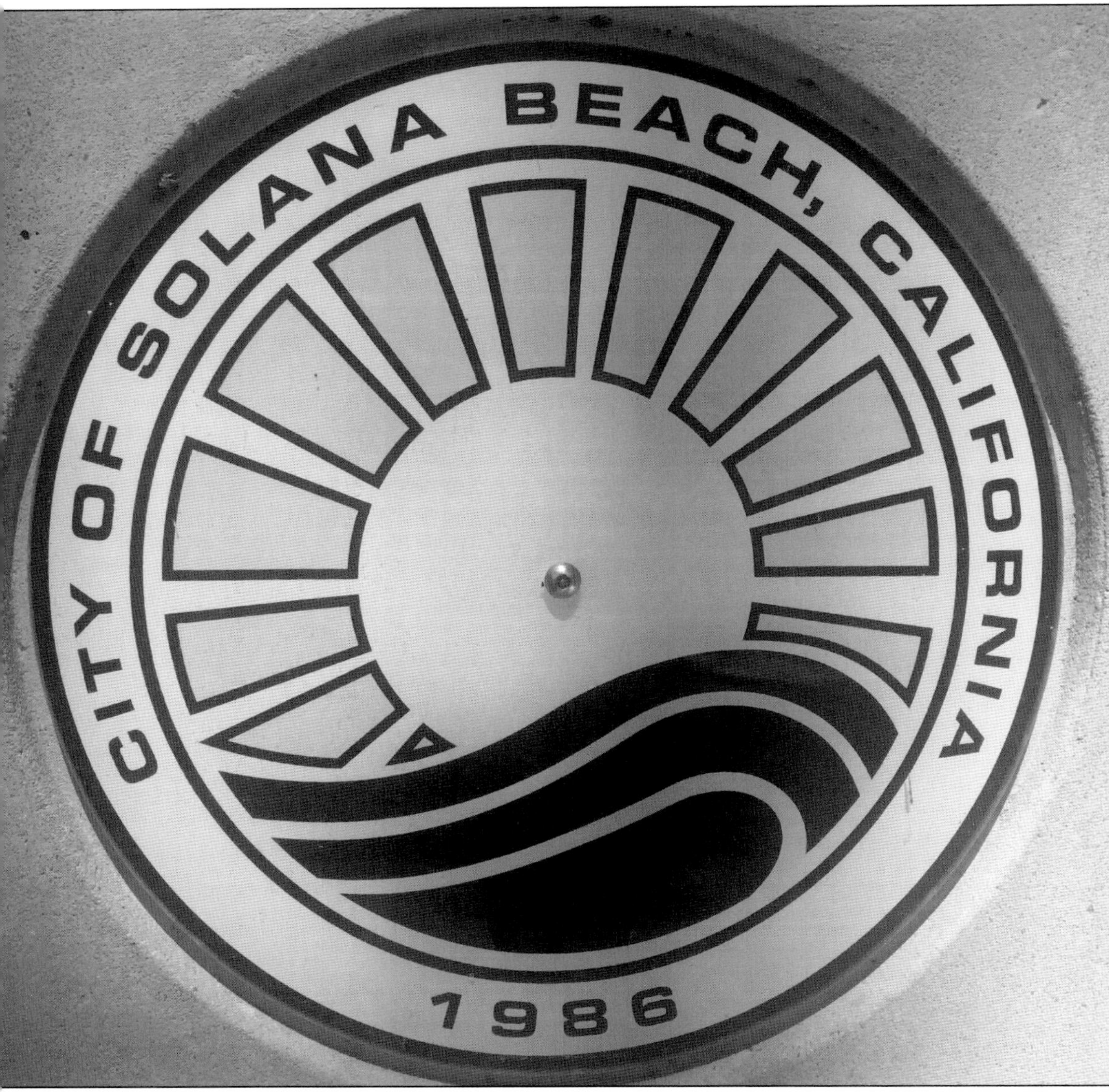

This is the seal for the city of Solana Beach.

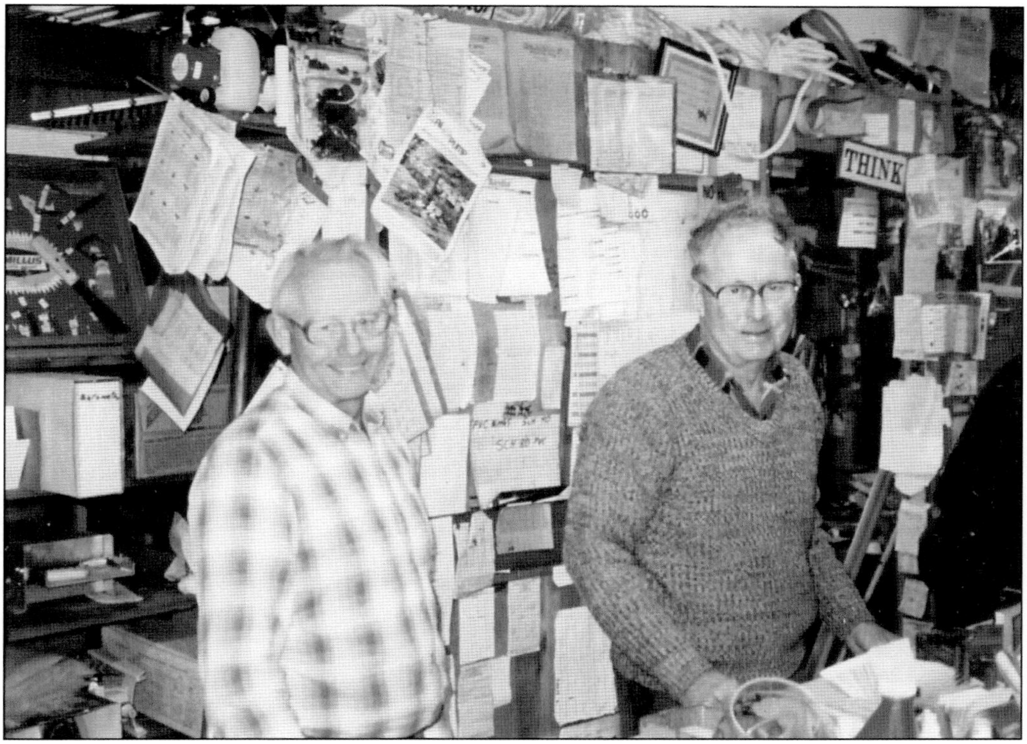

George (left) and Bob Wilkens are pictured in G.G. Wilkens Ranch and Garden Supplies, the store their father opened in 1937. The store remained active in the family until 1986.

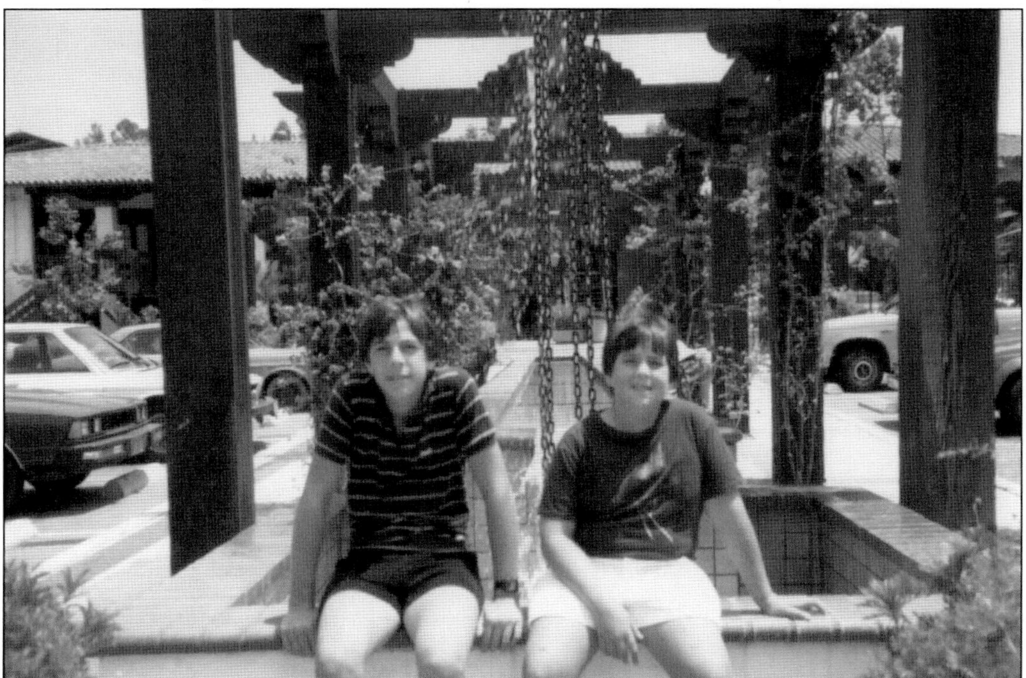

This 1986 photograph shows two boys posing in front of the newly constructed Lomas Santa Fe Shopping Plaza just east of Highway 5. (Courtesy of Tom Thompson.)

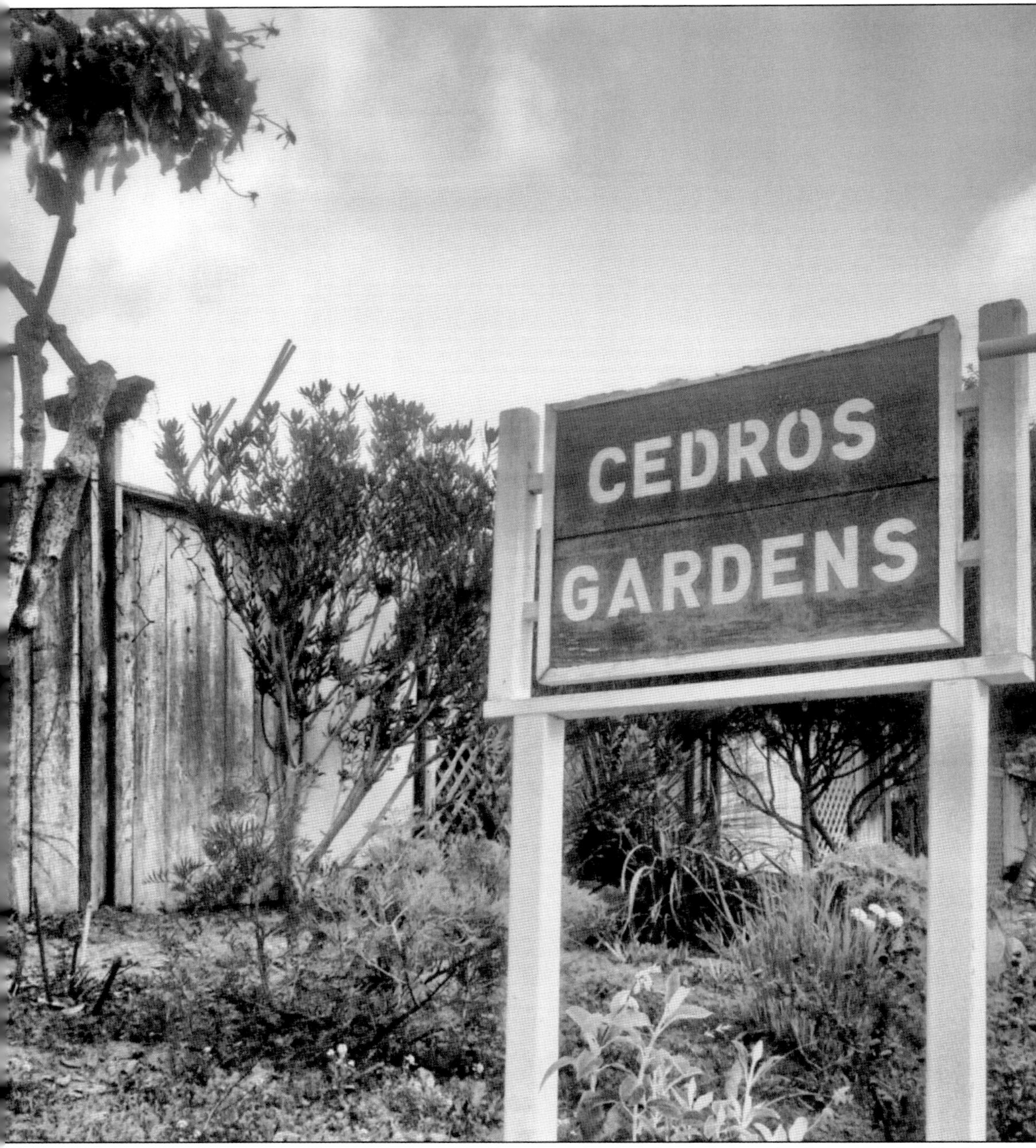

Cedros Gardens opened on March 17, 1994, at its current location in the heart of the Cedros Design District in Solana Beach.

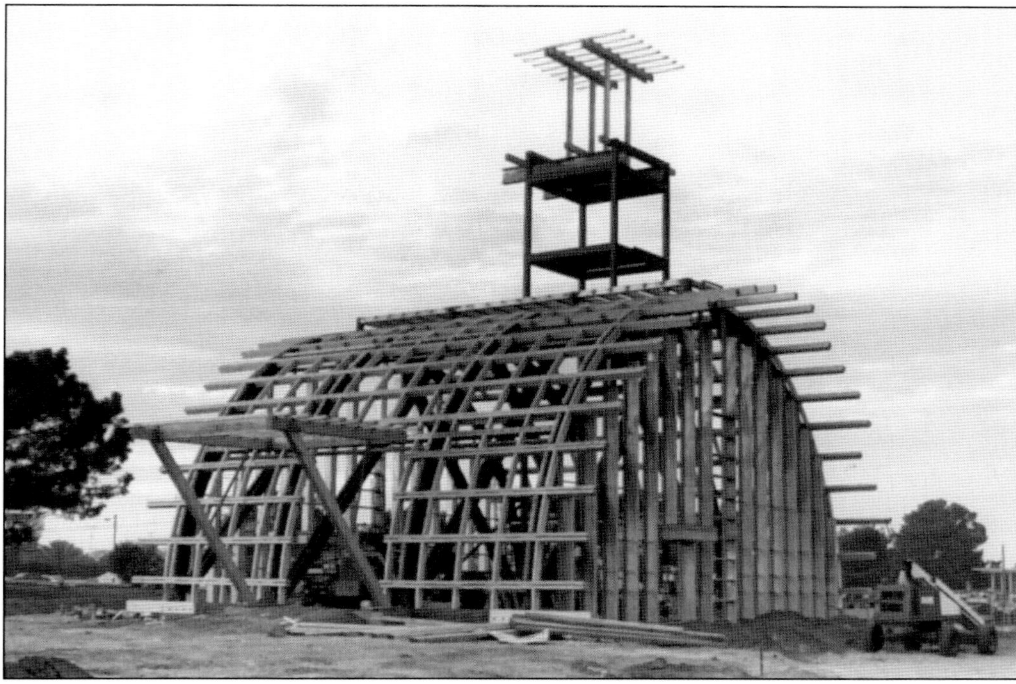

This 1994 photograph shows the train station under construction about 100 feet away from the original train station that was shut down. (Courtesy of the Solana Beach Civic and Historical Society.)

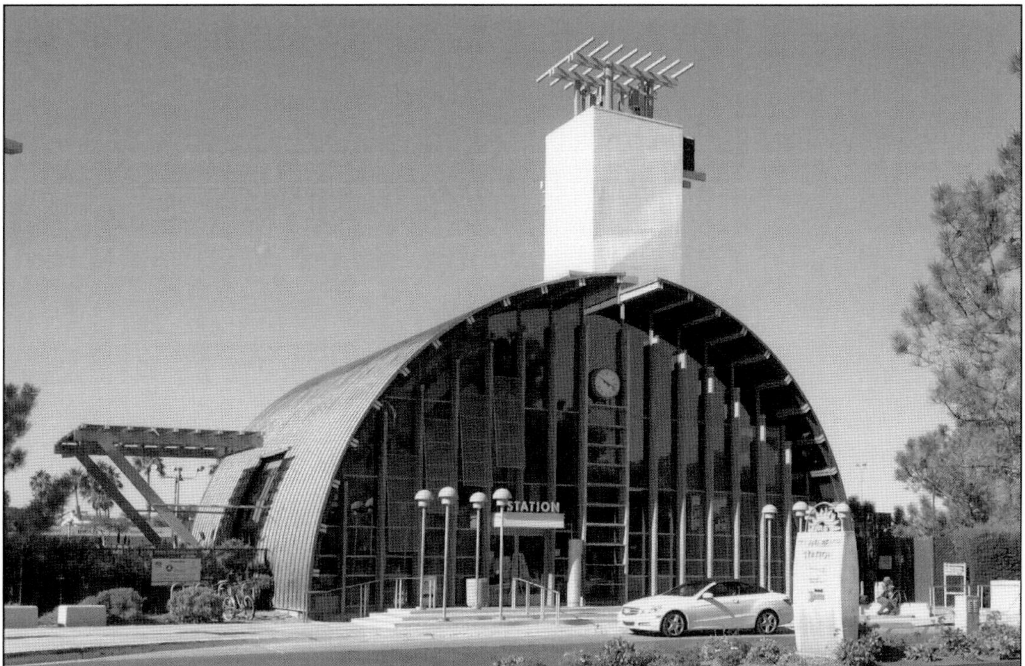

In 1995, the Santa Fe train station was moved from Del Mar to a new station in Solana Beach. The depot was designed by San Diego architect Rob Wellington Quigley. For the Solana Beach Station, Quigley drew inspiration from the Quonset huts first used by Bill Jack.

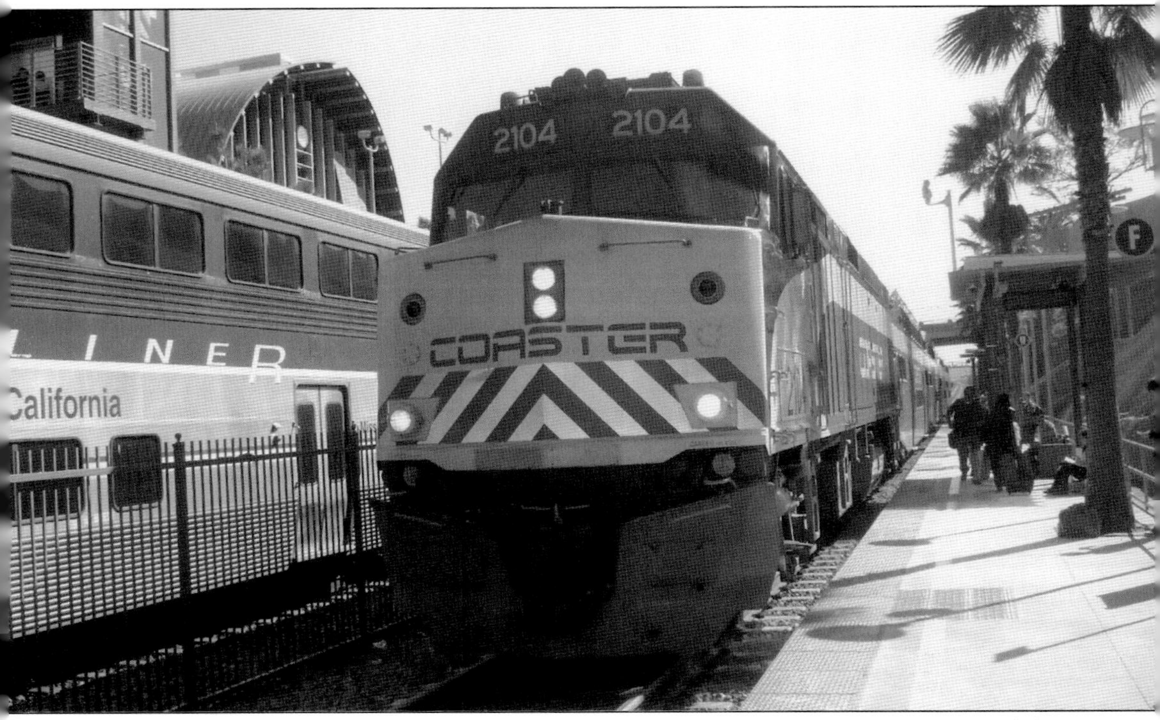

In 1999, the North County Transit District, operator of the *Coaster* commuter train, and the City of Solana Beach completed a multimillion-dollar project to lower the train tracks below grade level under Lomas Santa Fe Drive.

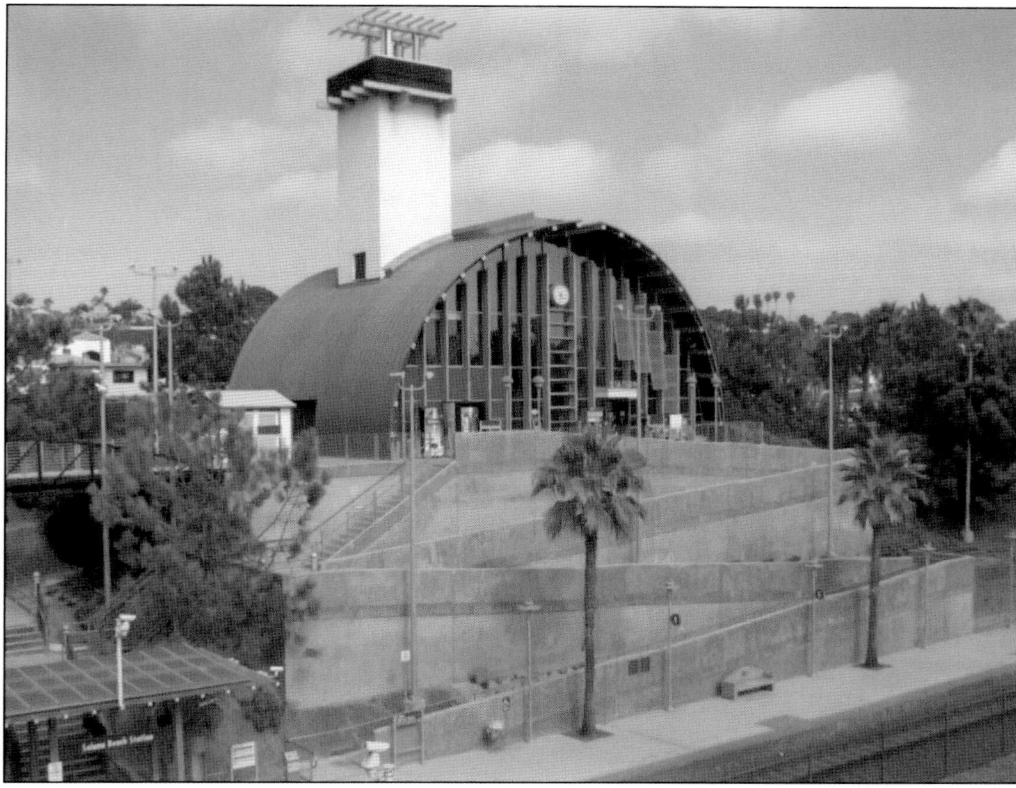

Solana Beach Train Station is one of the busiest commuter hubs in San Diego and serves *Coaster* and Amtrak trains.

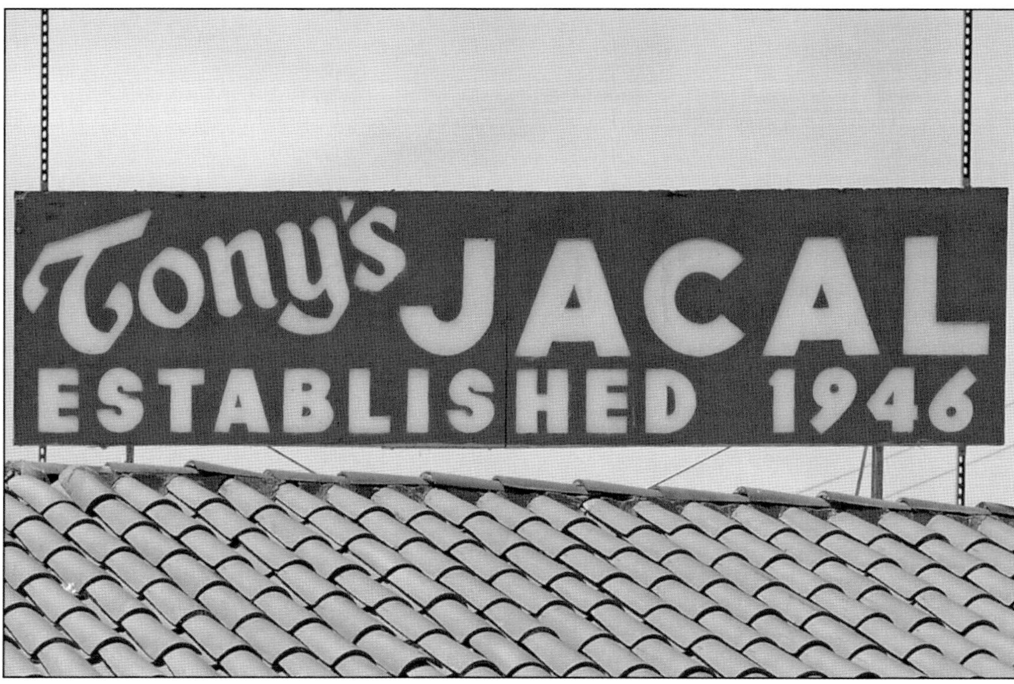

Pictured here is Tony's Jacal, a family-run Mexican restaurant established in 1946.

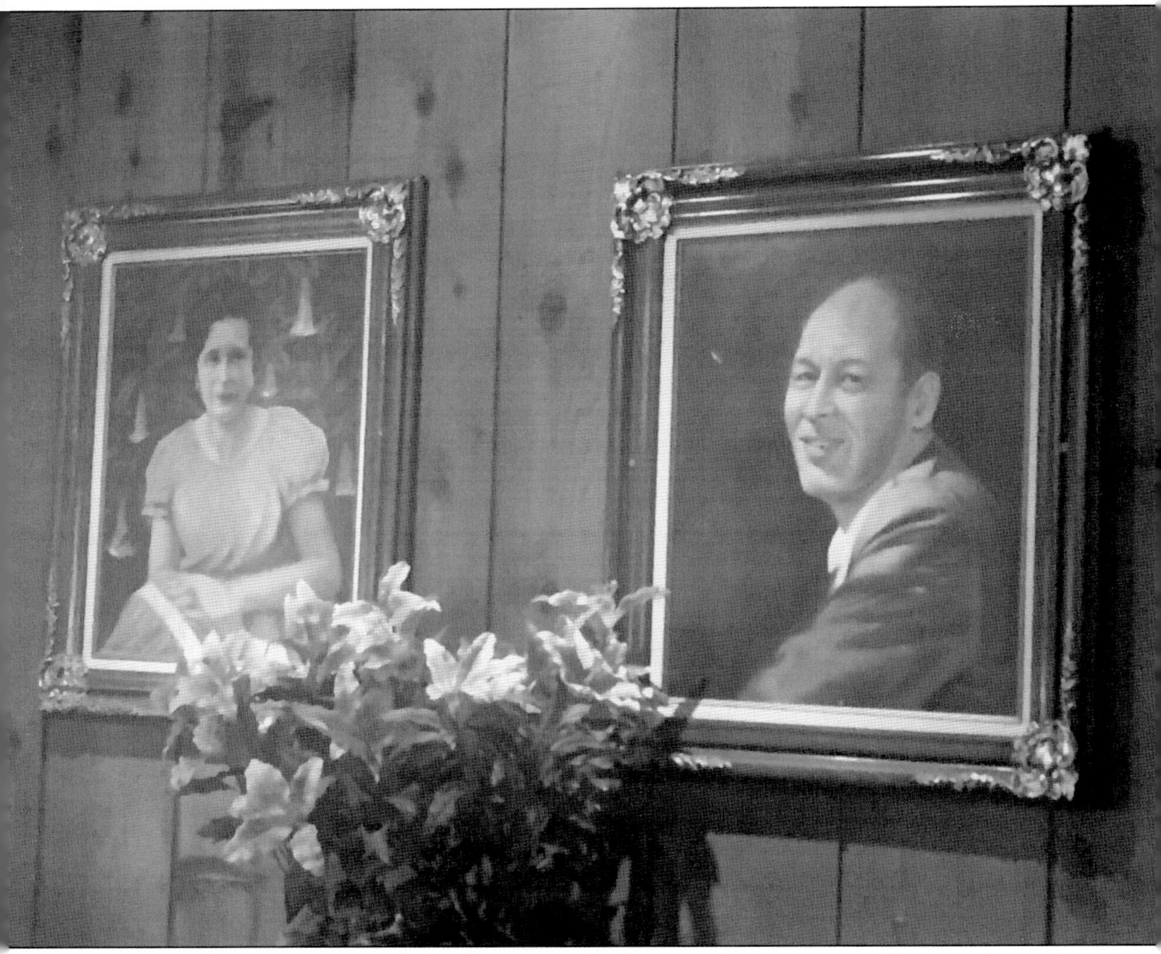

Portraits of owners Tony and Catalina Gonzales hang in the restaurant. Open at first only on weekends, the modest establishment could seat just 26 people. Catalina did the cooking, and Tony helped serve the food.

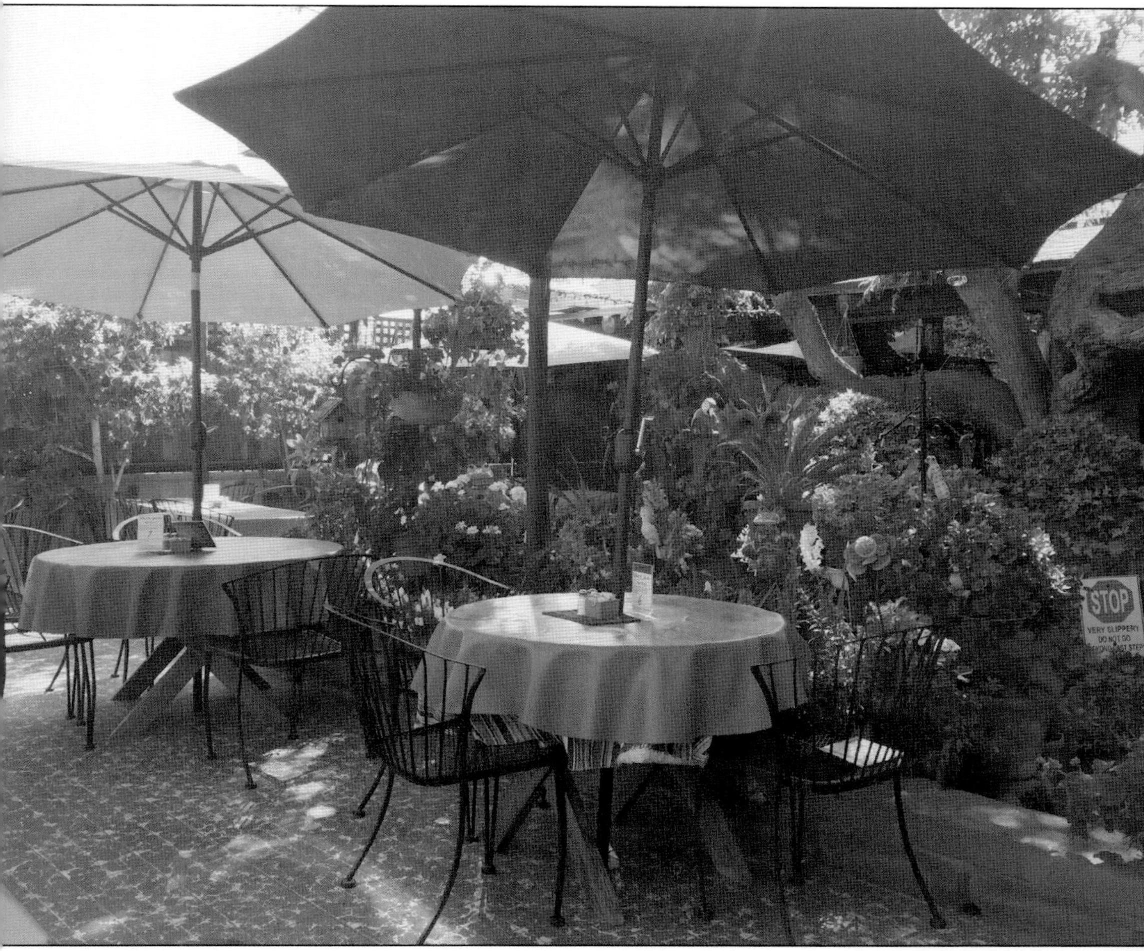

This is the festive patio at Tony's Jacal. The restaurant has been active for 42 years in establishing college scholarships for local Mexican American youth. Teresa Rincon and her sister Catalina Salgado, daughters of Catalina and Tony, were honored at the Encinitas Senior and Community Center in a tribute event recognizing their longtime efforts to keep their parents' generosity alive.

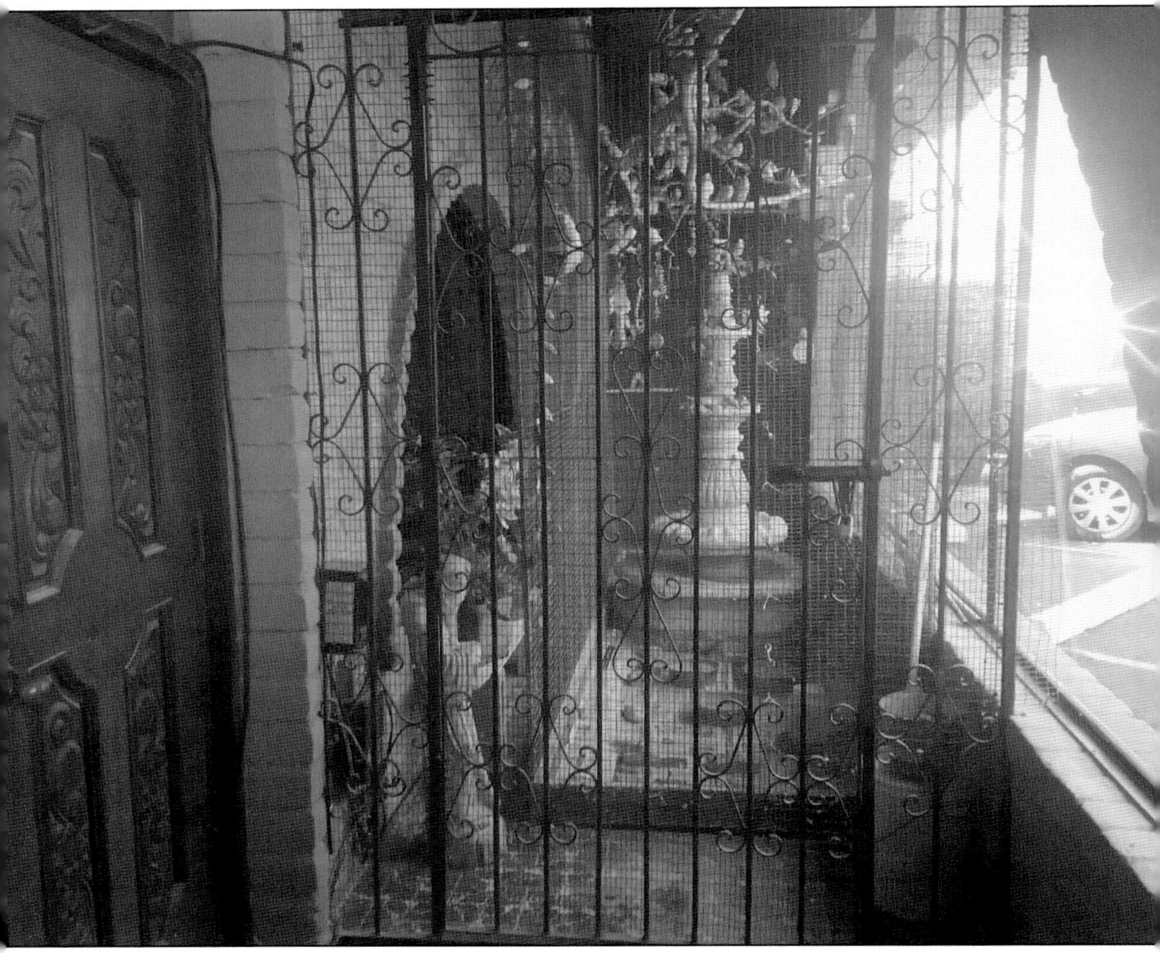

An aviary with dozens of chirping birds surrounding the bar lends a tropical feel to the establishment.

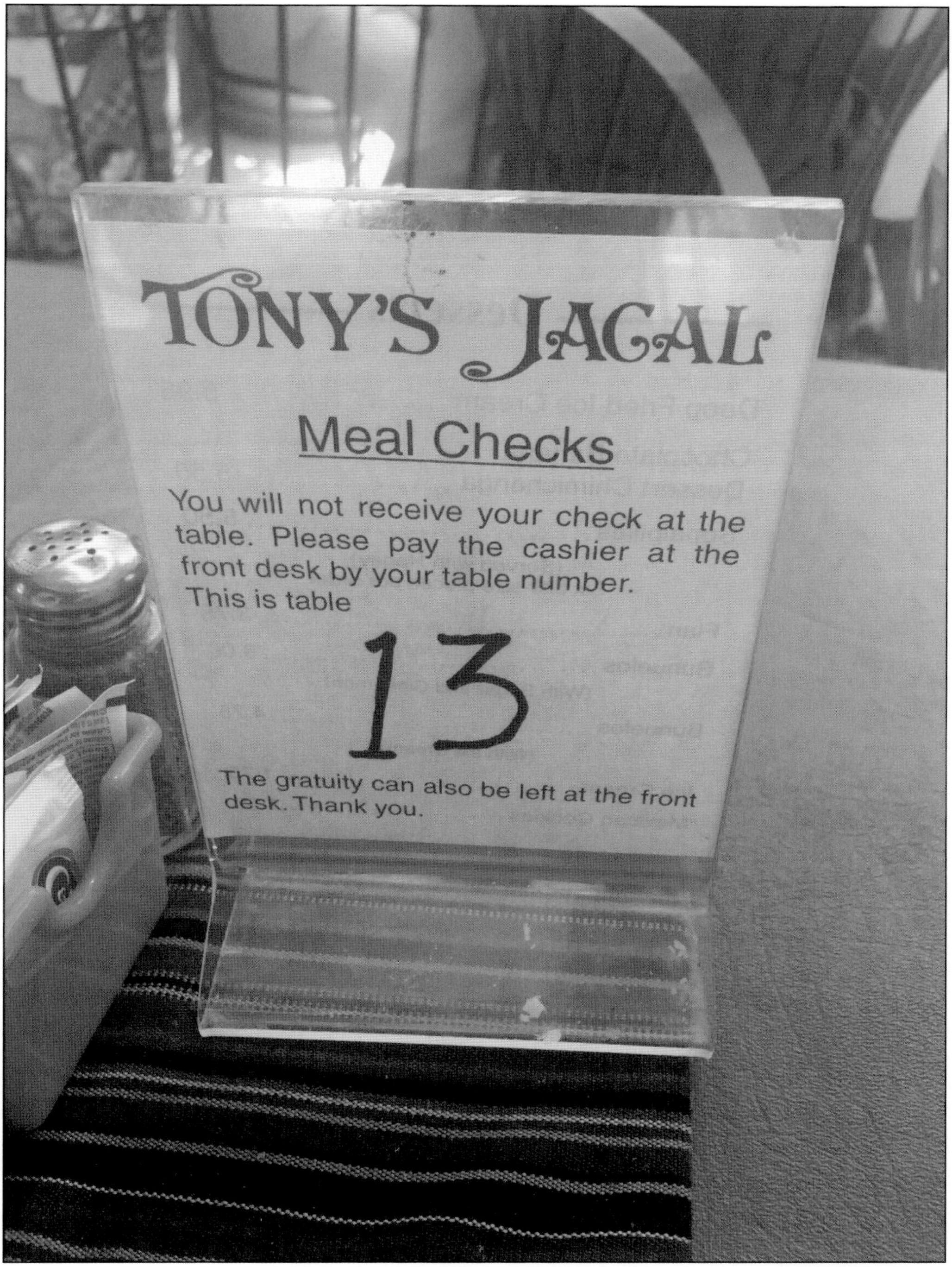

This is a meal ticket from Tony's Jacal that patrons use to pay their checks at the cashier's desk.

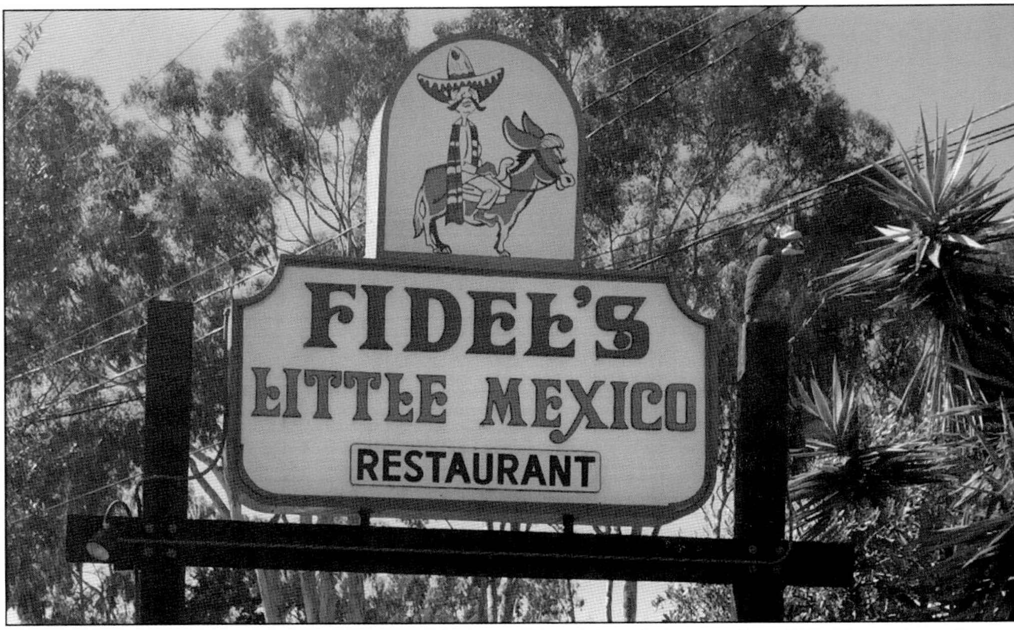

Fidel's Little Mexico opened right next door to Tony's Jacal. Located at 749 Genevieve Street, the restaurant has been a San Diego landmark since the early 1960s. Owner Fidel Montanez came up with the idea to serve tacos at his busy barbershop. The shop was located in the heart of Eden Gardens, a small neighborhood in Solana Beach that was home to a number of Mexican American families.

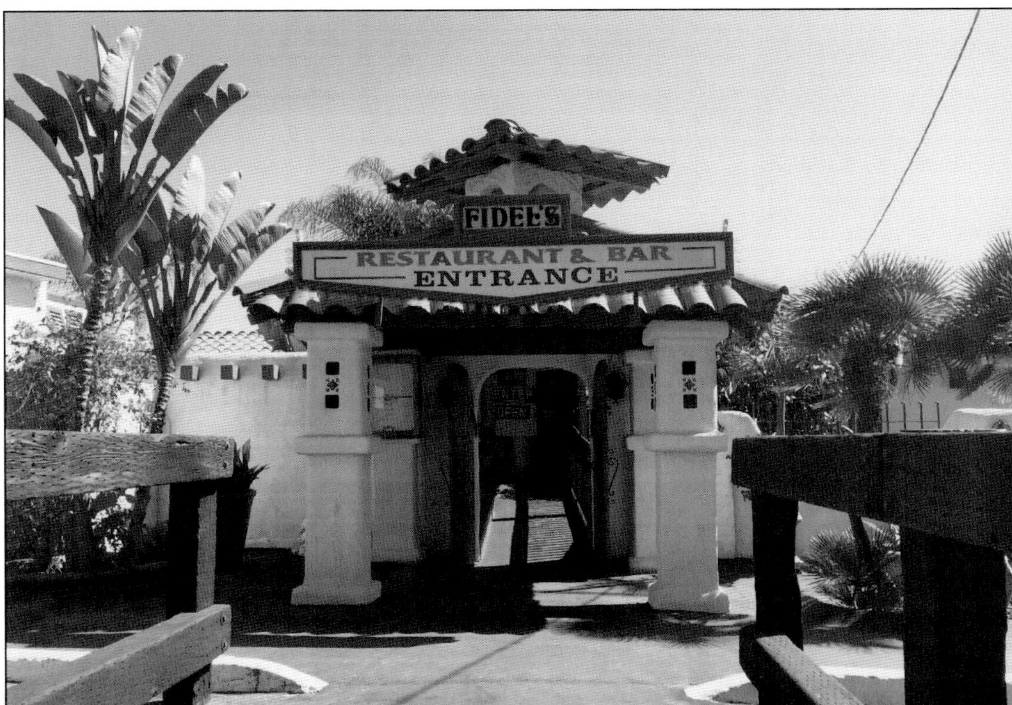

The business thrived and expanded as Fidel converted his two-story residence into three different levels, including a festive courtyard, a couple of bars and outdoor patios, and a taco bar.

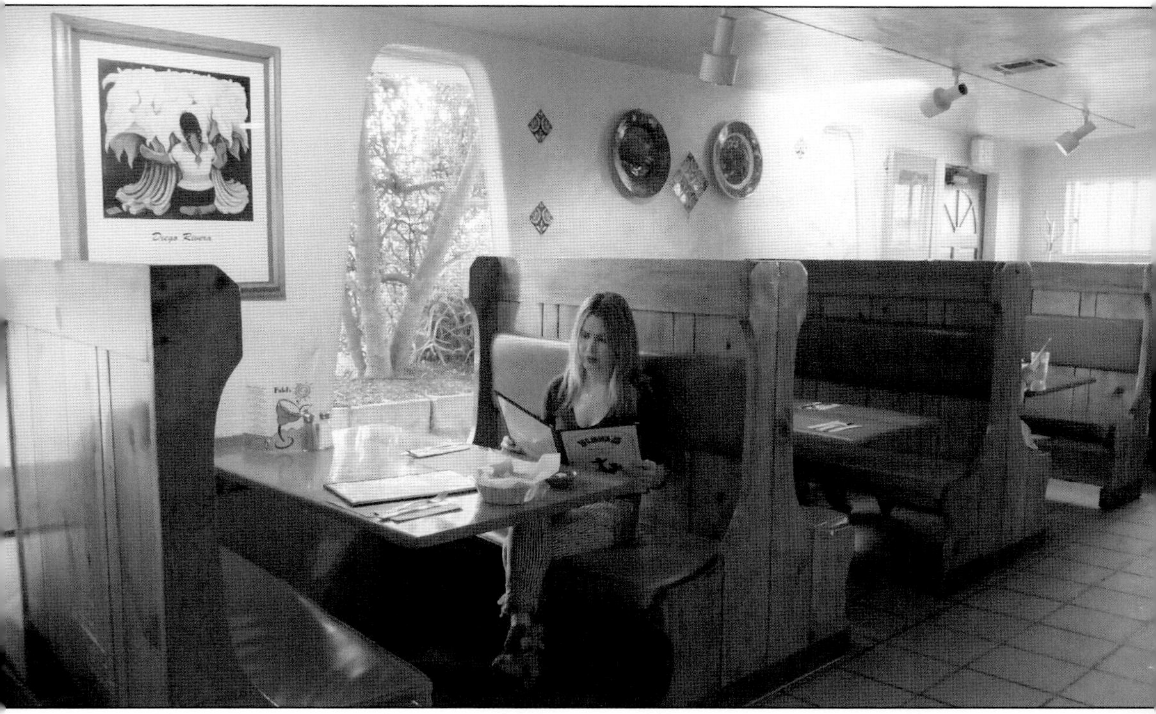

Today, Fidel's Little Mexico ranks among the top restaurants in San Diego County.

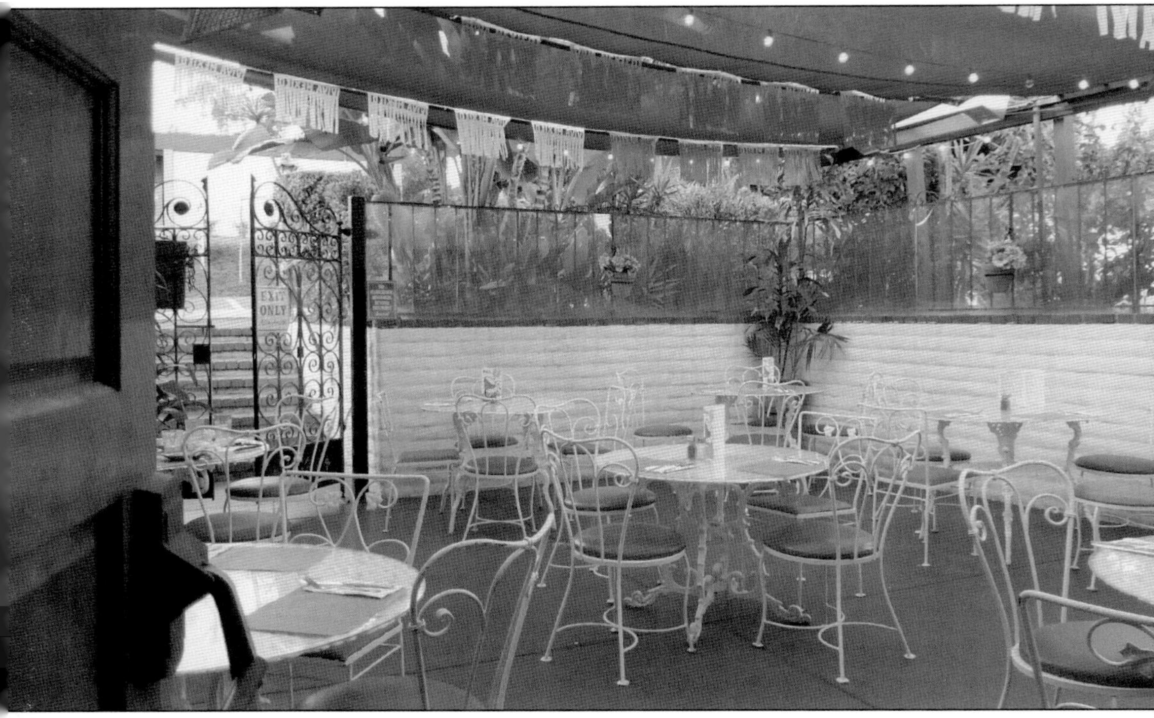

Pictured here is a brightly colored patio at Fidel's Little Mexico.

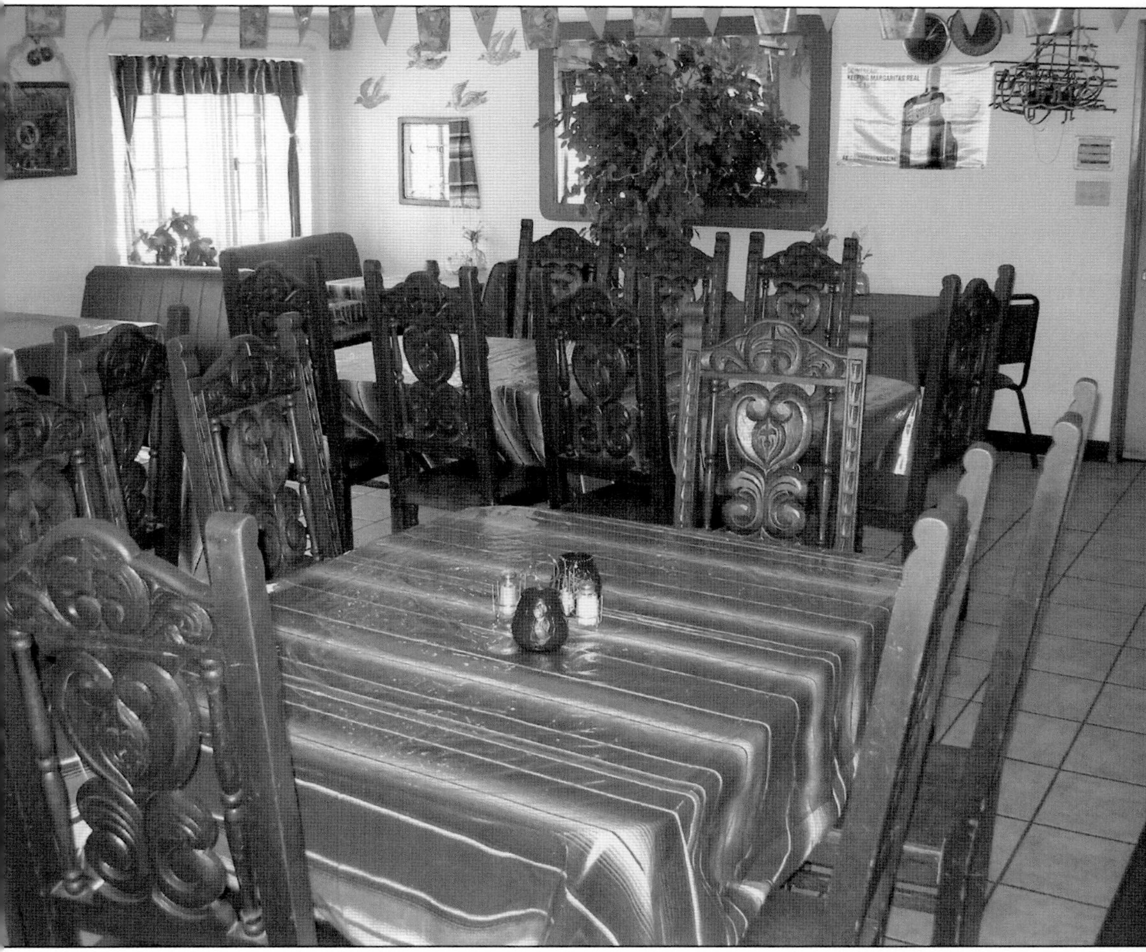

The Granados Market closed its doors in 1970. Several years later, the Granados family decided to renovate it and established a new restaurant dubbed Don Chuy. Mike Dalton, of the Solana Beach Civic and Historical Society, prepared a plaque to be mounted in front of Don Chuy Mexican Restaurant. Starting in 1932, Jose and Elvira Granados built and operated this establishment for several years as a grocery store, servicing residents of Eden Gardens.

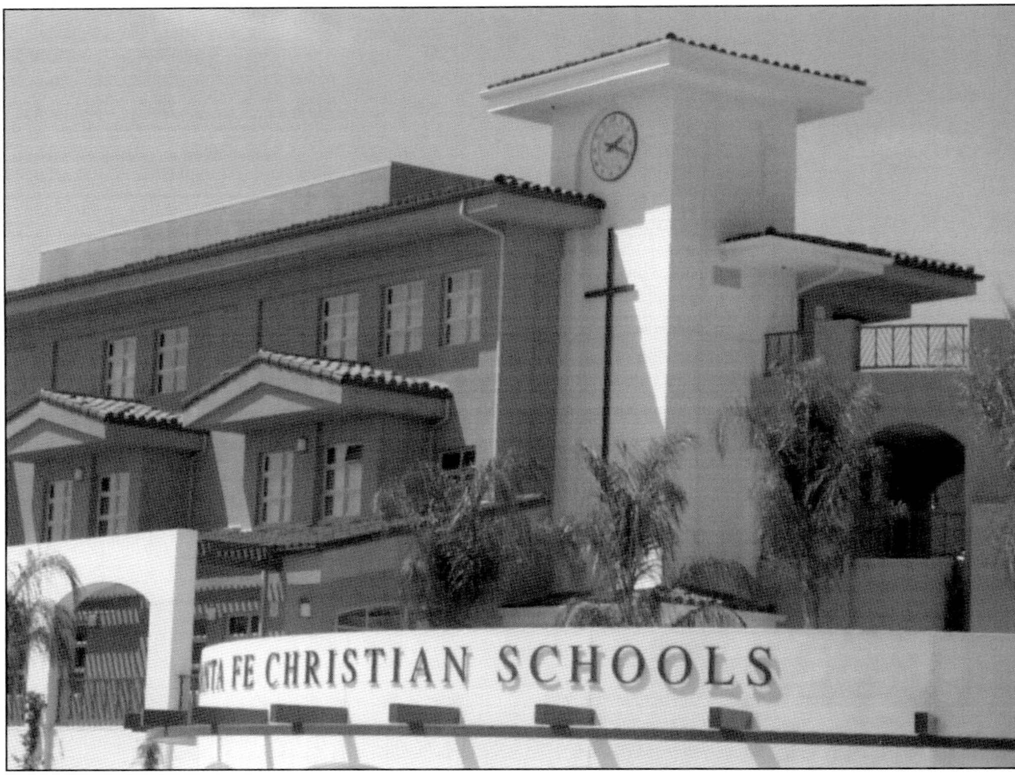

Founded in 1977, Santa Fe Christian Schools is a coeducational, independent college-preparatory school. The lower school serves students from kindergarten to fifth grade, the middle school grades six through eight, and the upper school grades nine through twelve.

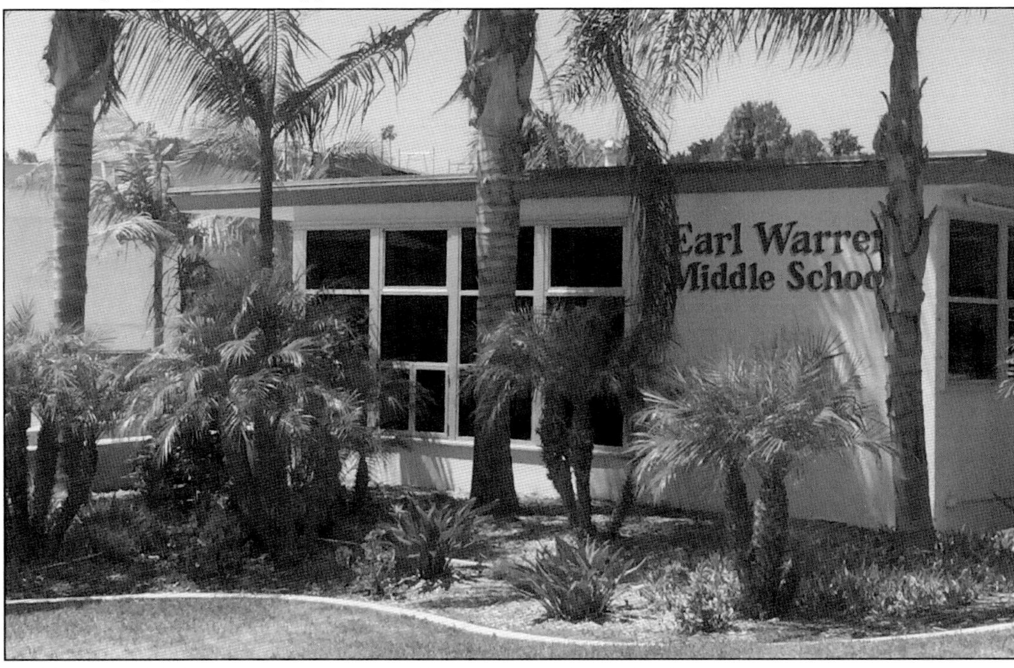

Earl Warren Middle School in Solana Beach was built in the 1950s.

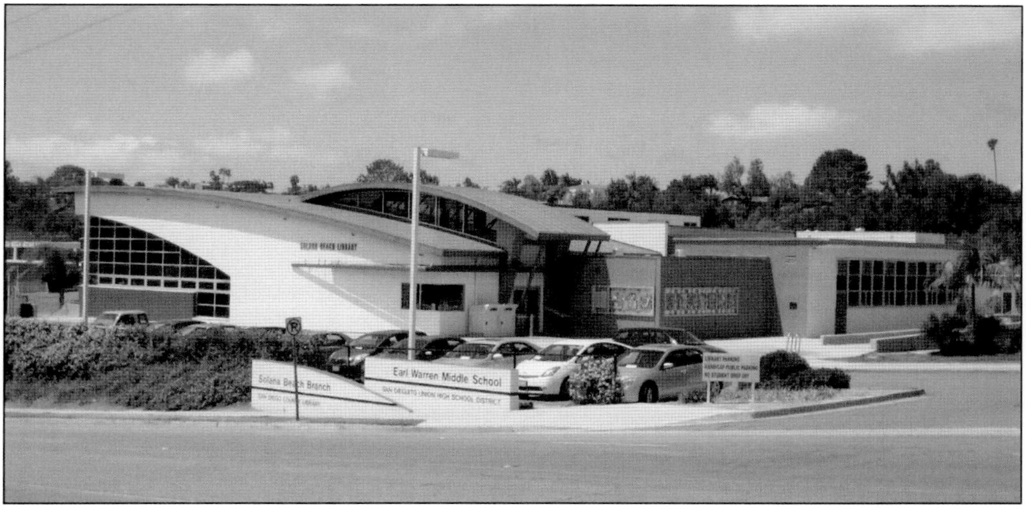

Solana Beach Library is located on the same site as Earl Warren Middle School, at 157 Stevens Avenue.

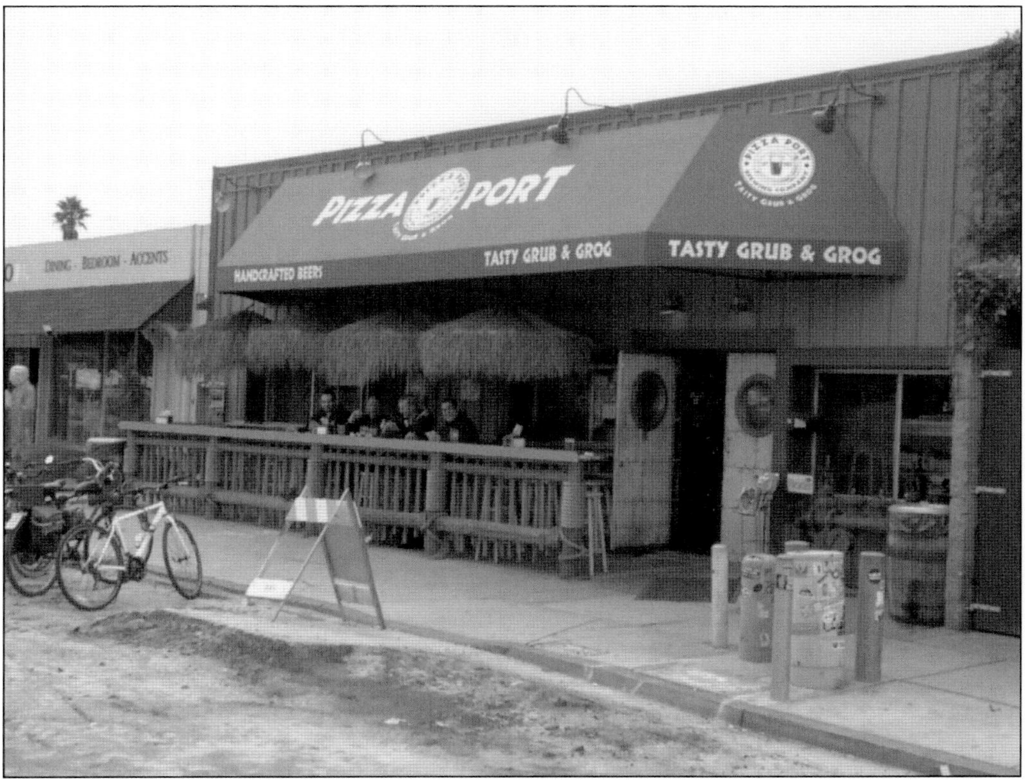

In March 1987, Gina and Vince Marsaglia bought a struggling pizza place and renamed it Pizza Port, now a fixture with several locations throughout the county. This photograph shows the popular restaurant during the redesign of Highway 101 through Solana Beach, completed in 2013.

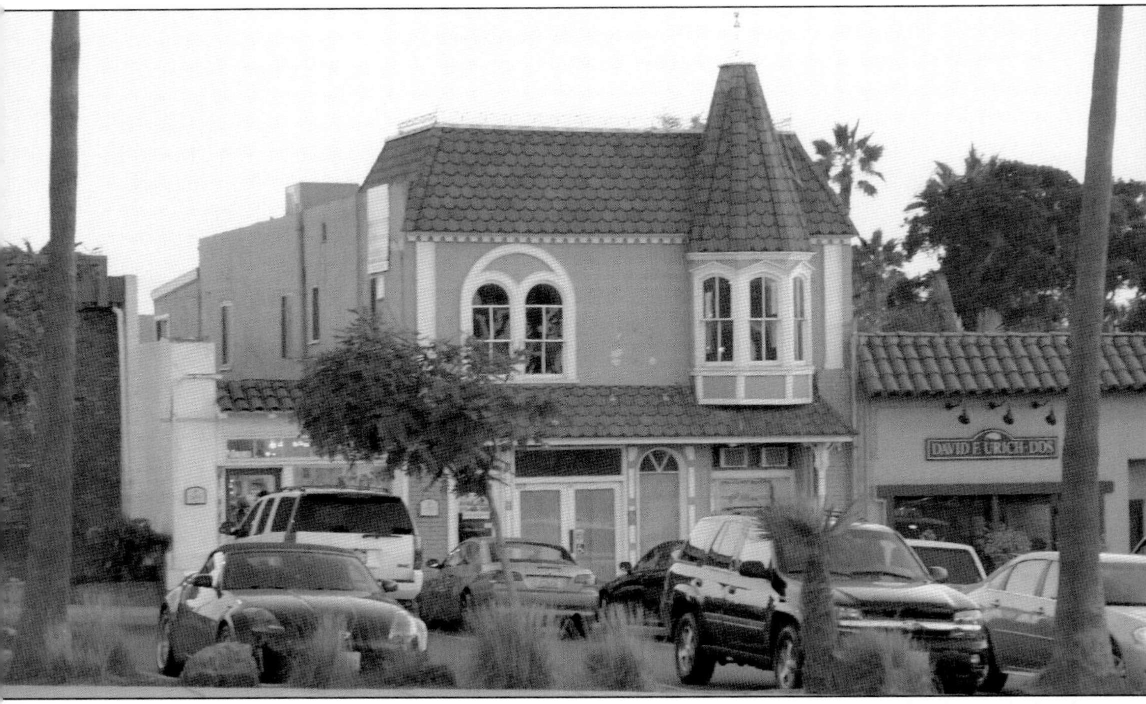

This 2013 photograph shows some of the original structures of the Solana Beach Plaza Ed Fletcher created in the 1920s that are still standing despite changing hands many times in the interim. (Courtesy of Julianne Eggold.)

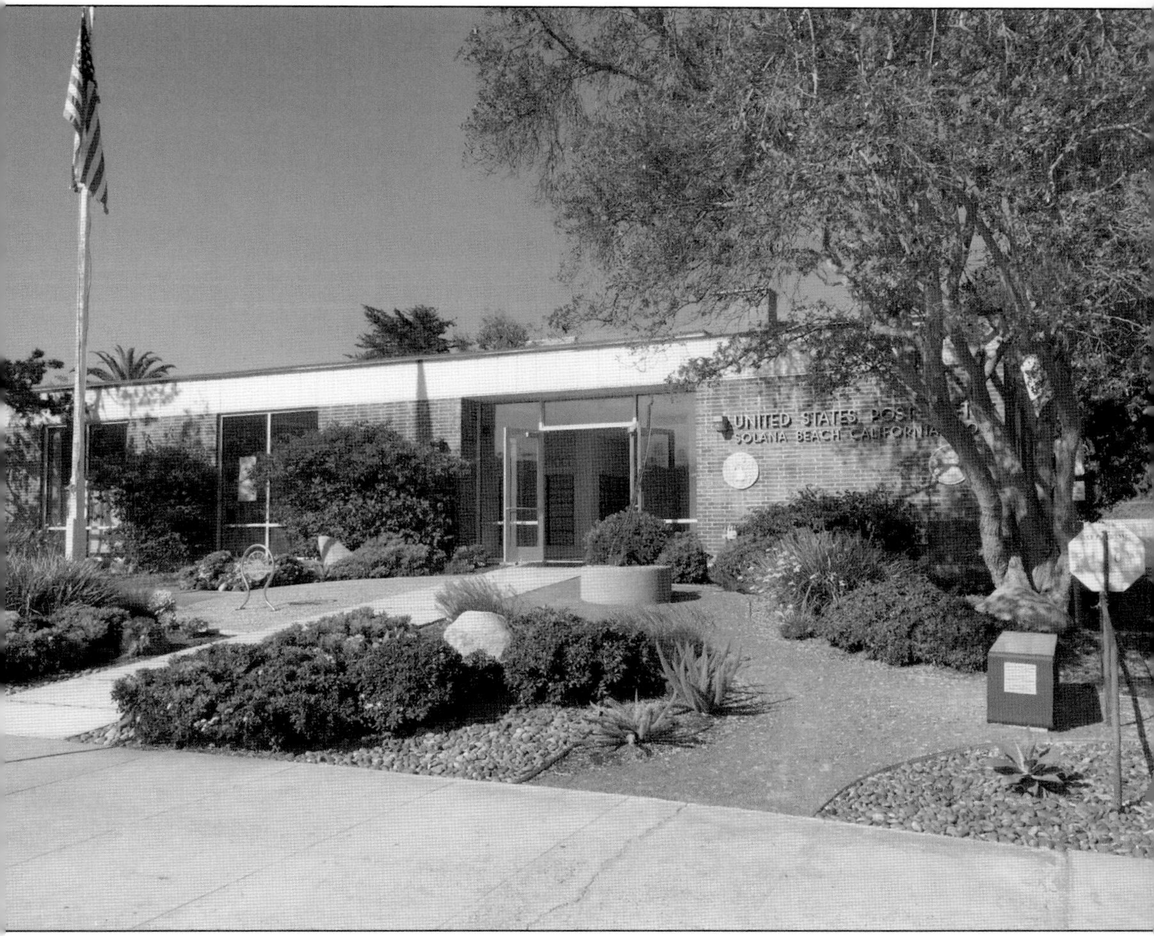

The Solana Beach Post Office, located at 153 South Sierra Avenue, received a renovation during the 1980s.

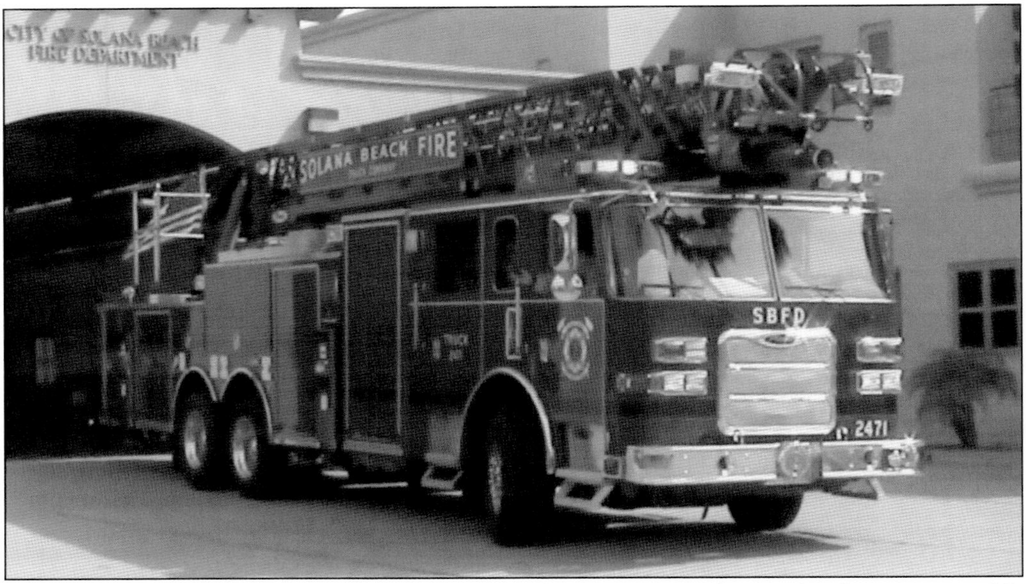

Pictured here in 2002 is a Solana Beach fire truck. Since 1986, the city has been responsible for managing its own fire services, while police services are still contracted through the City of San Diego.

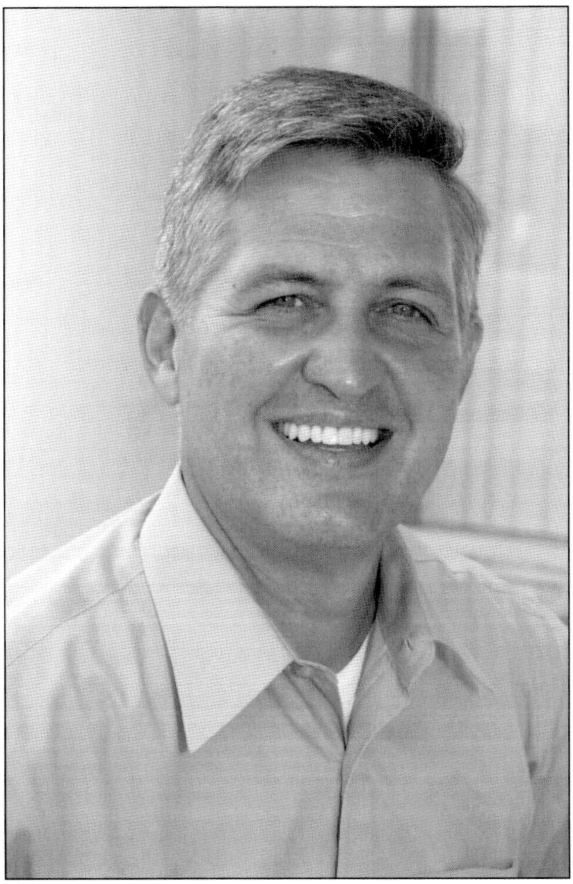

This is Dave Roberts, supervisor for San Diego County. Roberts previously completed two terms on the Solana Beach City Council and served as the city's mayor and deputy mayor.

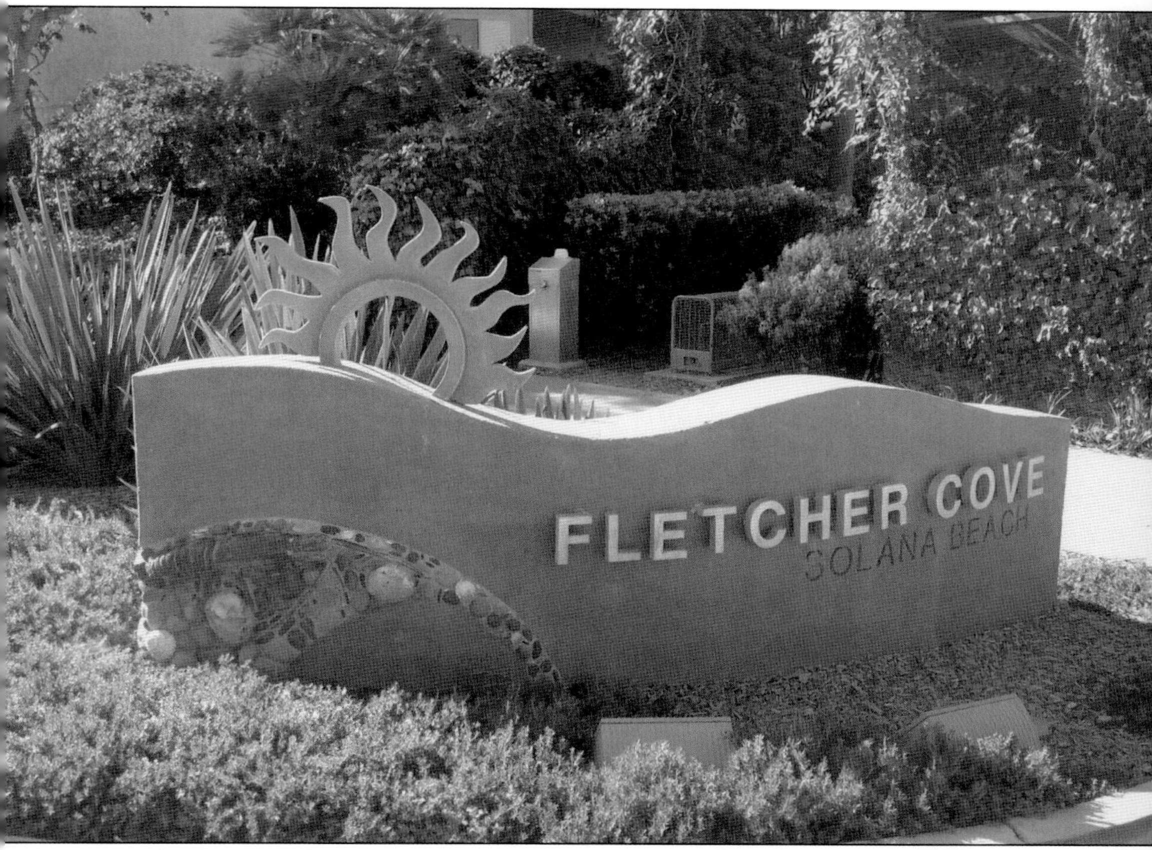

In 2011, Fletcher Cove began a major restoration, including beautifying its pathways, adding signage, and establishing a park area, play center, and a miniature amphitheater.

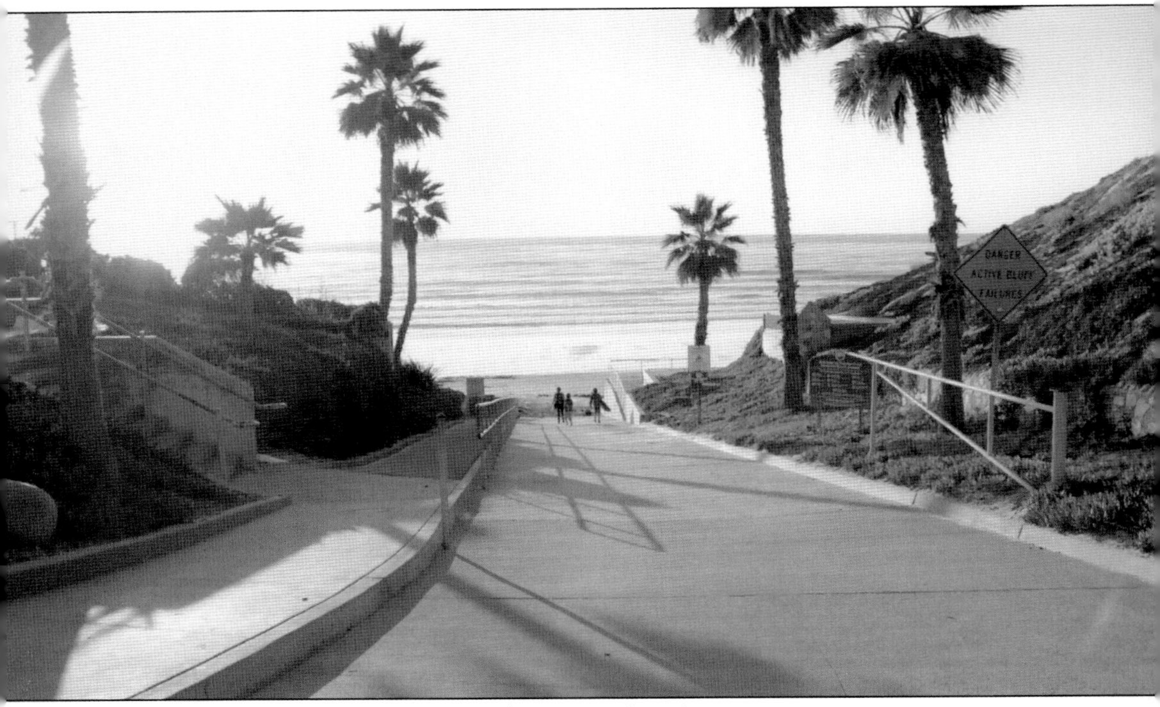

The entrance to Fletcher Cove is seen here around 2013.

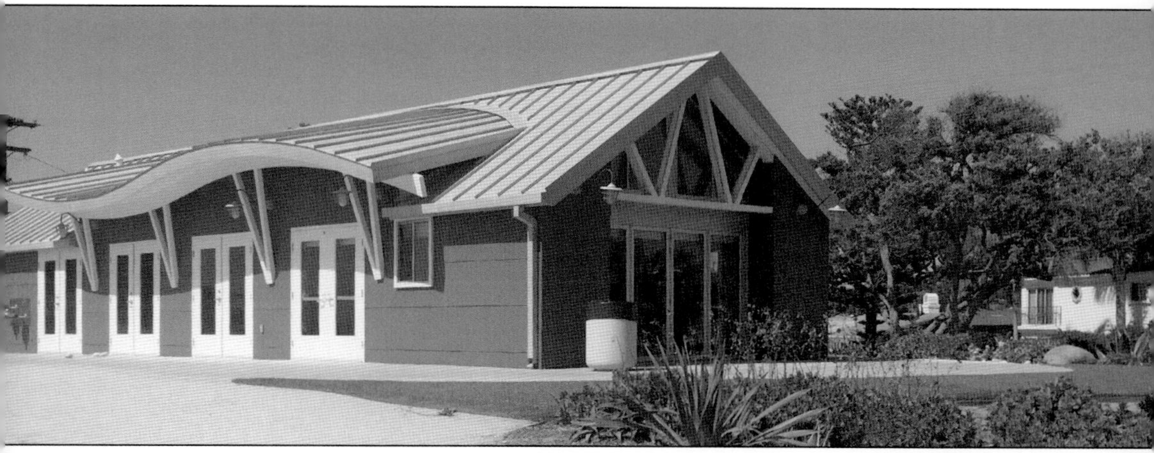

Pictured is the newly renovated Fletcher Cove Community Center in 2013. (Courtesy of Julieanne Eggold.)

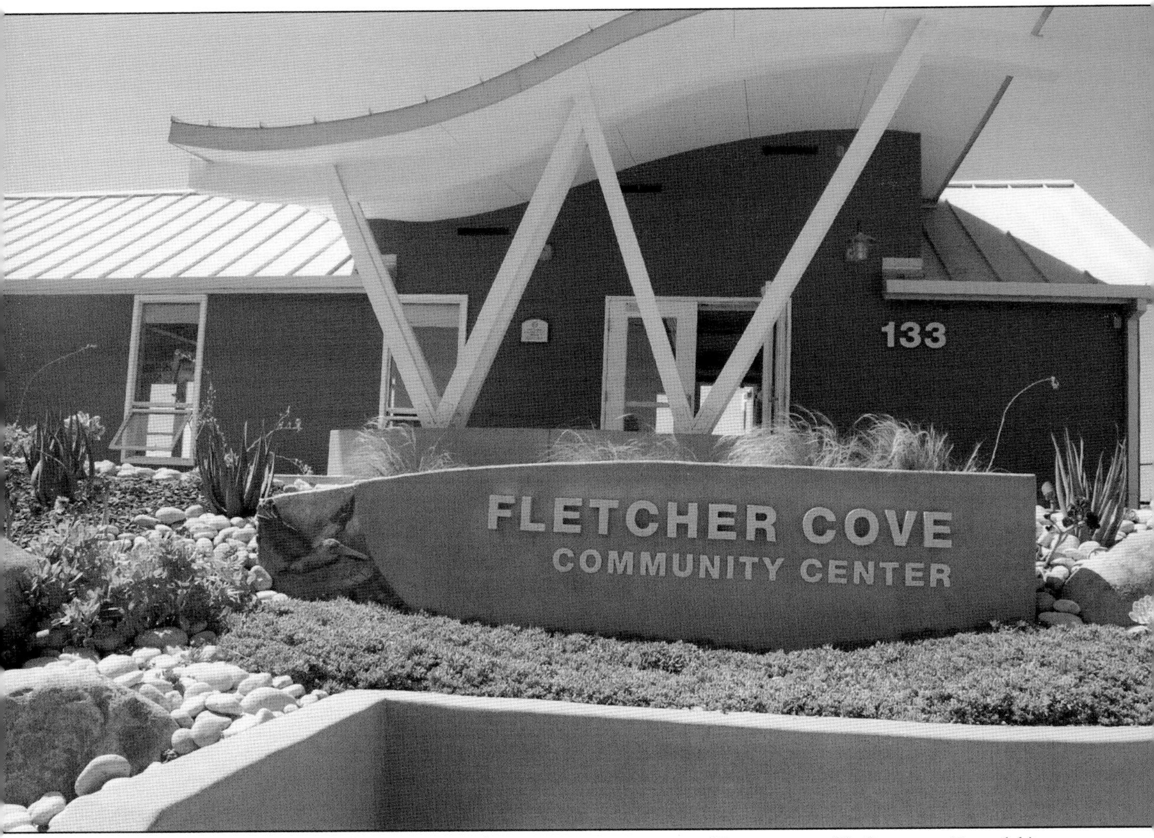

This is another shot of the renovated community center. (Courtesy of Julieanne Eggold.)

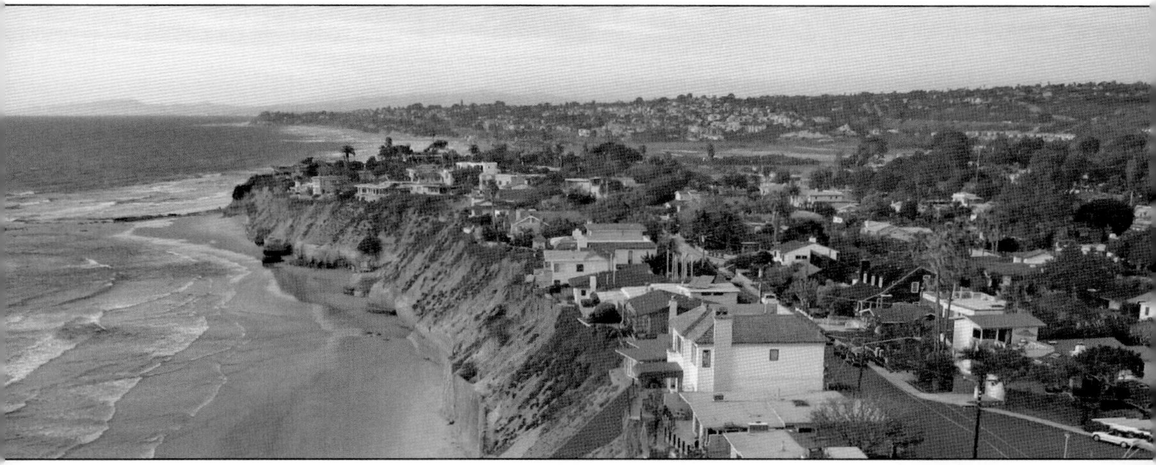

An aerial view of this charming seaside community highlights its 1.7 miles of coastline.